Beginning Oracle® Application Express

W9-BAP-289

Beginning
Oracle® Application Express

Rick Greenwald

Wiley Publishing, Inc.

Beginning Oracle® Application Express

Published by
Wiley Publishing, Inc.
10475 Crosspoint Boulevard
Indianapolis, IN 46256
www.wiley.com

Copyright © 2009 by Wiley Publishing, Inc., Indianapolis, Indiana

Published simultaneously in Canada

ISBN: 978-0-470-38837-2

Manufactured in the United States of America

10 9 8 7 6 5 4 3 2 1

Library of Congress Cataloging-in-Publication Data

Greenwald, Rick.
 Beginning Oracle Application express / Rick Greenwald.
  p. cm.
 Includes index.
 ISBN 978-0-470-38837-2 (paper/website)
 1. Oracle Application express. 2. Application software--Development. I. Title.
 QA76.76.A65G7437 2009
 005.1--dc22
                        2008045553

Everything I do benefits from the love and support I get from my family — LuAnn, Ellie, Josie, and Robin.
I am truly a lucky guy to be surrounded by such extraordinary people.

About the Author

Rick Greenwald is the author of more than 15 books, primarily focusing on Oracle technology, including *Professional Oracle Programming* from WROX and *Oracle Essentials* from O'Reilly, as well as several books about some of the ancestors of Oracle Application Express. Rick is a veteran of over 20 years in the IT industry, as a technologist and evangelist, but his real preoccupations are his family and music.

Credits

Executive Editor
Robert M. Elliott

Development Editor
Ed Connor

Senior Production Editor
Debra Banninger

Copy Editor
Foxxe Editorial Services

Editorial Manager
Mary Beth Wakefield

Production Manager
Tim Tate

Vice President and Executive Group Publisher
Richard Swadley

Vice President and Executive Publisher
Joseph B. Wikert

Project Coordinator, Cover
Lynsey Stanford

Compositor
Craig Johnson, Happenstance Type-O-Rama

Proofreader
Nancy Carrasco

Indexer
Johnna Van Hoose Dinse

Acknowledgments

I would like to thank two people from Oracle Corporation who were the guiding lights of this project: Judson Althoff, who was the executive sponsor of this book, and whose vision of introducing Oracle Application Express to a broader audience led to the volume you are holding; and Nick Kritikos, who not only took that vision and made it a reality, but was kind enough to include me as a partner in the creation of that reality, and guided the process through the labyrinth that the Oracle Corporation can sometimes be. Thanks, Judson and Nick.

Certainly, David Peake has been the most important contributor to this book. David is the product manager for Oracle Application Express, and he has been a constant presence throughout the long process that led to the publication of the book. David has been there for technical advice and guidance, as well as being a sounding board for ideas and direction. In fact, David is nothing less than the "hidden" coauthor of this book. It has been my real pleasure not only working with David but also coming to know him as a friend. Thanks, David — without a doubt, this would not have happened without you.

I would also like to call out two people from Wiley who have been instrumental in this book. I will always remember the first time I spoke to Bob Elliot more than 15 years ago from a pay phone in Hawaii. It took a decade for that initial introduction to result in a book, and a few more years to get to this one. Bob has always been there to listen to ideas, guide them in the right direction and offer practical and accurate advice. You should all be so lucky as to have a friend and colleague like Bob.

Finally, I would like to thank Ed Connor for his stewardship of the project and editing contribution. This book was not the easiest effort, but Ed brought it through the process with a smooth and steady hand. Thanks, Ed, hope we get to do this again.

Contents

Contents

Contents

Foreword

My name is David Peake, and I am a true believer in Oracle Application Express.

As principal product manager for Oracle Application Express, I devote countless hours of my working life to this product, reveling in its virtues and trying to constantly improve its breadth and reach. Even with this involvement, not a week goes by when I don't hear of someone using this product in a way that stretches my concept of its capabilities.

But the one thing that has dogged my involvement with APEX from the beginning is the misleading impression that the mere label of "Oracle" attached to the product means that APEX must be far too complex for mere mortals. Nothing could be further from the truth; Oracle products are becoming easier for everyone to use and attain the best results with. From installing and managing the Oracle database right through to development tools such as APEX, SQL Developer, and JDeveloper, we have made great strides in making Oracle easier to learn and become proficient in, so that you can concentrate on exceeding your business requirements.

That's why I was excited to hear that Rick Greenwald was going to be writing a book introducing APEX to the broader community of developers. Rick has a terrific ability to place even sophisticated technology issues in an easy-to-understand framework, which he has done admirably with the volume you are holding. Irrespective of your experience, even if you have never used Oracle before, you should find this book easy to follow. Rick has done a masterful job of explaining both the concepts and practical steps involved in building a web application from the ground up.

I am confident that, once you try it, you will learn to love APEX. And once you join the ever-expanding community of APEX developers, I am sure our paths will cross, on the discussion boards or at Oracle events.

Welcome to the world of APEX!

Introduction

Oracle Application Express is an easy-to-use application development environment built on the Oracle technology stack. There are two aspects of that previous sentence that you may find jarring — that Oracle, a company widely known for its database technology, has an application development environment, and that Oracle, a company thought of as delivering high-end, enterprise-ready technology, has anything that is easy to use.

But, as this book will show, the introductory statement is completely accurate. Oracle Application Express, commonly known as Oracle APEX or simply APEX, does benefit from the long-established enterprise-class robustness that is the hallmark of Oracle technology. The applications you build will be able to support hundreds of users and many terabytes of data, scalability far beyond even the imagination of most other development environments.

And Oracle APEX, with its declarative, wizard-driven methodology, is truly easy to use. In the course of the few hundred pages of this book, you will not only learn about how to use APEX, you will create a usable order entry system. The fast learning curve presented in these pages is a consequence of many years of development and refinement of the APEX product, which began life almost a decade ago within Oracle.

By the end of this volume, you will know enough to create your own applications, as well as having the knowledge and understanding of Oracle APEX and the world of Oracle technology to explore further refinements on your own.

Best of all, you can use APEX with absolutely no cost — either in a hosted environment, as suggested in Chapter 1, or with a free version of the Oracle database.

Welcome to the world of Oracle Application Express!

Who This Book Is For

This book is aimed at a particular group of users — those who are not familiar with Oracle Application Express. The book assumes that you have a basic knowledge of application development, the type you could get from playing around with a personal database such as Access. In fact, this book was written with an Access developer in mind — an Access developer looking to step up to a more scalable and reliable environment, with reduced maintenance overhead and greater integration between application systems.

What This Book Covers

This book covers the use of Oracle Application Express. Although the book is based on the 3.5 version, you can use the book with older versions as well. However, since the book will use a hosted version of Oracle Application Express, and since both the Oracle database that supports the product and the product itself are available as free downloads from http://otn.oracle.com, you should be able to use the latest version easily.

How This Book Is Structured

This book is structured to give the reader a gradual introduction to the essentials of development with Oracle Application Express. The book contains the following chapters:

Chapter 1: Welcome to Oracle! — This chapter contains an overview of Oracle Application Express, as well as instructions on how to set up a hosted development environment for performing the exercises used in the book.

Chapter 2: Jumpstart Oracle Application Express — In this chapter, you will leap into creating applications with Oracle Application Express and finish a simple application by the end of the chapter.

Chapter 3: Extending Your APEX Application — This chapter will introduce you to the options in Oracle APEX that let you ensure that your users will enter correct data while using your application.

Chapter 4: Validation, Calculation, Navigation, and Lists — This chapter continues the exploration of the aspects of APEX that help you to ensure that data used in your application is correct. Additionally, the chapter covers basic navigation options for your application.

Chapter 5: Reporting and Charting — This chapter covers the powerful and flexible reports you can create with Oracle APEX, and introduces you to the graphical capabilities of APEX reporting.

Chapter 6: Components Working Together — This chapter extends your work with charts, showing how you can create charts that link to a more detailed view of the data they represent. You will also learn how to create a calendar page with links to the data shown as part of the calendar, and how to add images taken from the underlying database to an Oracle APEX report.

Chapter 7: Customizing User Interfaces — This chapter explores advanced options for customizing user interfaces, on individual pages as well as across your entire APEX application.

Chapter 8: PL/SQL — This chapter introduces you to PL/SQL, the underlying language used to implement your APEX application, and demonstrates how to use the power of PL/SQL to extend the logic in your application.

Chapter 9: Security — This chapter covers how security is implemented for your APEX environment.

Chapter 10: Deployment and Administration — This chapter covers the options you have for deploying an APEX application to another environment and walks you through one of those options. Additionally, this chapter introduces you to the administrative functionality you can use to monitor and manage your APEX applications.

Chapter 11: Packaged Applications — This chapter gives an overview of packaged applications available for Oracle Application Express, with a more detailed look at a select few.

Chapter 12: Migration — This chapter describes how to migrate applications from Microsoft Access to Oracle Application Express.

What You Need to Use This Book

This book contains tutorials to guide you through the process of learning Oracle Application Express. You can use a hosted version of APEX to complete the basic exercises in this book, so all your really need is a browser and access to the Internet and you are ready to plunge into the world of Oracle Application Express.

Conventions

To help you get the most from the text and keep track of what's happening, I've used a number of conventions throughout the book.

Try It Out

The *Try It Out* is an exercise you should work through, following the text in the book.

1. They usually consist of a set of steps.

2. Each step has a number.

3. Follow the steps through with your copy of the database.

How It Works

After each *Try It Out*, the code you've typed will be explained in detail.

> **Boxes like this one hold important, not-to-be forgotten information that is directly relevant to the surrounding text.**

Notes, tips, hints, tricks, and asides to the current discussion are offset and placed in italics like this.

As for styles in the text:

❑ I *highlight* new terms and important words when I introduce them.

❑ I show keyboard strokes like this: **Ctrl+A**.

❑ I show file names, URLs, and code within the text like this: `persistence.properties`.

❑ I present code in two different ways:

```
A monofont type with no highlighting is used for most code examples.
```

```
Grey highlighting is used to emphasize code that's particularly important in the
present context.
```

Source Code

As you work through the examples in this book, you may choose either to type in all the code manually or to use the source code files that accompany the book. All of the source code used in this book is available for downloading at www.wrox.com. Once at the site, simply locate the book's title (either by using the Search box or by using one of the title lists) and click the Download Code link on the book's detail page to obtain all the source code for the book.

> *Because many books have similar titles, you may find it easiest to search by ISBN; this book's ISBN is 978-0-470-38837-2.*

Once you download the code, just decompress it with your favorite compression tool. Alternately, you can go to the main Wrox code download page at www.wrox.com/dynamic/books/download.aspx to see the code available for this book and all other Wrox books.

Errata

We make every effort to ensure that there are no errors in the text or in the code. However, no one is perfect, and mistakes do occur. If you find an error in one of our books, such as a spelling mistake or faulty piece of code, we would be very grateful for your feedback. By sending in errata you may save another reader hours of frustration, and at the same time you will be helping us provide even higher-quality information.

To find the errata page for this book, go to www.wrox.com and locate the title using the Search box or one of the title lists. Then, on the book details page, click the Book Errata link. On this page you can view all errata that has been submitted for this book and posted by Wrox editors. A complete book list, including links to each book's errata, is also available at www.wrox.com/misc-pages/booklist.shtml.

If you don't spot "your" error on the Book Errata page, go to www.wrox.com/contact/techsupport .shtml and complete the form there to send us the error you have found. We'll check the information and, if appropriate, post a message to the book's errata page and fix the problem in subsequent editions of the book.

p2p.wrox.com

For author and peer discussion, join the P2P forums at p2p.wrox.com. The forums are a web-based system for you to post messages relating to Wrox books and related technologies and interact with other readers and technology users. The forums offer a subscription feature to email you topics of interest of your choosing when new posts are made to the forums. Wrox authors, editors, other industry experts, and your fellow readers are present on these forums.

At http://p2p.wrox.com you will find a number of different forums that will help you not only as you read this book but also as you develop your own applications. To join the forums, just follow these steps:

1. Go to p2p.wrox.com, and click the Register link.

2. Read the terms of use, and click Agree.

3. Complete the required information to join as well as any optional information you wish to provide, and click Submit.

4. You will receive an email with information describing how to verify your account and complete the joining process.

> *You can read messages in the forums without joining P2P, but in order to post your own messages, you must join.*

Once you join, you can post new messages and respond to messages other users post. You can read messages at any time on the web. If you would like to have new messages from a particular forum emailed to you, click the Subscribe to this Forum icon by the forum name in the forum listing.

For more information about how to use the Wrox P2P, be sure to read the P2P FAQs for answers to questions about how the forum software works as well as many common questions specific to P2P and Wrox books. To read the FAQs, click the FAQ link on any P2P page.

Part I

Introducing Oracle Application Express

Chapter 1: Welcome to Oracle!

Welcome to Oracle!

Welcome to the world of Oracle technology. The book you are holding will give you all you need to start creating powerful, flexible, highly productive applications for yourself and your users. And the software included with this book will give you the path to even greater capabilities through a broad range of Oracle software. You are going to like it here.

This chapter will introduce you to the core technology you will be using to create applications, Oracle Application Express. The rest of the book will walk you through the process of creating an application with a hosted version of this product, finishing up with information on expanding your environment with packaged applications and migrating existing applications to your new platform.

But first, a few basic questions and their answers.

What Do You Need?

You need to be able to respond to the needs of users. And you need to respond rapidly, which means your development platform of choice has to be highly productive. You also need to retain that productivity over the life of these applications, as demand for new applications and functionality never seems to slow down.

These requirements are the minimum — your development platform must deliver in these areas. You cannot even consider any options that would impede the velocity of your work.

Why Don't You Have It?

But these table stakes are not, by themselves, enough. These requirements have led, over the years, to an approach that frequently used tools and platforms that were designed for personal use, such as Microsoft Access or spreadsheets. Initially, these user- and developer-friendly tools seemed like a great idea — a good developer could create applications very rapidly.

The problems arose after that initial deployment. Because of inherent limitations with the scalability and functionality of these tools, organizations ended up with a mess — hundreds of different applications, and dozens of sources of data and versions of the truth. This jumble of systems led to enormous maintenance requirements, which created a lot of extra overhead. Sometimes these overhead requirements were so high that standard practices were just abandoned, leaving critical data unprotected and insecure — or led to the development of even more systems, compounding the problem even more. Couple this with increasing regulatory demands, and you have a recipe for an unmanageable mess that could potentially put mission-critical data at risk.

This brief description only summarizes the acute pain that you and your client base feel. What this list of problems doesn't cover is the lost opportunity that comes from such a fragmented set of systems. The value of data grows as that data grows, through continued use and, more significantly, through integration with additional data to create a broader view of the overall organization. This value is trapped inside the welter of discrete systems. You could spend a significant quantity of resources trying to bring this data together with the same tools, but the proliferation of moving parts makes this a patchwork solution at best — if it's even possible.

So the need is clear — you don't want to sacrifice the advantages of rapid development in a productive environment, but your situation is growing more untenable by the day, as every new system only increases the problems springing out of a vast, unintegrated pool of systems.

Why Oracle?

You have two problems, and both of them require solutions. But why would you look to Oracle for both of those solutions?

Of course, Oracle is widely known for their enterprise strength database. You would expect systems built on the robust foundation of this database to be highly scalable, and for each database system to be able to support many different applications. But isn't this sophisticated technology both complex and expensive?

As you will see throughout the remainder of this book, the answer to both of these questions is a resounding "No!" The folks at Oracle have indeed included a host of advanced features in their database and supporting technology for decades. This leadership has given their technology a significant advantage in the market, and in the ever-increasing ease of use of their products. Typically, Oracle introduced features into their technology years ahead of other products, and has refined and simplified the interface to that technology, in cooperation with their user community, while others strove to catch up. At this point in time, Oracle has simplified the use of their standard features to the point where you get their advantages with virtually no effort on your part. The exercises in this book are an illustration of this approach — although the application you will create is robust and flexible, with the ability to transparently scale to thousands of users, you will not have to perform any special configuration or management tasks to gain these benefits.

Even better, there is still a vast domain of advanced functionality in Oracle technology that you can choose to add to your application stack if you wish. From analytical capabilities to clustering solutions and everywhere in between, Oracle technology has all the features you need, regardless of how demanding your requirements are.

Oracle technology provides a great on-ramp to the highest levels of technical capabilities. You can easily use Oracle technology to create your systems, with all the power and functionality of Oracle products right there when you need it. But, you say, surely all this capability must be expensive, right?

Once again, the answer is no. In this book, you will be creating an order entry system, and all you will need is a browser. You will use a hosted Oracle environment that is available to you without any charges. If you want to create the same application using your own installed software, everything you need is either available in the hosted version of primary tool you will be using, Oracle Application Express, or ready for you to download from the Oracle site.

In fact, the primary tool you will be using, Oracle Application Express, is included with every Oracle database as a no-cost option. Once you become acquainted with the productive potential of Oracle Application Express, you can create almost any application using this tool and deploy that application onto any production Oracle database.

In other words, the best reason to use Oracle technology is that there are no reasons not to — the question should be "Why *not* Oracle?" And, with this book, you have the perfect introduction to using that technology to implement your own IT solutions — at least, that is what this author hopes!

What Is Oracle Application Express?

The focus of this book, like its title, points to Oracle Application Express. What exactly is Oracle Application Express, also known as Oracle APEX?

Oracle Application Express is a rapid application development (RAD) tool built on Oracle technology. Oracle APEX runs in an Oracle database instance and comes as a no-cost option with all Oracle databases.

APEX runs entirely in a browser and does not require any software to be loaded onto your client machines. You develop your applications from a browser-based environment, as shown in Figure 1-1, and deploy your applications to a browser-based environment.

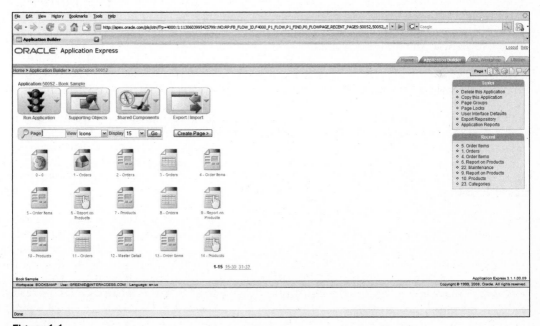

Figure 1-1

Oracle Application Express is a declarative development tool. As you will see throughout this book, APEX development consists of assigning values for properties which describe the various components of your applications. The Oracle APEX environment does the rest for you.

For most components, you will use wizards to guide you through the process of creating those components. After this initial creation, you have access to these properties to modify or shape the operation of your applications, combining ease-of-use and productive maintenance in the same development tool.

All APEX development is data-driven. Tight integration with the Oracle database which hosts APEX means that your applications will naturally flow from your data designs. For instance, APEX applications automatically understand and implement relationships between tables, generating fully-featured applications without additional programming overhead.

Oracle Application Express is an all-in-one development tool. You use the same techniques to create forms, reports, and charts, as well as integrating these components together with navigation methods.

Your Oracle APEX environment gives you all you need to create virtually any application through an easy declarative development process. However, APEX is also extensible, so you can use HTML to modify the presentation of your APEX-generated client interfaces and Oracle's standard PL/SQL procedural language to supply additional logical operations on the back end.

When you start to use Oracle APEX, you will quickly discover that you are not alone. The Oracle Technology Network (OTN) has a vibrant community of APEX users and experts, who regularly contribute leading to continual improvement in best practices and technical solutions. In addition, you will find a large collection of application packages that have already been created with APEX, readily available for you to integrate in with your own applications.

Last, but certainly not least, Oracle Application Express gives you a way to protect the investment you have in all those personal applications spread throughout your organization. You can upload data from an Excel spreadsheet with a few simple mouse clicks, moving crucial information into an Oracle database. You can even generate a complete application to interact with that data with a few more clicks, completing the task in less than 10 minutes.

Oracle also provides a migration tool to help you move your Access applications to Oracle APEX, migrating from a personal database with limited scalability to the world's most powerful database.

Ready to start yet? This book contains all you will need to jump into the world of APEX-created applications. But first, a little bit about the application you will be creating in the remainder of this book.

What Are You Going to Do?

So far, so good. You've got a handle on Oracle Application Express, the tool you will be using to accomplish the task laid out in this book.

That primary task is to build an order entry system from scratch. You will be creating the data structures to hold the order information, loading data into those structures, creating maintenance tools for administrators to use to access and modify this data, and creating a browser-based user interface for your application.

The application itself will have all the features you would expect in a robust application:

❑   Ability to enter data, while ensuring that the data contains appropriate values

❑   Ability to search for data, according to user-specified conditions

❑   Ability to report on that data, both at the detail level and through higher-level approaches, such as graphs and charts

❑   An easy-to-use, attractive interface that will enhance user productivity

You can see a couple of views of this application in the following figures. Figure 1-2 displays one of the key pages in your completed application, where users will see their orders and the items in those orders, along with the ability to add new items and modify or delete existing items.

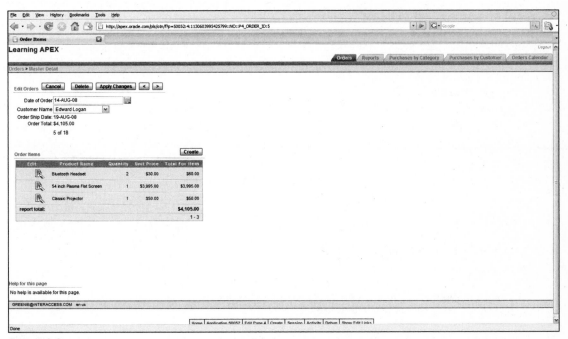

Figure 1-2

Figure 1-3 shows you an example of using the charting capability of Oracle Application Express. Although you cannot tell from this one image, the chart shown has built-in drill-down functionality, so that a user can get more detailed information on any of the sections of the pie chart with a simple mouse click.

Although this application is fully functional and scalable, you hopefully are interested in this book for more than just the order entry application you will build. The order entry application you will create was chosen as an example because you can learn most of the techniques you will need for your own future work. The primary purpose of this book is to teach you how to use Oracle Application Express to realize your own development goals, rather than arriving at the end product of a complete order entry application. But by the time you reach the end of the examples in this book, you will be able to extend the application you have built in almost any direction your requirements dictate.

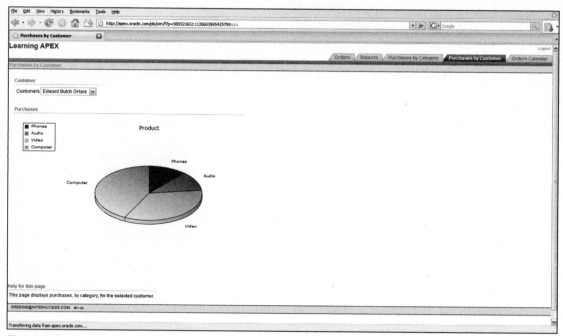

Figure 1-3

You will build this application over the remainder of this book. You can also get script files, and instructions on how to use them at the web site for this book, www.wrox.com.

How Will You Do It?

The format of this book is to teach you about Oracle APEX while iteratively developing the sample order entry application. Each chapter explores a basic area of functionality and the development techniques you will need to achieve that functionality.

Oracle Application Express runs within the Oracle database environment. You have a few choices on how you want to use APEX.

❑ You can download a free copy of a developer edition of Oracle Database 11g and Oracle Application Express. If you wish, you can load that software following the installation instructions that accompany the software. These installation instructions also include information on how to access your Oracle APEX software.

❑ If you already have an Oracle database within your organization, you could use Oracle Application Express from that environment. If APEX is not already installed on your server, the APEX home page at http://otn.oracle.com/apex has a link to download the software for your database. The only requirement is that your Oracle database be version 9.2.0.3 or higher.

This book is based on Oracle Application Express version 3.1.2. All the examples in the book have been tested against that version, so you should be fine if you are running that version or a later version.

❑ You can also use a hosted version of Oracle Application Express. This book is designed for this remote access to APEX, although the examples should work with either of the other two options.

The next section will describe exactly how to sign up for your hosted Oracle APEX account.

How to Sign Up for a Hosted APEX Account

Oracle Corporation provides free hosted APEX accounts for your trial use. Signing up is an easy process that will take you less than 2 minutes.

Open your browser and go to `http://apex.oracle.com`, which is shown in Figure 1-4.

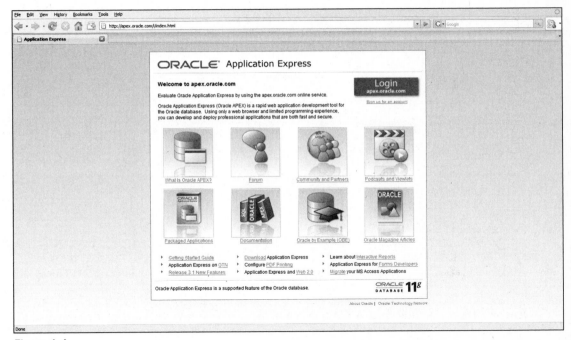

Figure 1-4

❑ Click on the `Sign up for an account` link underneath the big red Login button, which will bring up the first page of the Signup Wizard, shown in Figure 1-5. This page is also your first view of an APEX application.

❑ Click on Next to move from the Welcome page to begin the process.

❑ Your first step, shown in Figure 1-6, is to identify the person who will be the administrator of the hosted Oracle APEX account. Enter your name and email address, and click Next.

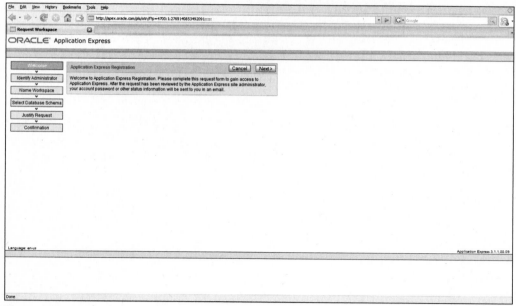

Figure 1-5

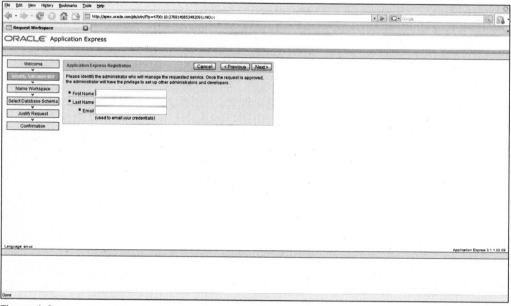

Figure 1-6

❏   Oracle Application Express can support multiple workspaces to give you and your organization the
ability to segregate work on different applications. The next page of the Signup Wizard prompts you
for a workspace. Enter a name you can remember, and click Next. If the workspace name you enter
is not unique, you will receive an error message and be prompted to enter the name again.

❑ In the next step, you are prompted for the name of a *schema*. Oracle Application Express exists within an Oracle database. An Oracle schema is a collection of tables and objects — similar to the concept of a database in Access. Give your schema an appropriate name, the easiest being the same name as your workspace.

The schema name must not exceed 30 characters, cannot contain spaces or quotation marks, and must be unique for the hosted version. If you select a schema name that violates any of these restrictions, you will get an error and be prompted to select another name.

❑ Leave the default initial space allocation of 10MBs. Although an Oracle database can scale to handle many terabytes of data easily, you will not need that much space for your initial explorations of APEX. Click Next.

❑ The final step in your signup process is to let the folks at Oracle know why you want to obtain a hosted APEX account. Enter your reason, which is to work on the exercises in this book, and click Next.

❑ The final step should be familiar to web users. You are asked to enter a verification code, which ensures that a human is making the request, rather than an automated program. Match the text and click Submit Request, which will bring up the page shown in Figure 1-7.

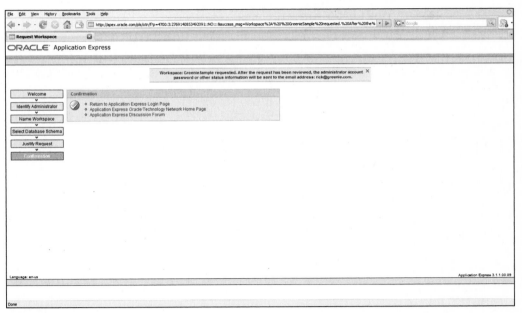

Figure 1-7

This page informs you that you will receive an email once your request has been reviewed. This review process typically only take a few minutes. The email message you will receive contains a summary of your request and an activation link.

❑ Click on the activation link in your email. This action will create a workspace for you in the hosted APEX environment. Once the workspace has been created, the hosted environment will send credentials for that workspace to your email address.

❑ Click on the link to go to the login page for your hosted account, shown in Figure 1-8. Enter your workspace name and your user name, which is the email address. Check your email for your credentials, and enter the password sent to you. Click Login, which will bring you to Oracle Application Express, your development destination, shown in Figure 1-9.

And that's it! You are ready to start creating APEX applications — which you will begin in the next chapter.

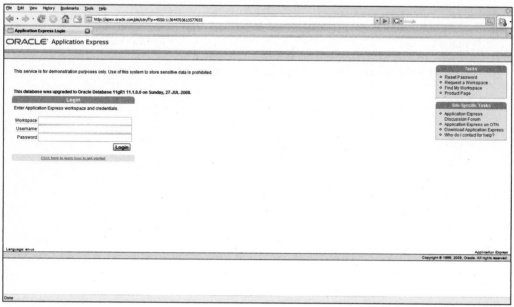

Figure 1-8

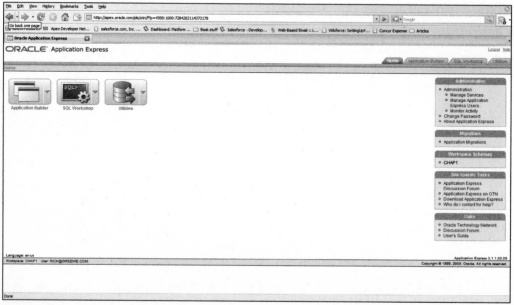

Figure 1-9

Script Files for This Book

You can get those at the web site for this book, www.wrox.com, which also includes a script to create the entire application from scratch. At this web site, you will find links to a wide variety of other materials that you may find helpful, including additional tutorials on APEX. You will also learn how to get loads more interesting stuff, like Oracle software, tutorials, white papers and other collateral.

Summary

Oracle Application Express will give you the power to create robust and scalable applications in an easy, highly productive environment. This chapter introduced you to the basics of APEX, including:

❑   What is APEX?

❑   What application will you be building in this book

❑   How will you build that application

This book will walk you through the process of creating a sample order entry application, which will teach you the techniques you need to create your own applications. Without further ado, on to the world of APEX!

Part II

Building an Application with Application Express

Jumpstart Oracle Application Express

Oracle Application Express, more commonly known as Oracle APEX or APEX, gives you a highly productive environment to create applications from start to finish. You can use APEX to create the structures for your data and quickly build interactive HTML-based pages to give users access to this data.

This chapter will get you right into the mix. In the next few pages, you will learn about the basic data design for the sample application used in this book, create the tables specified in that design, and create your first few pages to interact with that data. By the end of the chapter, you will have the bulk of the functionality you saw in the previous chapter ready for actual use.

So let's get going!

Data Design

In the old days, our field was called "data processing"—a term that has been superseded by more descriptive phrases but that still carries an important message. Although applications and reports may be the visible aspects of our work as developers and business analysts, the entire system rests on a foundation of data.

Given this foundation, you should begin your process of development by creating a design for your data. A good data design is the natural outgrowth of a thorough understanding of the business processes that your application system will be implementing. You will need to understand not only the discrete pieces of data that you will require to store and manipulate but also how to organize this data into logical units, and how to relate those units to each other.

You are probably aware that Oracle is one of the leading enterprise databases in the world — if not *the* leading one. Based on this heritage, Oracle Application Express is built to leverage good data design. In order to use APEX most effectively, you should fully understand the data requirements of your business scenario before beginning, which is the focus of this chapter.

Application Needs

The application we will be building is an order entry system. The multiple pages that make up this application will have to deal with a number of data areas, including:

❑   Orders, which will include data identifying the overall order

❑   Order detail lines, which will indicate the quantity and pricing of a particular product within an order

❑   Products, which will carry descriptive information about the products offered by your company

❑   Customers, those wonderful people who will be ordering products

You will need to collect and process data about these four entities in the application that you will be designing for this book. Later in the book, you will be adding some other groups of data to support the operation of your application, but these four groups of data are all you need to create the main portion of your functional application.

Data Structures

Oracle Application Express is built on top of an Oracle database. The Oracle database is a classic relational database. In a relational database, groups of data are implemented as *tables*. A table is the core component of a database. All data activity centers on tables; you read and write all individual pieces of data as operations on rows within one or more tables.

> *Depending on your background, you might be more used to referring to rows as records. A row within a table is the relational database equivalent of a record within a file or personal database. Since Oracle Application Express is built on top of Oracle, and since some readers may be coming from a relational background, this book will use the terminology of tables and rows.*

Creating the data structure for this application will require the creation of four tables to implement the four functional data groupings listed above.

Figure 2-1 shows the four tables, as well as the relationships between them.

You can see the four tables, as expected, as well as lines connecting those tables. The lines indicate relationships between the tables. The tables connected by straight lines — Orders and Customers, Order Items and Products — have what is called a *one-to-one relationship*, with each row in a table being connected to a single row in the other table. One set of tables — Orders and Order Items — are connected by a line with what looks like a fork at one end. This line represents a *one-to-many relationship*, with the fork indicating the many end of the relationship. Each Order row can have one or more Order Items rows.

As you will see by the end of this chapter, the data groupings and relationships within this simple data design are more than a simple way of grouping data. Oracle Application Express uses the structure implemented in your data design to automatically create powerful functionality.

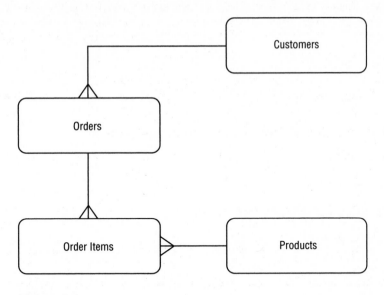

Figure 2-1

Your First Page

Data design should always come first in your development process, since no amount of clever code can correct for an invalid or inefficient data design. For the purposes of the sample application you will be creating in this book, the four tables in the current data design are enough to get started creating your application. By the end of this short section, you will have moved from the concept illustrated in the data design to a highly functional application. You understand your data design, so you can start right in on creating your application.

Creating a Table

You have a high level data design. The first step towards a working application is the creation of a table. If you are creating an application to work on data that already exists in some form, you probably want to also populate the table with that existing data as soon as you create it.

APEX gives you several ways to quickly create and populate the tables that will be used in your application. In this chapter, you will use the following methods:

❑   Automatic table creation and population directly from a spreadsheet

❑   Manual creation of table structure and population from a spreadsheet

❑   Automatic creation of related tables from data in an existing table

There are other methods you can use to bring data into the Oracle database that works with APEX, including standard Oracle utilities for loading and unloading data, as well as other potential data sources, such as text or XML files. You can explore these other options through the online help in APEX.

The fastest and easiest method for table creation is to import both structure and data from a spreadsheet. You are going to use this method for one of the core tables for the application, Orders.

Try It Out   Importing a Table from a Spreadsheet

APEX makes creating and populating a table from a spreadsheet easy — just a few clicks and you are done. This example will use the ORDERS.csv file from the sample files for this book to create the core table for the sample application.

You can get all the files needed for the examples in this book at the web site for the book – http://www.wiley.com/go/greenwald.

1. Log into your APEX-hosted account to bring up the page shown in Figure 2-2.

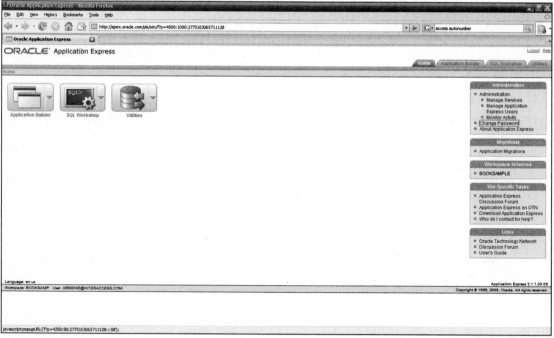

Figure 2-2

2. Click on the Utilities icon, and use the cascading menus to select Data Load/Unload, and then the Load choice, as shown in Figure 2-3.

3. Click on the Load Spreadsheet Data icon in the Load page, which will bring up the page shown in Figure 2-4.

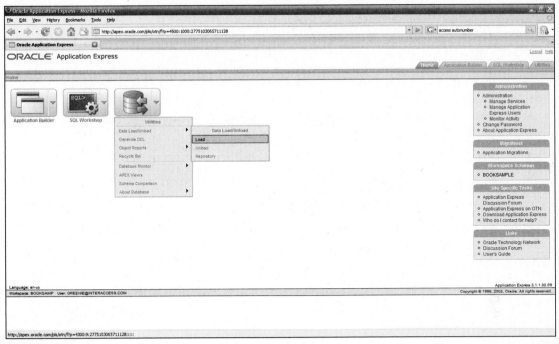

Figure 2-3

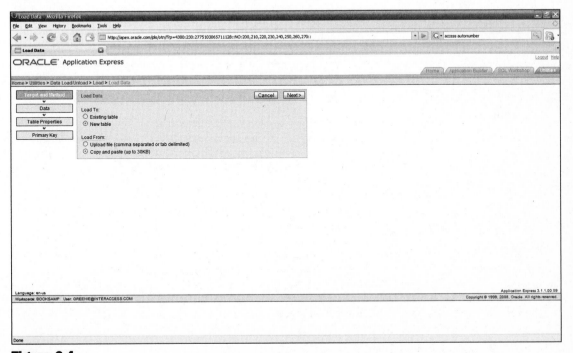

Figure 2-4

4. On this page, accept the (Load To) New table choice, but change the Load From choice to Upload File. Click Next once you have made this change.

5. The next page, shown in Figure 2-5, prompts you for the name of the file to use as a data source. Click Browse and locate the ORDERS.csv file. The default values for other choices on this page can be left with their default values for this file. Click Next to bring up the next page.

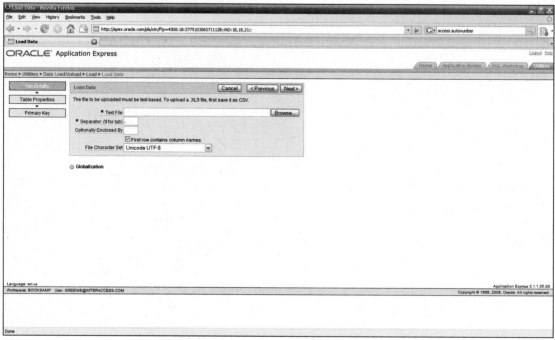

Figure 2-5

6. The next page, shown in Figure 2-6, gives you a lot of information about the comma-separated file you indicated in the previous page. You can see that the column names, data types, and even first set of values slated to be loaded into the table are shown. All that is left for you to do is to add a name for the tables, which should be ORDERS, and click Next.

You can also see a dropdown box asking for a schema. In Oracle terms, a schema is equivalent to a database —— a set of tables that can be directly accessed, without further name qualification. You defined a schema when you created your online account in the last chapter.

The next page, shown in Figure 2-7, has a few choices that control how APEX will implement logic for this particular table. In relational terms, every row in a table must have a *primary key*. The primary key is used to identify the particular row of the table. On this page, you identify either a new or existing column to hold the primary key value. APEX also asks for the name of a *constraint* to use to implement the primary key. A constraint is simply a database specification that indicates, in this case, that the particular column is a primary key.

You will learn more about constraints in Chapter 4.

Figure 2-6

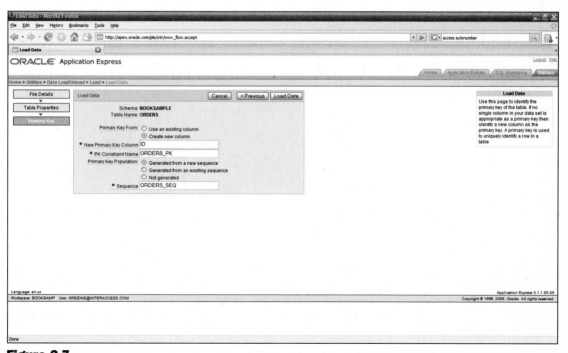

Figure 2-7

Finally, the page asks if you want to use a sequence to generate primary keys. APEX applications require that each row in a table will have a unique primary key value. The Oracle database includes an object that is ideal for generating unique values — a sequence, which is roughly equivalent to an Autonumber data type field in Access. A sequence object performs a simple task––each time you ask the sequence for a number, the sequence provides the next consecutive number.

The page shown in Figure 2-7 allows you to specify the creation of a new sequence to generate a primary key, use an existing sequence, or not generate a sequence, which requires you to provide your own unique primary key value.

7. For this data load, accept the default value of Create new column for the Primary Key From: choice, but change the name of the New Primary Key Column to ORDER_ID. You can leave the other choices with their default values and click Load Data.

8. After the data load has completed, you will be presented with a page that lists the most recent data loads into the repository, the Oracle database that underlies your APEX environment.

With these few steps, you have both created a table and loaded data into your Oracle database.

How It Works

You can now go and take a quick look at your data through the standard APEX data-browsing tools.

1. Start by clicking on the SQL Workshop tab in the set of tabs in the upper-right area of the page, which will bring up the page shown in Figure 2-8.

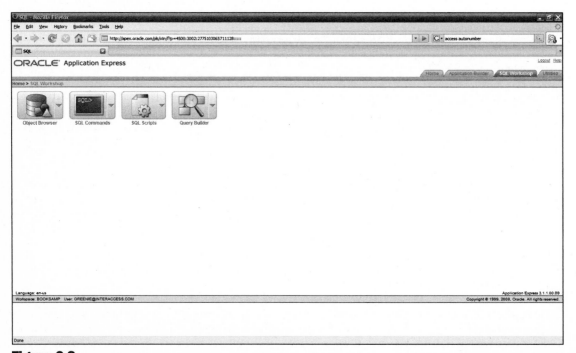

Figure 2-8

2. As with your initial step above, click on the down arrow in the Object Browser icon, and then select Browse and Tables from the cascading menus.

The Object Browser has a picklist at the top of the left-hand panel that allows you to select the type of database object you want to view, as well as giving you the option to search for instances of that object based on a search string. Below these two entry fields is a list of all the objects that match the type and search criteria.

3. Click on the ORDERS table to bring up the Object Brower window, as shown in Figure 2-9.

Figure 2-9

You can see you have a lot of options available for a table in the Object Browser. If you are familiar with SQL data definition language (DDL), you will recognize the lower row of options as a part of standard SQL syntax for the overall table. You will be using some of these options in this and subsequent chapters. Right now, you want to take a quick look at the data in the ORDERS table to make sure that the import from the spreadsheet succeeded as described.

4. Click on the Data option in the top line of choices in the right-hand panel to bring up the page shown in Figure 2-10.

This page displays the initial set of data for the table. If there were more rows, you would have the option to scroll through the rows. You can also see that there is a link labeled Download in the lower-left corner of the data display window. This link gives you the ability to download the data in the table into a .csv file — one of several ways to extract data back out of the Oracle database underlying the APEX environment.

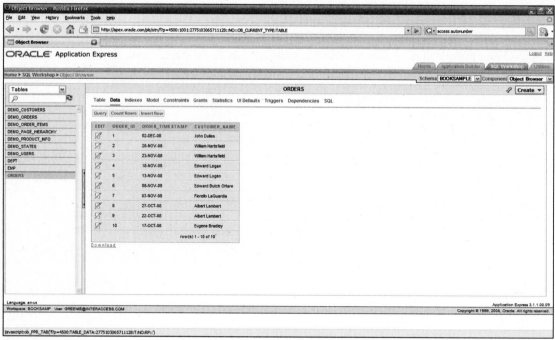

Figure 2-10

To the left of each row of data, you can see an icon that will take you to an edit page for that row of data. You can click on it to see the editing interface, but with APEX, you can quickly create a page in an application to accomplish the same tasks with just a few clicks — as you will do in the next section.

Creating an Application

Now that you have data in your database, the next step is to create a way to manipulate that data. In this section, you will create an application with half a dozen clicks and a tiny bit of typing.

Try It Out   **Creating an Application**

You will use the first of many Oracle APEX wizards to create an application.

1. Click on the Home tab of the APEX environment, and then click on the down arrow in the Application Builder icon to select Create Application. This action will bring up the page shown in Figure 2-11.

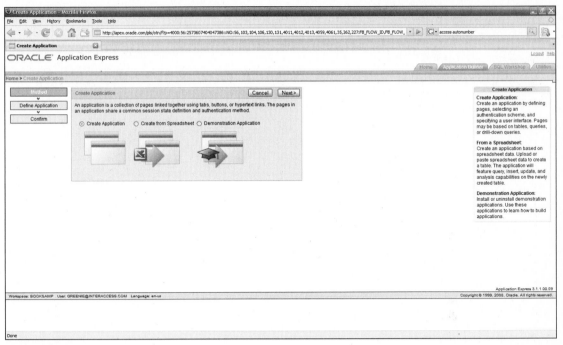

Figure 2-11

On this page, you select whether you will be creating an application from scratch, creating it from a spreadsheet, or installing one of the demonstration applications. Creating an application from a spreadsheet essentially combines the steps you took in the previous section with the steps in this section. In addition, you have the ability to define a few standard reports. In the interests of combining the rapid creation of an application with the process of learning how to use APEX, this chapter has taken the slightly longer route.

2.   Select the Create Application option, and click Next to bring up the page shown in Figure 2-12.

The main requirement of this page in the Application Creation Wizard is to give a name to your new application. You also can see that the application is assigned a number. An APEX application is created with code stored in the underlying Oracle database. Each application is identified by a unique number. The number assigned by default on this page is unique, but it is also somewhat meaningless. You could give your application a more meaningful integer to identify it, but that integer would have to be unique within your Oracle database.

For the purposes of this book, you should just accept the assigned number.

You can give the application any name you like, but the examples in this book will refer to this application by the name of Book Sample.

You can also see that you can create application design templates, which can be used to create default applications that use a structure you have designed.

3.   Give the application a name and click Next to bring up the page shown in Figure 2-13.

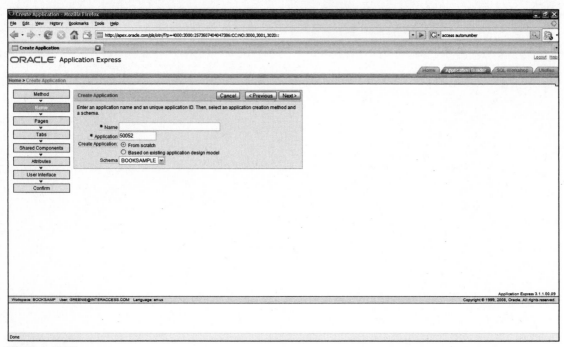

Figure 2-12

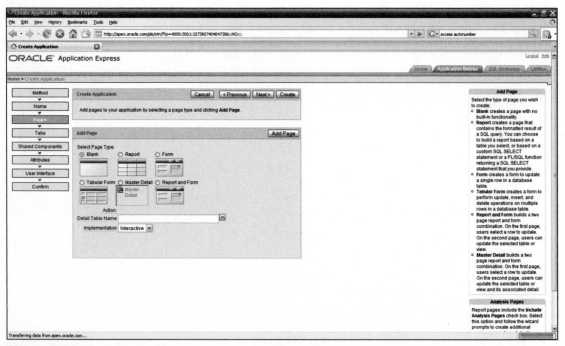

Figure 2-13

You can accomplish a lot on this page. You can specify any number of pages that will be part of your application with just a few clicks. Since you only have one table available right now, you will only create one set of pages but with a more fully populated database, you could create fairly sophisticated application systems with the point-and-click methods of this page.

4. Select the Report and Form option in the Add Page box.

5. Select the ORDERS table as the Table Name, and click Add Page. The result is shown in Figure 2-14, with two pages, the report and the edit form, added to the page list above.

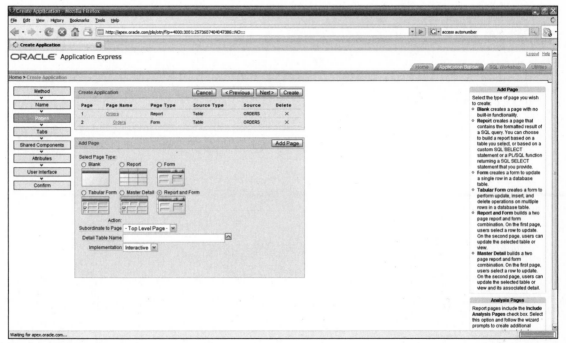

Figure 2-14

6. Click Create.

That's it! You will be presented with the Summary page shown in Figure 2-15, listing the defaults applied to your application. These defaults include specifying one level of tabs, a standard method of authenticating users, and a standard template. You can change any of these, or you could have selected them during the application creation process by clicking Next on the Create Application page shown in Figure 2-14. You can also access the edit pages for these choices by using the Previous button on the page.

7. Click Previous, which will bring up the page shown in Figure 2-16.

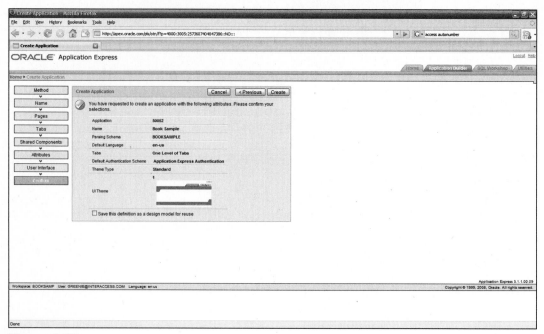

Figure 2-15

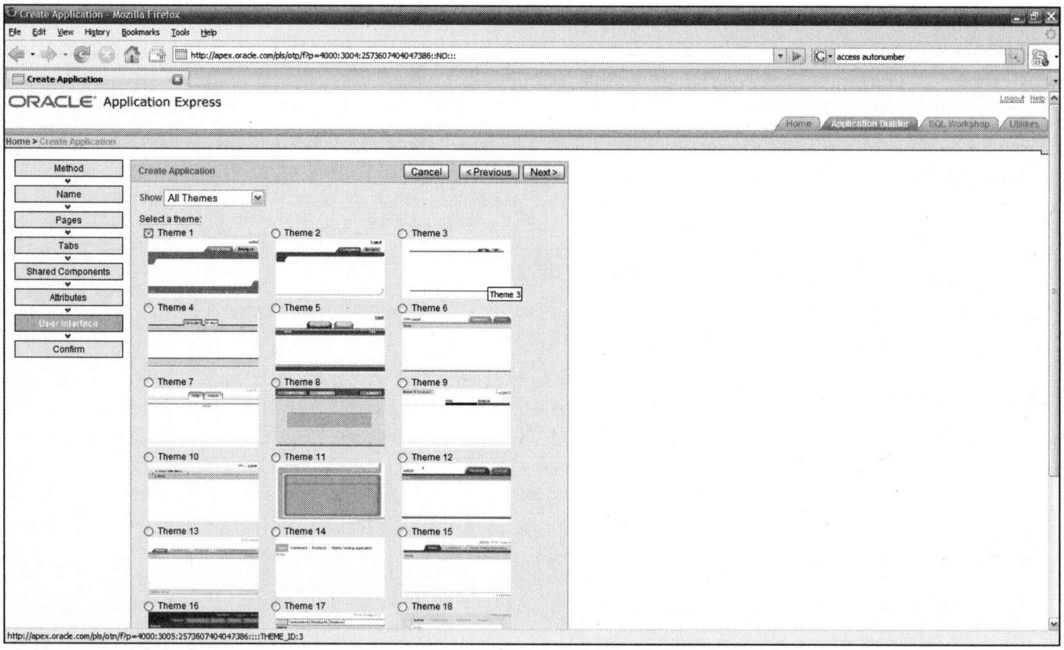

Figure 2-16

This page gives you the option of changing the template for the application, which provides the basic look and feel for the end user. The examples in this book will use Theme 13. Later in this book, you will learn more about templates and how to use them.

8. Select Theme 13 and click Next.

9. Click Create, which will create the application and take you to the development home page for the application, as shown in Figure 2-17.

Figure 2-17

That was pretty easy, and, as you will see in the next section, the application you created has a significant amount of built-in functionality. Oracle APEX provides you with both wizards (to speed the development process) and loads of automatic functionality (to reduce the amount of development you will have to do yourself).

How It Works

The ease of application creation is nice, but the default functionality provided in that application is even nicer.

To run your new application, you can click on the traffic light icon, either in the big button at the top of the page or as the little icon, just under the main tabs, to the right of the Page 1 label.

1. Click on the traffic light icon to run the application, which will bring up the page shown in Figure 2-18.

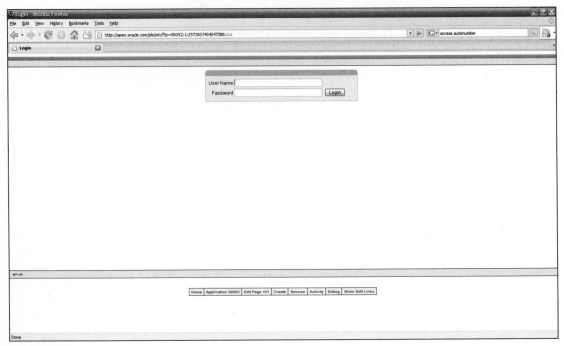

Figure 2-18

If you are coming from the world of single-user databases and applications, you might be a bit surprised to see a login page for a simple application like the one you just created. But APEX is designed from the ground up to support multiple users. The designers of APEX know that multi-user applications require security, so APEX applications leverage the built-in security of the Oracle database for all applications.

You could create an application for public use that did not require any login to access.

The page shown in Figure 2-18 also has a number of links at the bottom of the page in what is called the Developer's Toolbar. As its name implies, these links are only visible to developers, not to end users running the application. These links make it easy for you to quickly move between the runtime environment of the application and the development view of the application, and to gather information about the runtime environment. As a developer, you will be using these links frequently throughout the cycle of development, and you will learn more about them over the coming sections and chapters.

2. Enter the name and the case-sensitive password you use as a developer, and click Login to bring up the page shown in Figure 2-19.

The page you see has everything you would expect and quite a bit more. The page includes the look and feel from the template you chose in the previous exercise, and a tab with the name of the table displayed by the page. The data in the ORDERS table is shown in a list, with an icon on the left side of the row that will take you to an edit page for that row.

Figure 2-19

The page also includes built-in search capabilities, with a text box for entry of a search string. This search box does a little bit more than your everyday average search function.

3. Enter `la` into the search box, and click Go to bring up the page shown in Figure 2-20.

Now, you can see that the search function limited the display to those records that had the character "`la`" somewhere in their columns. You could have limited the number of rows returned with the selection list to the right of the search term field. But notice that the search term now appears below the search header, along with an icon to indicate that the search term limits the rows, a check box to indicate whether the search term is used, and an icon to delete the search term. There is a lot of power in this little display, which you can see by adding another search condition.

4. Enter `b` into the search box, and click Go to bring up the page shown in Figure 2-21.

You can now see that both search conditions are listed and have been applied to limit the results. You can simply uncheck the check box next to either condition to remove that criterion from the search. You could even collapse the search conditions by clicking on the little minus sign to the left of the conditions. Although these types of multiple search conditions are not that impressive with a single table with a handful of rows, you can imagine how useful this could be in a production environment.

Figure 2-20

Figure 2-21

But there's even more here.

5.   Click on the column heading labeled Order Timestamp to bring up the popup shown in Figure 2-22.

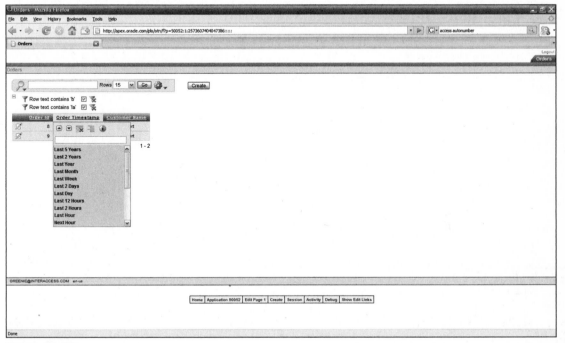

Figure 2-22

The popup you see brings a lot more functionality into every interactive report. The icons at the top of the popup allow you to sort based on this column, by either ascending or descending values. You can hide the column, create a control break on the column, or get information about the specification for the column. You can even select a search condition based on actual data values. Since APEX knows that the column is a date field, you are presented with the choices based on the age of the value.

6.   Click on the value Last Year in the popup.

Notice that the condition you just specified with a single click now appears as one of the search conditions at the top of the page. All this functionality is automatically built into all APEX interactive reports.

You will be learning much more about reports in Chapter 5.

7.   Click on the Edit icon on the left-hand side of a row to bring up the page shown in Figure 2-23.

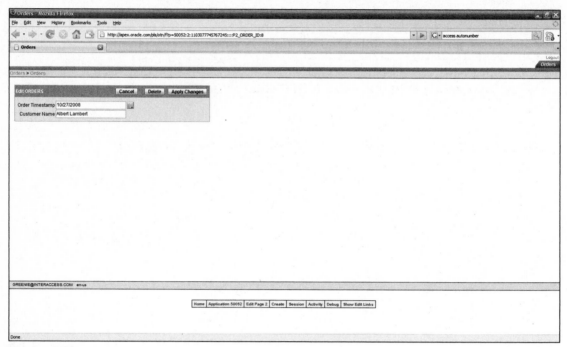

Figure 2-23

The edit page for the row presents you with all the editable columns for the row. The same page would appear if you clicked Create on the previous page but without values for any of the fields.

You might be thinking that there could be a more user-friendly way of editing some of these values, such as picklists or lookups. Don't worry, you will be learning how do modify this default edit page in the next chapter.

You have the option of canceling or applying changes you make to the row in this page, or deleting the selected record.

8. Click Cancel to return to the previous page.

9. Return to the development environment by clicking on the Home link at the bottom of the page.

Expanding Your Application

The basic "work" of creating an application framework and the first few pages is done. Now you can add more data and pages to the application. For the purposes of learning about APEX development while building this sample application, your next task will be to add a table with data related to the ORDERS table.

Importing Order Items

The ORDERS table contains information that pertains to the overall order. The ORDER_ITEMS table contains details about individual products ordered. It makes sense that the ORDER_ITEMS table would somehow be connected with the ORDERS table. In this section, you will import data for order lines, establish the connection to the ORDERS table, and see how APEX automatically incorporates that relationship into the default pages you can use to access both the master and detail tables.

Try It Out   Importing and Linking Another Table

The order entry application that is the focus of this book requires more than one table. Now that you have imported the ORDERS table, performing the same operation for the ORDER_ITEMS table is simple. But once you create the table through the import process, you can then link the data in that table to related rows in the ORDERS table

1. Go to the Utilities page, and then to the Load page under the Data Load/Unload icon.

2. Select the Load Spreadsheet Data icon.

3. Change the Load From: choice to Upload File, and click Next.

4. Select the ORDER_ITEMS.csv as the source, and click Next.

5. Give the new table the name of ORDER_ITEMS, accept all the defaults, and click Next.

6. Accept the default of New Primary Key column for the Primary Key From: option, but change the name of the primary key to ORDER_ITEMS_ID, then click Load Data.

Once again, the ORDER_ITEMS table will require a primary key, like all tables in an Oracle database. But you will have to add another constraint to this table to establish the relationship between ORDER_ITEMS and the ORDERS table.

7. Return to the SQL Workshop page.

8. Select the Browse and Tables choices under the Object Browser icon.

9. Select the just imported table ORDER_ITEMS, and select Constraints from the choices at the top of the right-hand panel.

10. Select the Create option, to bring up the page shown in Figure 2-24.

This page allows you to create any of the Oracle supported constraints. Oracle APEX has already created primary key constraints for the ORDERS and ORDER_ITEMS tables as part of the import process. You will now create a *foreign key* constraint.

A foreign key constraint links two tables in a parent-child relationship. The foreign key column is in the child, and the connection links to the primary key of the parent. As you will see in a few steps, the APEX environment is aware of foreign key constraints and implements default options to handle them.

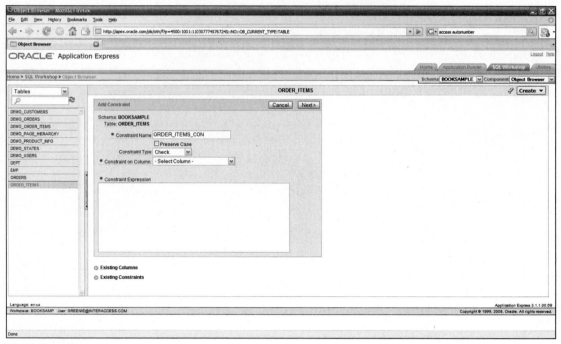

Figure 2-24

11. Change the `Constraint Type` to `Foreign Key`, which will change the appearance of the page to look like the completed page shown in Figure 2-25.

The `Constraint Type` specifies the action taken on the child data if the parent row is deleted. You can prevent deletes of parents that have children, automatically delete the children of a parent if the parent is deleted, or simply set the value of the foreign key to `NULL` if the parent is deleted. For the purposes of this demonstration application, you should choose the most common implementation of the constraint, but in the real world, this decision would be based on the business process the data is supporting.

12. Choose `Cascade Delete` for the `Constraint Type`, which would cause the related rows in the `ORDER_ITEMS` table to be deleted when their associated `ORDERS` row is deleted.

13. Select `ORDER_ID` for the `Foreign Key Column(s)`.

14. Select `ORDERS` for the `Reference Table Name` and `ORDER_ID` from the `Reference Table Column List`.

15. Click Next and then Finish on the next page.

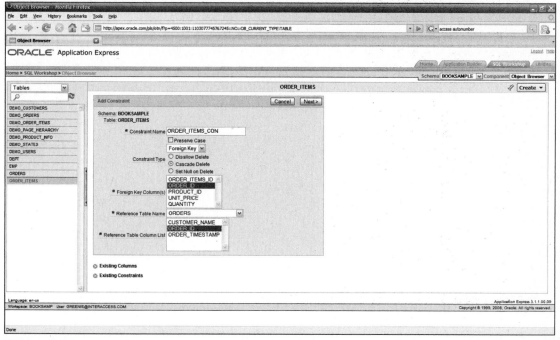

Figure 2-25

You have created a foreign key constraint. The constraint will work in this case because the value stored in the ORDER_ITEMS table matches the value in the primary key of the ORDERS table. The foreign key constraint is implemented within the Oracle database, so you can see it in the Object Browser. But the real payoff comes when you create a page for the ORDER_ITEMS table, and you can see how APEX handles the defined relationship.

Creating Another Page

It won't take long to generate another page in your APEX application to handle interactions with both the ORDERS and the ORDER_ITEMS tables.

Try It Out	Creating Pages for Master-Detail Tables

1. Return to the Application Builder page, and double-click on the Book Sample application you just created, which will bring up the page you saw before, as shown in Figure 2-26.

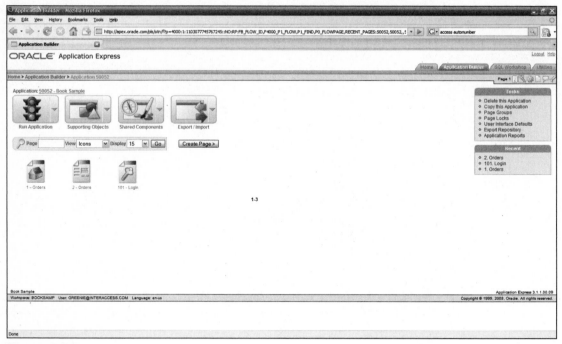

Figure 2-26

At the top of this page, you can see four icons used to run your application and deal with administrative tasks connected with the application. You will learn more about the three icons for Supporting Objects, Shared Components, and Export/Import later in the book.

You can also see the pages that were automatically generated for you when you created the application. You could double-click on any of these pages to modify its appearance or functionality, which you will be doing in the next chapter. Right now, you want to create a new page for the application.

> **2.** Click Create Page to bring up the page shown in Figure 2-27, which is where you will begin the process of creating a new set of pages to handle the ORDERS and ORDER_ITEMS tables together.

> **3.** The page shown in Figure 2-27 gives you a number of choices for the type of pages you want to create. Select the Form choice and click Next.

> **4.** The next page gives you a number of choices for the type of form you want to create. Select Master Detail Form and click Next, or simply click on the Master Detail icon.

You will have to go through a few steps to completely define the functionality implemented in the master-detail forms. Although each step is quite easy, the left-hand panel displays a list of the steps, and where you are in the process, to keep you informed of your progress.

> **5.** The next page, shown completed in Figure 2-28, collects information about the master table. Select the ORDERS table from the selection list.

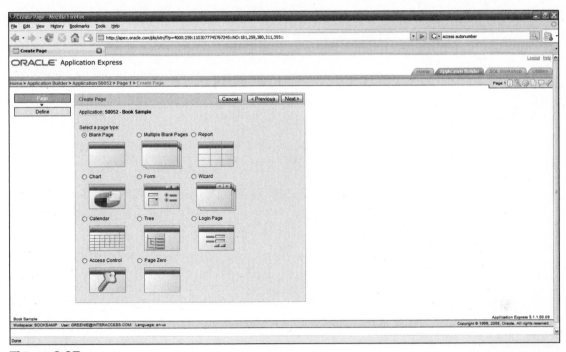

Figure 2-27

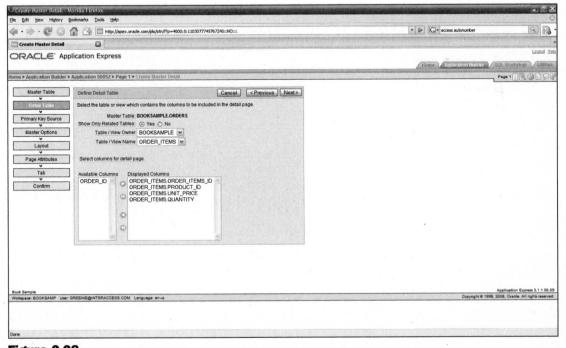

Figure 2-28

6. Select all the columns in the Available Columns list, and click on the right arrow button to move them to the Displayed Columns list. Click Next.

7. The next page asks you for the same information about the detail table. Select the ORDER_ITEMS table in the selection list and move all the columns to the Available Columns list. Click Next.

The next two pages will confirm the source of the primary key value for each of the tables. Both tables use a sequence to produce the primary key.

8. On the next page, shown in Figure 2-29, select Existing Sequence and the ORDERS_SEQ sequence from the selection list that appears. Click Next.

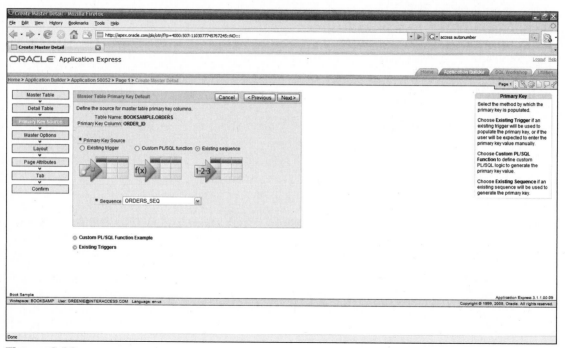

Figure 2-29

9. On the next page, make the same choice, except select the ORDER_ITEMS_SEQ sequence from the selection list. Click Next.

10. The next page, shown in completed form in Figure 2-30, allows you to specify how you want the user to navigate through the rows of the master table. For this example, you want to have a report on the rows of the master table, so leave the choice for Include master row navigation? set to the default of Yes. Select ORDER_ID as the Master Row Navigation Order to allow navigation by ORDER_ID, and click Next.

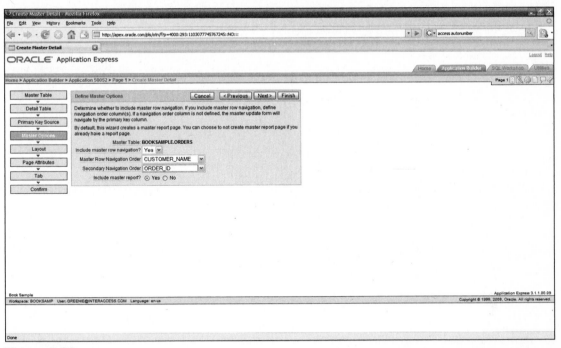

Figure 2-30

11. The next page gives you the option of editing detail records in a multi-row table on the same page as the master record, or on a separate page. You should change the value to Edit detail on a separate page, since this is the most common choice for web-based applications. Click Next.

12. The following page, shown complete in Figure 2-31, gives you the option to change the default text associated with the pages APEX will create. The upper panel lets you set the title for the pages and regions within the pages. Set the Page Title and Region Title for the Master form to Orders, the Detail page title to Order Items, and the region titles to Edit Order Items and Order Items Detail; set the Page Title for Detail 2 to Order Items and the region title for that page to Edit Order Items.

Your APEX application can use breadcrumbs, a series of links in the top left hand corner of the page representing the hierarchical path to this page, to provide easy navigation through pages. You can see breadcrumbs at work in the APEX development environment, because the APEX development environment is written in APEX itself.

13. Set the Entry Name to Orders, and click Next.

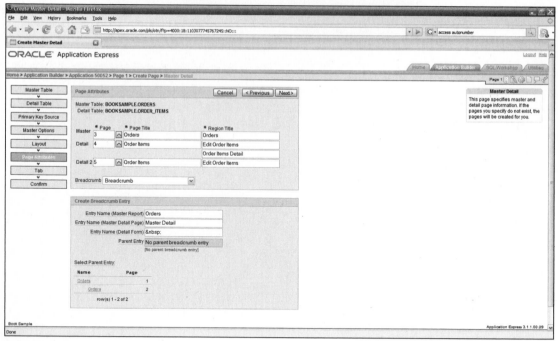

Figure 2-31

The last page of attributes for the master-detail pages asks how you want to use tabs to navigate to the page. Since these pages involve the ORDERS table, you will want to select that tab for the pages.

14. Select the third option to use an existing tab set and tab, and click Next.

15. On the next page, select the T_ORDERS tab, the only one available, and click Next.

16. The final page confirms the choices you have made and allows you to confirm the creation of the pages. Click Create to take this action.

When you have completed the process, you will see a success page with two icons. In the next section, you can see the functionality you have implemented with this small set of clicks.

How It Works

The pages you have just created do more than the simple report and edit pages for the ORDERS table.

Click on the Run Page icon. If you have logged out of your browser session since the last time you ran the application, you will be prompted to log in to the application again. The initial page, shown in Figure 2-32, with the report for the ORDERS table, is not that impressive. In fact, it's just a simple report, not even as cool as the interactive report you created last time. But the cool stuff begins once you go to edit an order.

Does the interactive report on the ORDERS table seem nicer than the simple report that is part of the master-detail pages? Later in the book, you will learn how to substitute the interactive report for this report.

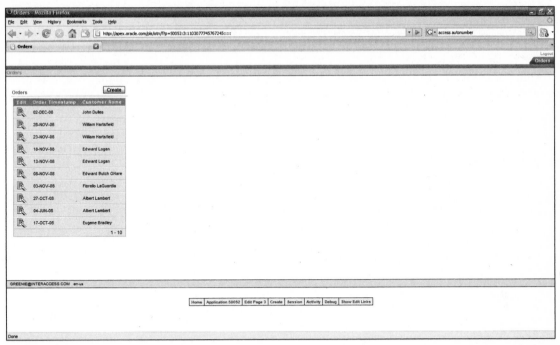

Figure 2-32

1. Click on the Edit icon for the first order, which will bring up the page shown in Figure 2-33.

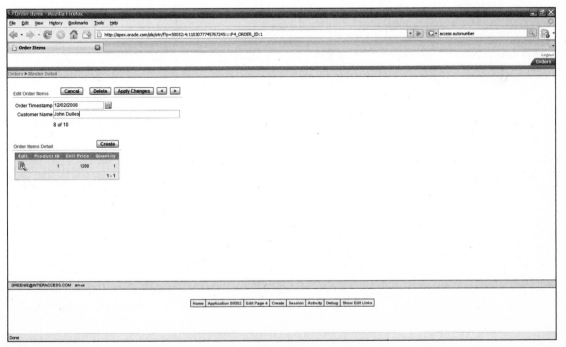

Figure 2-33

You can see a lot more in the way of buttons and other elements on this page. At the top of the page are buttons that give users the ability to delete records, save changes, and scroll through the master records. You can also see that the date field of Order Timestamp has a little calendar icon next to it, which will bring up a date picker.

Below the fields for the ORDERS table is an area where you can display one or more records of order items associated with this order. There is a button that allows you to create a new row. You can display multiple detail rows or add rows until you fill up the space allotted for the detail table.

2. Click on the Create pushbutton to bring up the page shown in its completed state in Figure 2-34. Set the Product Id to 3, the Unit Price to 40, and the Quantity to 3. Click on Create to add the new record and return to the page for the main Order.

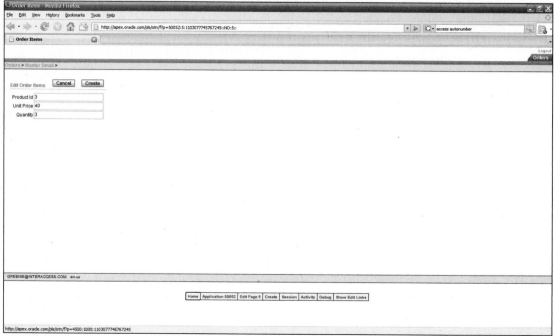

Figure 2-34

You can use these master-detail pages to edit values for either of the tables, or to delete rows from the ORDER_ITEMS table by going to the edit page for the existing record and deleting the row with the Delete button, which will be present.

Rounding Out Your Data Set

Before moving on and modifying your basic application in the next chapter, you still have to load one final table to complete the initial loading of your data set. Before jumping into this task, you should consider the implications of the foreign key you created in the previous section.

For that foreign key constraint, the value in the ORDER_ID column for the ORDER_ITEMS pointed to the value in the primary key of the ORDERS table, ORDER_ID. But you might remember that this column was created automatically when you loaded the table from the spreadsheet. Why did the values in the ORDER_ITEMS column match the appropriate values in the ORDERS table?

Well, this data is sample data, specifically designed for demonstrations like the ones in the book. The values for the ORDER_ID in the ORDERS table were nicely created to be sequential from 1 to 11, and the values in the corresponding column in the ORDER_ITEMS table matched that simple scheme. In the real world, however, you probably won't be so lucky. In fact, a common task might involve breaking one spreadsheet up into more than one table, and loading the same column value into both tables involved in the foreign key restraint.

On one hand, this scenario is easy to deal with. When importing the table, you simply say that the value for the primary key is in an existing column. The issue arises with the use of a sequence to assign further values automatically. By default, the sequence defined as part of the loading process starts numbering from 1. This default choice means that you will eventually run into a primary key conflict, when the sequence tries to assign a value that already exists as a primary key, which must be unique.

There is an easy way to avoid this issue — create a sequence before loading the table, and ensure that the starting number for the sequence is greater than the maximum number currently existing in the primary key column of the table you are going to create.

You will take this minor detour as you load the table containing information about products.

Try It Out   Create a Sequence and Use It for a New Table

You will start out your new task in the now familiar Object Browser within the SQL Workshop.

1. Return to the APEX environment main page by clicking on the Home link at the bottom of the runtime page.

2. Using the dropdown menus from the SQL Workshop icon, select Object Browser, Create, and Sequence to bring up the page shown in Figure 2-35 with the values you will enter.

3. Give the sequence the name of PRODUCTS_SEQ, a starting value of 12, a minimum value of 12 and a maximum value of 99999. Click Next and then Create.

You don't actually have to assign a minimum and maximum value to the sequence. If no values are present, the defaults are 1 for minimum and a string of 9s for the maximum.

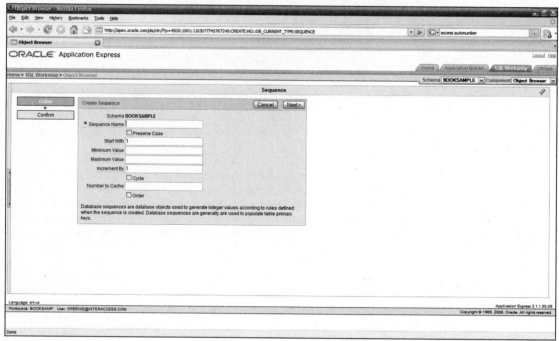

Figure 2-35

Now that you have a sequence created, you can use it when you are loading your new table.

1. Click on the Utilities tab and use the drop down menu to select the Load choice from the Data Load/Unload menu.

2. As you did before, select the Load Spreadsheet Data icon.

3. Select the Upload file choice, and click Next.

4. On the next page, select the PRODUCTS.csv file with the browser, and click Next.

5. On the next page, give the table the name of PRODUCTS. Note that the first field listed in the display is the PRODUCT_ID field, which contains the current value for the primary key for the product row.

6. Click Next.

7. On the next page, you want to change two default choices. First, change the Primary Key From: choice to Use an existing column. Leave the Primary Key selection list on the PRODUCT_ID column, which is the default.

8. For Primary Key Population –– Choice, select Generated from an existing sequence, and then select the PRODUCTS_SEQ you just created from the Sequence selection list.

9. Click Load Data to complete this operation.

The next step is to create a foreign key constraint linking the PRODUCTS table to the ORDER_ITEMS table.

1. Go to the SQL Workshop by clicking on the appropriate tab.

2. Use the dropdown menus to browse a table.

3. Select the ORDER_ITEMS table, since this table will be referencing the PRODUCTS table to get more information about the products entered as part of the order line.

4. Click on the Constraints label over the table, and then click Create to start the process.

5. Change the name of the constraint to ORDER_ITEMS_PRODUCT_CON, since you already have a constraint with the default choice offered.

How can you tell you have a duplicate constraint name? You may have noticed that many of the pages in the development environment have shortcuts at the bottom of the page — in this case, Existing Columns and Existing Constraints. You can simply click on one of these labels to display a list of the related values.

6. Select Foreign Key from the top selection list, Cascade Delete from the Constraint Type, PRODUCT_ID as the Foreign Key Column(s), PRODUCTS as the Reference Table Name and PRODUCT_ID from the Reference Table Column List, to end up with the values shown in Figure 2-36.

7. Click Next and then Finish to create the new constraint.

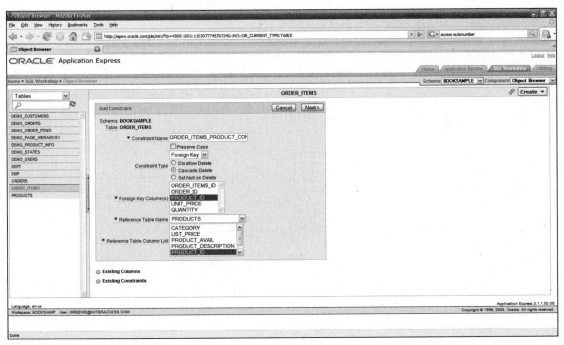

Figure 2-36

You have done everything you need to do to create a relationship between the ORDER_ITEMS table and the PRODUCTS table, although you will not be linking them together until you learn a bit more in the next chapter.

The last step is to create a page for the PRODUCTS table, for which you will use a different wizard to create another set of pages.

1. Return to the main development page by clicking on the Application Builder tab.

2. Double-click on the Book Sample application to add more pages to the application.

3. Click Create Page.

4. On the following page, select the Form option and click Next.

5. Select Form on a Table with Report, and click Next.

6. Accept the default schema of BOOKSAMPLE (or whatever you named your schema), and click Next.

7. On the next page, select the PRODUCTS table from the selection list and click Next.

8. You can accept the defaults on the following page, although you might want to change the Page Name and Region Title to a more user-friendly version with initial caps instead of all caps. Click Next.

The next page allows you to specify how this report and form will use tabs. This application already has a default tab set, with a tab for Orders, which was used for both previous sets of pages. You will want to use the same tab set but create a different tab within the set.

9. Change the Tab Options: choice to Use an existing tab set and create a new tab within the existing tab set. Accept the default Tab Set, and enter Products as the name of the new tab. Click Next.

10. The next page shows you the columns available for the report. Select all the columns except the PRODUCT_ID column, which is only used internally by the application.

11. Click Next.

12. Accept the default icon edit choice, and click Next.

13. Change the Page Name and Region Title to Products, and click Next.

14. Accept the default primary key on the next page, and click Next.

15. On the next page, select Existing sequence, and PRODUCTS_SEQ from the Sequence selection list. Click Next.

16. Select all the columns to include in the form, and click Next.

17. Accept the defaults to display the Insert, Update, and Delete buttons, and click Next.

18. The final page summarizes the choices you have made. Click Finish to create the pages.

19. You can play around with the Products page, as shown in Figure 2-37, by clicking on the Run Application icon.

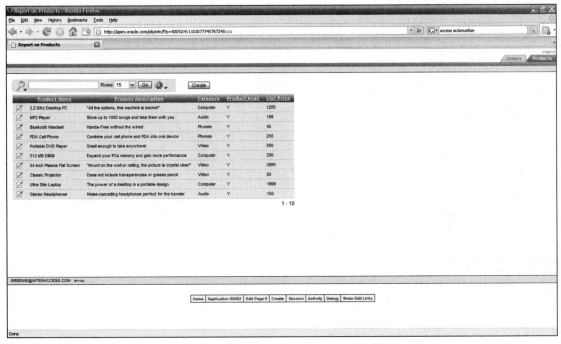

Figure 2-37

Summary

In this first hands-on chapter, you have come a long way. You have:

❑ Created the core tables for the application, ORDERS, ORDER_ITEMS and PRODUCTS and filled them with data.

❑ Created the application and added a few pages to allow your users to interact with this core data.

❑ Started to learn your way around the APEX development environment.

Keep in mind that this chapter has been designed to teach you how to use APEX, rather than focusing on creating applications in the most productive way. You could have created all the pages for this application when you created the application, a process that would have taken you less than five minutes to get where you are now in terms of application development.

In the next chapter, you will learn more about the capabilities of Oracle Application Express and add more functionality to your existing application.

Extending Your
APEX Application

In the last chapter, you quickly created the beginnings of a complete application. The Oracle Application Express wizards gave you the ability to make APEX pages with a fairly broad range of basic functionality, which is required by pretty much every application. But any particular application will require some additional customization and functionality, which you will add, in part, in this chapter.

In this chapter, you will extend your application by adding some formatting to some of the fields on your pages. More importantly, you will learn about some of the features of the APEX environment that allow you to protect the integrity of your data, guiding your users to avoid entering information that just doesn't make sense in the context of the application.

Along the way, you will learn more about the APEX development environment and some of the features you can use to improve your basic application.

APEX Page Attributes

In the previous chapter, you created pages with the help of wizards built into the APEX development environment. The wizards walked you through the process of specifying values for a variety of parameters. Once you assigned these values, Oracle Application Express used them to generate code which presents and processes your pages.

The code itself is generated with PL/SQL, the Oracle procedural extension language for SQL. You will see, in this and later chapters, that you can add your own PL/SQL code to an APEX page to extend the standard logic, but you need not concern yourself with the actual code that is generated. The APEX environment allows you access to the same parameters you entered through the wizard, and many, many more, which you can use to shape your own applications.

The focus of this book is to get you productively using APEX to create your own applications, rather than giving you a comprehensive description of every possible way you can use every feature within the environment. But you will still have to become familiar with the way you can access those features in the APEX development environment.

Accessing APEX Page Attributes

You have already seen a bit of the APEX development environment. Now it's time to drill down into the capabilities of an actual APEX page.

1. Go to the main APEX development page, and click on the Application Builder tab or icon. You will see the page shown in Figure 3-1.

Figure 3-1

On this page, you will immediately see the application you created in the previous chapter, represented by an icon in the main part of the page. Just above that icon, you can see a search bar, which you could use to find one application among many in your APEX workspace. You can also directly import or create applications with the buttons to the right of the search bar.

You can also see a couple of boxes of links on the right. The upper box has links for tasks that you would commonly want to perform when on this page. Just below that is another link box with the most recently accessed applications. These two boxes, with different entries, are common features across the APEX development environment — they can help you be more productive by putting your most frequently used destinations a single click away.

2. Double-click on the application you just created, which will bring up the page shown in Figure 3-2.

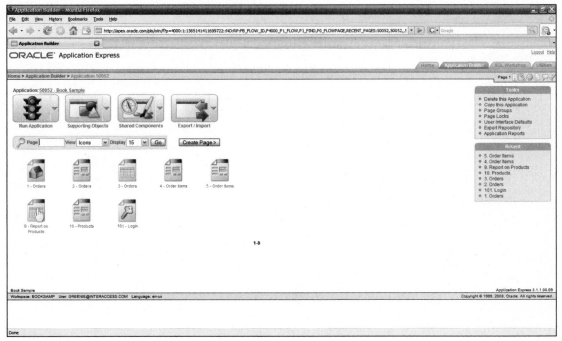

Figure 3-2

This Application Builder page shows the pages you have created for your application. The large icons at the top of the page let you quickly run the application as well as export and import application definitions. You can also see icons for supporting objects and shared components. Both of these types of entities are used across the whole application, so they are not listed on the Application Builder page for your specific application. You will be creating some shared components later in this chapter and learning about supporting objects later in this book.

This main development page for your application also includes a search box and a button to create additional pages.

The next level of detail for your application is to look at a page definition for one of the pages you have created.

3. Double-click on the first of two pages labeled Order Items. If you have followed the instructions in the previous chapter, the page should be number 4. This action will bring up the page shown in Figure 3-3.

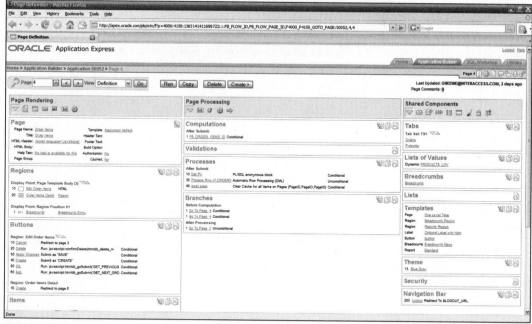

Figure 3-3

Whoa! Now this looks a little intimidating at first. You should not be too overwhelmed by all the choices on this page; instead, you should understand that these choices give you an enormous amount of flexibility in creating your APEX pages. And once you understand the basic sections of the page, you will be able to easily move around the choices to quickly perform your modifications.

At the top of the definition page is the now familiar search box, and some buttons that allow you to run, copy, or delete the page, or to create another page. You should also note the set of breadcrumbs at the top of the page, which chart the path you took to get here, from the home page to the Application Builder page to the specific application to this particular page. Each of these breadcrumbs also acts as a link to give you quick navigation back to any page in the trail. Breadcrumbs, by default, are also included in all your APEX pages for the same purpose.

The main portion of the page is divided up into three columns:

❑ **Page rendering:** Controls the objects that appear on a page and how they are displayed.

❑ **Page processing:** Describes processes that are run in response to different user actions on the page .

❑ **Shared components:** Lists the shared components used on the page.

Be aware that each column has a set of icons in the heading of the column. There is an icon for each section in the column, and clicking on any of these icons will hide all the other sections in the column, to allow you to focus on one particular section. Also, all of the attributes listed on this page are actually links that take you to development pages where you can change the attributes of a particular element of the page.

In this section, you will be learning a bit about the sections in the `Page Rendering` column. These sections are:

❑ **Page:** You can shape the overall appearance of the page, including the general text associated with the page, such as the page title.

❑ **Regions:** Lists the basic areas of the page. For this master-detail page, you can see there are two main regions defined — the Edit Orders region, for fields relating to the ORDERS master table, and the Order Items region, which has a report that lists the ORDER_ITEMS detail records for the master. You will be drilling down into this report later in this section. There is also a region used to display the breadcrumbs for this page.

❑ **Buttons:** Lists all the buttons for all the regions in the page. Buttons are used to call actions, and you can see a brief description of the actions for each button to the right of the button.

❑ **Items:** Lists the actual fields on the page. These items were generated based on the columns you specified for inclusion on the page.

There are a couple of things to notice about this section. First of all, you can see that the name of each of the items is prefixed with the letter P and the number of the page, followed by the name of the column that the item is bound to. You can also see that there are two arrows at the top of the list of items for the region that let you quickly change the order of the columns. The icon to the right of the arrows calls up a page, shown in Figure 3-4, where you can drag and drop the items, or even create new items for the page.

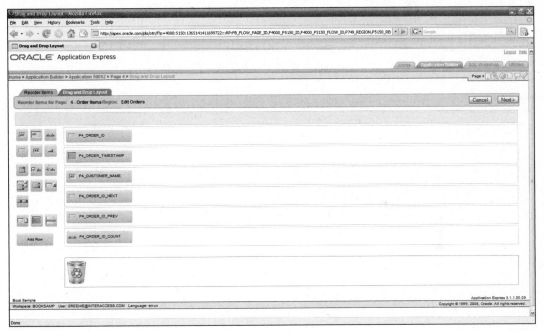

Figure 3-4

❑ **Computations:** Used to set the value of items on this page, another page, or at the application level.

❑ **Processes:** Runs in response to page level actions.

The Page Processing section includes computations and processes that are associated with the overall page, rather than specific regions.

These computations and processes fire in response to a user's submission of the page, as opposed to the same sections in the left-hand column, which fire when a page is loaded.

In addition, this column contains sections for validations, which are enforced when page-level actions occur, and branching, which controls conditional navigation. You will implement some validations later in this chapter and some branching in the next chapter when you learn about navigation.

You will learn about the sections and listings in the Shared Components column in a later chapter. For now, you will drill down into the report region of this page to see how report attributes are presented, and to change the appearance of a column in the report.

Formatting Data Fields

You are now ready to change the appearance of one of the fields in the report.

Try It Out   **Changing the Format of a Field**

You can change the format of a field on the report for the ORDER_ITEMS table by drilling down to the attributes for the column of the report.

1.   In the Order Items region, click on the Report link to the right of the region name, which will bring up the page shown in Figure 3-5.

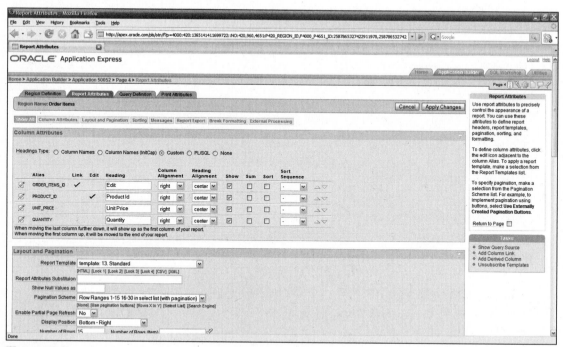

Figure 3-5

for the Order Items report once again has several sections. Since there is only one
...ge, there are buttons at the top of the page that allow you to show only one section at
...ay the icons did in the previous page.

...three tabs at the top of the page. For this section, you will only be working with one
...r the default middle tab, Report Attributes. You will be working with more sec-
...n the chapter that focuses on reporting.

...are labeled Print Attributes, which controls how the report will be printed, and
...which includes sections that affect the data retrieved for the report. You will be
...ection later in this chapter.

...t to do is to modify the formatting of one of the columns listed in the Column
... of this page.

...e Edit icon for the column named UNIT_PRICE, which will bring up the page shown
...6.

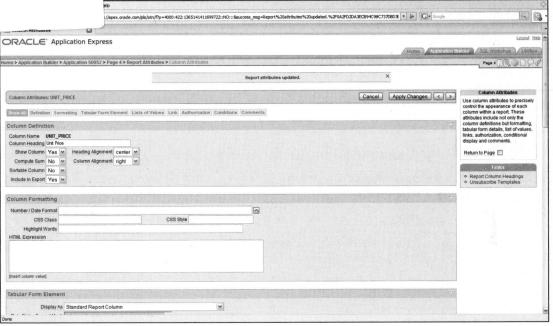

Figure 3-6

On this attribute page, the second section is labeled Column Formatting. This looks to be the right
section where you could change the formatting for the unit price. Sure enough, there is a field in this
section labeled Number/Date Formatting.

3. Click on the dropdown arrow for the Number/Date Formatting field.

The display list has examples of the type of formatting available for numbers and dates. The proper formatting for currency is the first choice, $5,432.10.

4. Click on the first formatting choice.

When you return to the Report Attributes page, you will see a cryptic listing for the format value. This is an internal value used by APEX to assign the formatting style you just chose to the number. The best way to see if your change had any effect is to run the page.

5. Click the Apply Changes button; you will receive a message informing you that the changes have been saved. Go to the breadcrumbs at the top of the page, and click on the breadcrumb for the current page.

Back on the main attribute page, notice that there is a series of icons in the upper-right corner, just below the tabs for the page. The first icon to the right of the Page 4 label looks like a traffic light and will immediately run the indicated page, just as the same icon did earlier.

6. Click on the traffic light to run the page.

This action will bring up the page directly, or, if you have closed your browser since you last accessed the application, it will bring up the login page to verify your identity before allowing you access to the page.

When the page comes up, you will notice that the page contains only the data fields for the upper part of the page for Orders, and it contains only Cancel and Create buttons. The reason the report for Order Items does not appear immediately is that the page was run without being passed a value to identify the Order. This scenario typifies exactly what happens when a user clicks the Create button on the previous report page.

7. Click Cancel to return to the report page for Order Items.

8. Click on the Edit icon for the first item listed, which will bring up the page shown in Figure 3-7.

You can see that the formatting for the Unit Price column has indeed been properly changed. The effect is what you were looking for, but it seems like the route to get to this result was a little bit too long. After all, you only wanted to change the formatting for a field, and you had to drill down through multiple pages.

The developers of APEX agree with you and have provided a much quicker route to change basic attributes of fields on a page. To use this direct method, you will have to go to another page in your application.

9. Click on the link at the bottom of the page shown in Figure 3-7 for the application.

This action will bring you back to the main development page for the application.

10. Double-click on the Products page, which should be the page in the application just before the login page.

11. Click on the traffic light icon to run the page.

Once again, you will see the page as you would if you were inserting a new Product record.

12. Click on the link at the bottom of the page on the far right labeled Show Edit Links, which will change the appearance of the page to look like Figure 3-8.

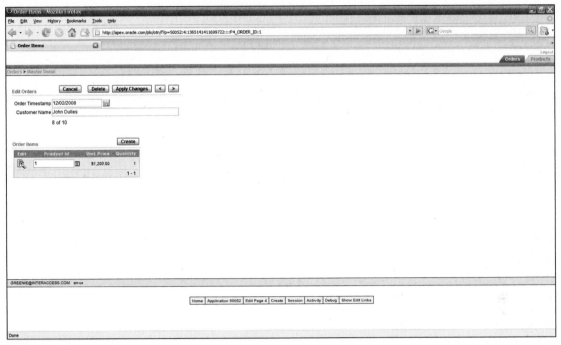

Figure 3-7

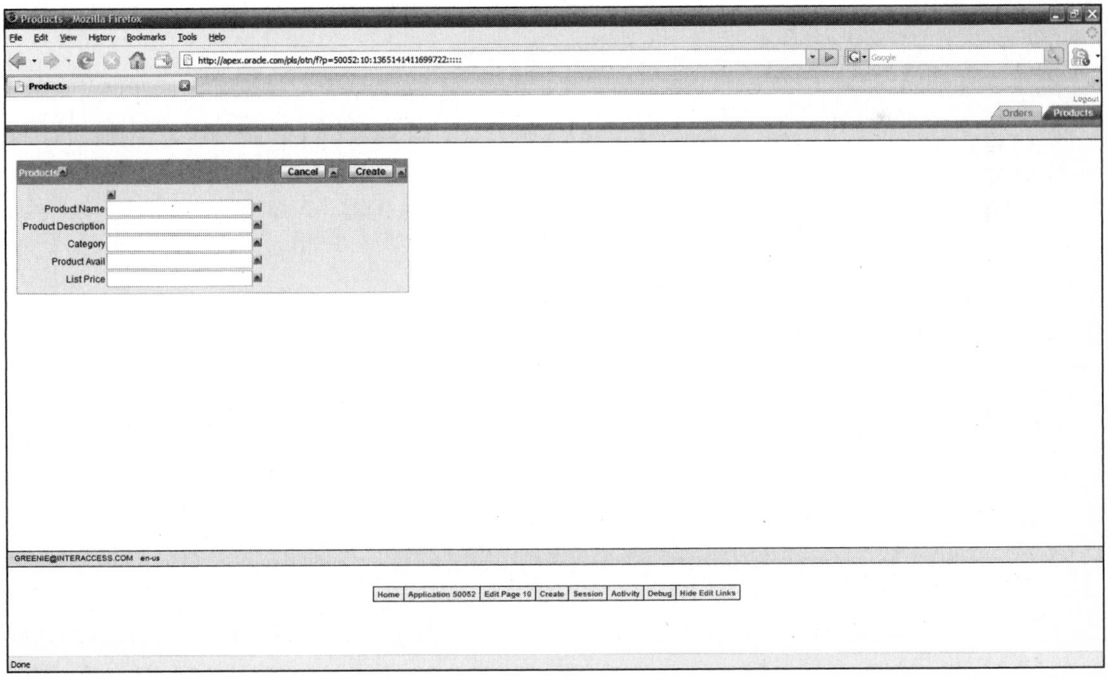

Figure 3-8

There is only one change in the page, but this change is very meaningful. You can see that there are little yellow arrow icons next to all the fields on the page. These icons, known as edit links, will bring up the attribute page for the particular item on the page.

13. Click on the edit link for the `List Price` item, which will bring up the page shown in Figure 3-9.

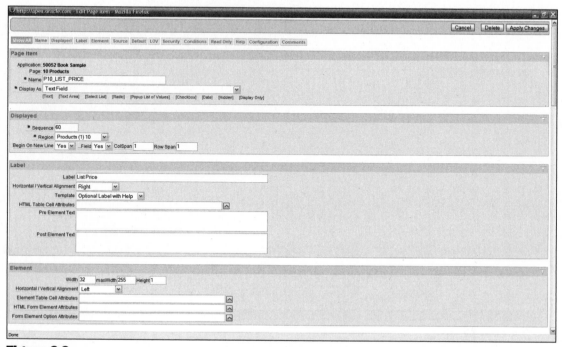

Figure 3-9

Yes, this is an attribute page that corresponds to the page you arrived at in the previous part of this section, except that this page has the attributes for an item on a page, rather than a column in a table. Because a page item has slightly different attributes than a report column, the formatting options are listed under the section labeled `Source`.

14. Click the Source button at the top of the page.

15. Click on the dropdown arrow for the `Format Mask` field, and select the currency format mask.

16. Click Apply Changes, and then close the window by clicking on the X in the upper-right corner.

You have now changed the formatting for this item, but you will have to return to the report and select a product before you can see the effects.

17. Click Cancel to return to the report on Products.

18. Click on the Edit icon next to the first product in the report to bring up the page shown in Figure 3-10.

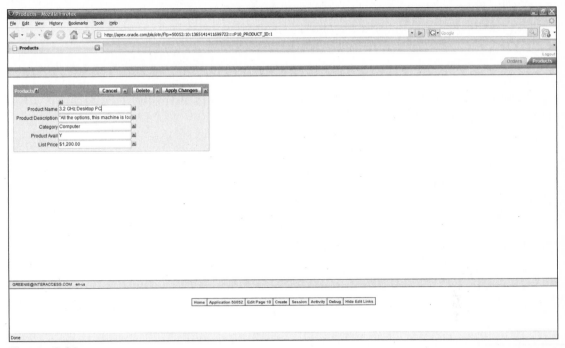

Figure 3-10

When you return to the page, you can see that the formatting has been properly changed.

How It Works

The APEX developers continually refine the APEX development environment to make it easier for you to do your work. You can use edit links to quickly access the attributes for items on a page — even when you are working with end users in a prototyping session. Once you turn edit links on, you will see edit links for all the pages you access from the development environment until you explicitly turn the edit links off. You will be using edit links throughout the rest of this book, where appropriate.

You may have noticed that you did not have edit links for individual columns in the report table. Edit links are not available for all objects in a page, so for things like columns in a table, you will still have to drill down in the development environment.

Changing formats for items was pretty straightforward. There are other items for which you might want to modify formats, which you can do at your leisure. For now, it is time to move on to another area of refinement for your application, adding default values.

Default Values

Your task is to create applications for your users, but those applications should also be easy to use for your clients. One of the ways you can help your users is to make it possible for them to skip data entry for any fields that will usually have the same value. You can specify a default value for these situations.

Try It Out   **Default Values**

A good candidate for a default value in the sample application is the ORDER_TIMESTAMP column, which would normally be the date the order is entered.

1. Return to the main development page for the application and select the master-detail page you created for ORDERS and ORDER_ITEMS, which would be the first page labeled Order Items, Page 4 if you are following along.

Rather than drill down to the detail page, you can use the Edit Link to go directly to the field from the runtime environment.

2. Run the page by clicking on the Run icon.

3. Click on the Edit Link for the Order Timestamp field, which is below the field.

4. Click the Default button to show the section of the page attributes related to default values, as shown in its completed form in Figure 3-11.

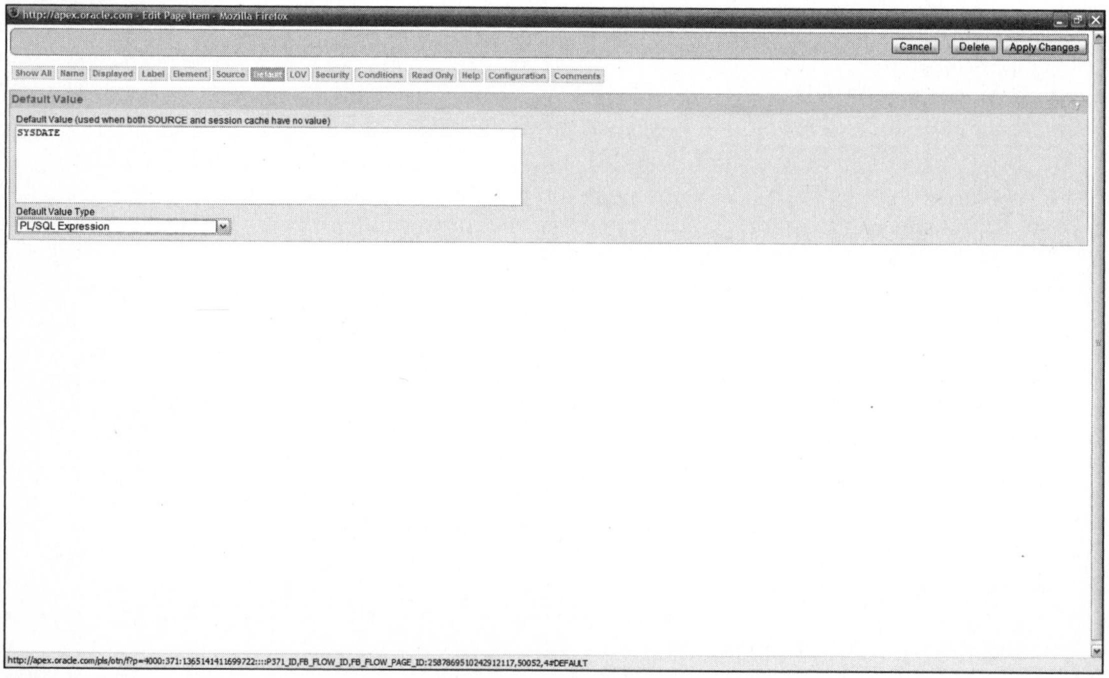

Figure 3-11

5. Enter SYSDATE in the Default Value text box, and change the Default Value Type to PL/SQL Expression.

SYSDATE is a function you can use with Oracle SQL or PL/SQL to return the current system date.

6. Click Apply Changes.

While you are making changes for this field, you might as well make the label for the field more meaningful.

7. Click the Show All button to bring up all the attribute sections. Change the Label in the Label section to Date of Order. Click Apply Changes.

8. Close the attributes window by clicking Cancel, returning to the application itself, and refresh the page. The new page should look like the page shown in Figure 3-12.

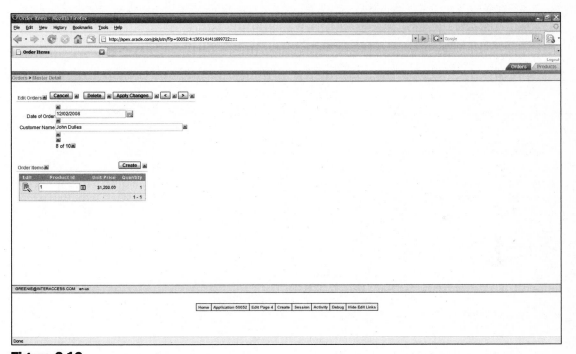

Figure 3-12

You have reduced the work your users have to do on this page, which also eliminates one source of potential data errors. The next section will cover more ways of ensuring that your users do not enter invalid data through your APEX application.

Ensuring Integrity

In the previous section, you added a default value to make data entry easy for your end users. Your users want ease of use, but your primary concern should be the accuracy of the data that is accessed by the application. You can add features to your application that not only make it easier to use but also ensure that the data entered has an appropriate value — that the data entered has complete data integrity. These features will be covered in this section.

Limiting Values

You have to start with the assumption that the users of your application want to do the right thing — they just may not know what that is. Thankfully, there are a number of standard user interface objects that make it possible to limit values, either to a set of known values or to a dynamic group of changing values.

The best place to start learning about these options is with a choice that is pretty simple — the column in the PRODUCTS table that specifies whether a product is in stock.

Radio Buttons

The PRODUCT_AVAIL field, in the PRODUCTS table, can logically accept one of two values — Y if the product is available or N if the product is not. Rather than expecting a user to know what values to use, your application would be both easier to use and more foolproof in terms of data integrity if you limited the user choices for data entry to those two values in a *list of values*. Lists of values underlie several different user interface choices, as you will see in this chapter.

The List of Values, commonly referred to in the APEX world as an *LOV*, is simply a logical representation of a two-column list, with the value displayed in an APEX page in the first column coupled with the value stored in the database table for that selection in the second.

Try It Out   **Creating a List of Values**

You can create an LOV in a couple of simple steps.

1. Return to the main attribute page for the application by clicking on Application Builder in the Developer Toolbar.

2. Double-click on the Products page with the form for the PRODUCTS table, which should be the last page before the login page.

3. Under the Items section in the Page Rendering column, select the P#_PRODUCT_AVAIL item link. (Substitute the number of the page in your application for the # symbol.) Change the Item Type from Text to Radiogroup by selecting the quick pick link labeled Radio under the Item Type field or by using the select list.

4. Click on the LOV button to isolate that section of the page, where the attributes of an LOV for the page will be displayed, as shown in Figure 3-13.

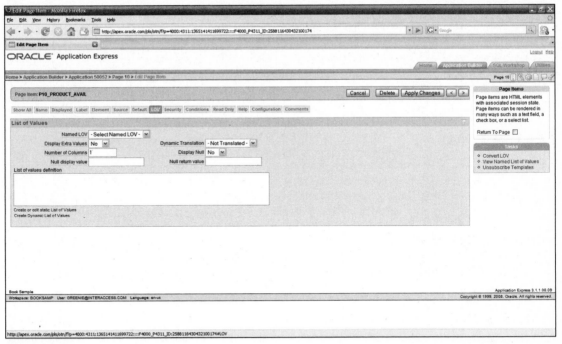

Figure 3-13

In this section, you can see a number of options which will shape the behavior of the LOV for this item. You could use an existing LOV, which could be selected in the Named LOV picklist, but since you have not defined any shared LOVs (yet!), you cannot use this option. Instead, you will want to create an LOV for this item.

5. Click on the link at the bottom of the section labeled `Create or edit static List of Values`, which will bring up the page shown, in its completed form, in Figure 3-14.

The definition page for a static list of values is pretty basic. For each value, you define a displayed value and a return value, the value that is returned to the database and stored.

6. In the first row, enter `Yes` and `Y` for the `Display Value` and the `Return Value`, respectively, and `No` and `N` for the same columns in the second row. Click Apply to close this page and return to the page for the item.

You should see some text in the `List of values` definition box — `STATIC2:Yes;Y,No;N`. This text indicates a static list of values, with each value in the pair separated by a semicolon and each pair of values separated by a comma.

You have now defined an LOV for the item and changed the way that the item is displayed so that it shows only the choices in the LOV.

7. Click Apply Changes.

8. When you return to the main development page, click on the Run icon to run the page and see the result of your changes, as shown in Figure 3-15.

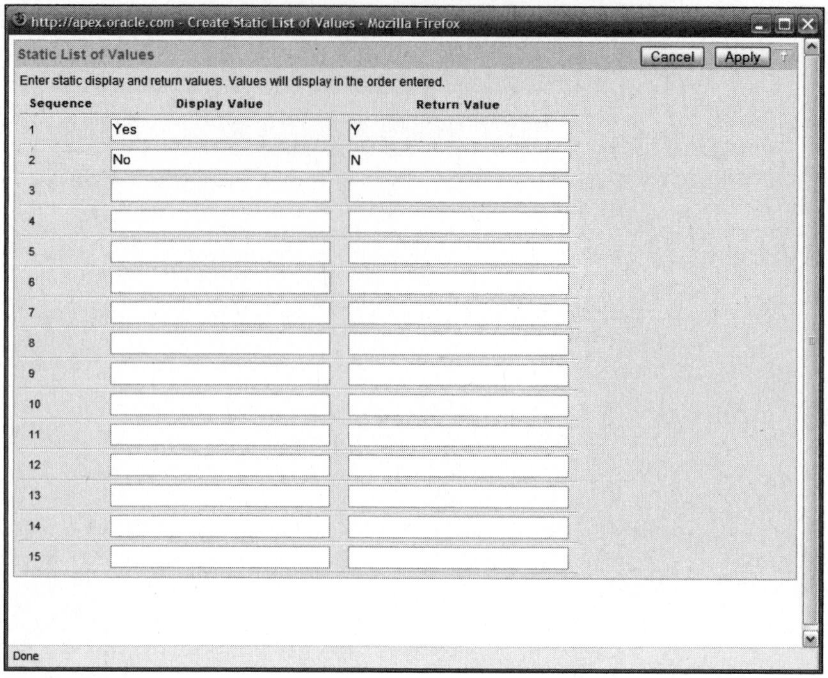

Figure 3-14

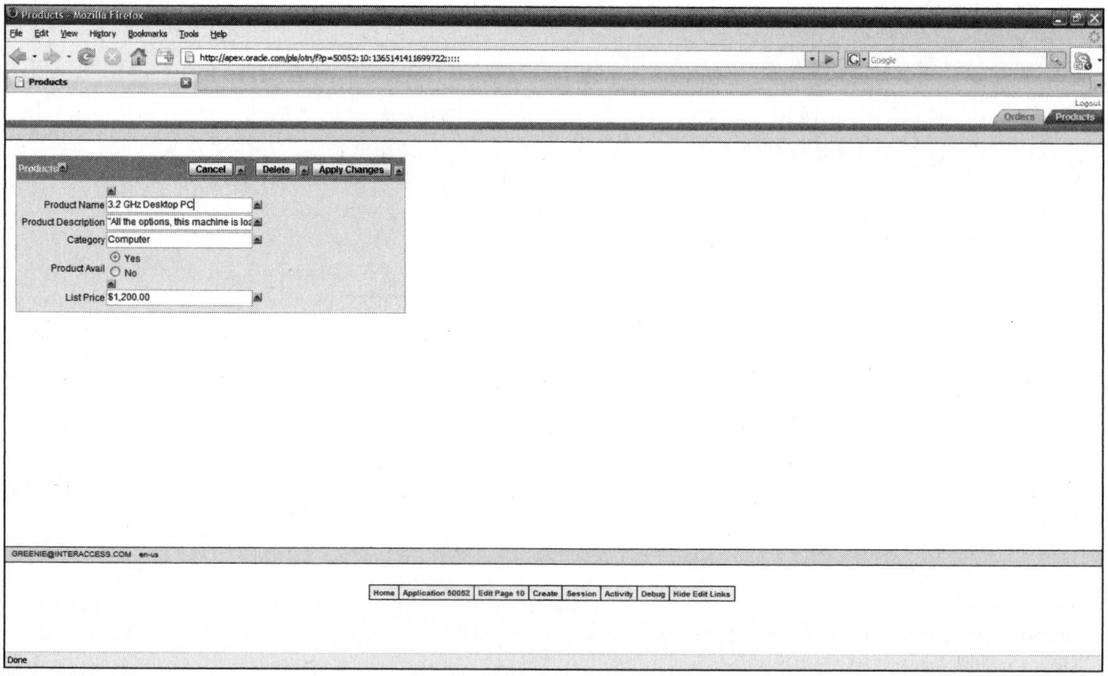

Figure 3-15

You can now see that the user has only two choices for this field — Yes and No. You have made the application a little more attractive and a little easier to use, and you have eliminated the chance that a user could enter the wrong data values.

What you have is fine for this particular item. But what if there were other columns in your tables that needed to be limited to the same choices? You could eliminate some extra work and standardize the use of simple binary choices by making this LOV available to other pages. Fortunately, this is accomplished easily.

1. Click on the Edit Page link at the bottom of the runtime page.

2. Click on the item that now has a list of values, the P#_PRODUCT_AVAIL field.

3. On the right-hand side of the page, you can see a link labeled Convert LOV in the Tasks list. Click on that link.

4. The resulting page contains the code for the list of values, as well as a field that forces you to give a name to the LOV. Give the LOV a descriptive name, such as Y/N.

5. Click Create, which will return you to the main development page for your page. If you look at the Shared Components column on the far right, you can see that the Lists of Values section now has the LOV you just created.

6. Click on the PRODUCT_AVAIL item and notice that there is now a named LOV for the item — the LOV you just named.

How It Works

You have just created a list of values for an item, and then converted that LOV into a shared object that can be used by other pages in your application. The LOV itself is not a user interface choice. Instead, there are a number of user interface options that require an LOV — groups of radio buttons and picklists, for example.

The LOV you created is about as basic as it gets — two distinct values. Remember, though, that you have already defined a number of relationships between tables through the use of foreign keys. You can create more powerful dynamic LOVs, and then use these as the basis for more flexible ways to improve the user interface and strengthen the data integrity of your application.

Dynamic Lists of Values (LOV)

There are times when you want to limit the values entered by a user, and there are a small, essentially permanent list of acceptable values — such as the Yes and No values in the previous example. However, if the list of acceptable values is longer, or if the values in that list might change over time, it makes sense to simply keep the values for that list in another table, and create a relationship from the field that will hold those values to that table.

It just so happens that you have already defined a relationship between two tables that would be an ideal candidate for this type of interaction — the ORDER_ITEMS table and the PRODUCTS table. There is an existing foreign key relationship between the PRODUCT_ID column in each table. And you may have noticed that the ORDER_ITEMS page displays a not very user-friendly ID number for the associated product, instead of the more comprehensible name of the product.

In this section, you will work with dynamic LOVs, which will both improve the user interface to your application and ensure data integrity by limiting the values entered for a field to those that exist on the related table.

Try It Out   Creating and Using a Dynamic LOV

In the previous section, your last step was to take an LOV you had created and make it a shared object. For this dynamic LOV, you can start by creating the shared object and then add it to one of your pages.

1.   Return to the main development page for the application, and click on the Shared Components icon to bring up the page shown in Figure 3-16.

Figure 3-16

2.   Under the User Interface section of the page, click on the Lists of Values link. Click Create.

3.   On the next page, leave the default selection, to create a list of values From Scratch, and click Next.

4.   Name the new LOV PRODUCTS_LOV, and change the type to Dynamic. Click Next to bring up the page shown in Figure 3-17.

Figure 3-17

This page shows you the form of the SQL statement you will use to create a dynamic LOV. The first column in the column list, `ename` in the sample code, is the column that will be displayed, which is indicated by the label `d` following the column name. The second column, `empno` in the sample code, is the value returned to be stored for the column, and it is indicated by the label `r`. These two columns are followed by the syntax to identify their table, as well as an optional ORDER BY clause to set the order.

You can easily modify this code for your own purposes.

5. Change the code in the `Query` box to the following:

```
select PRODUCT_NAME d, PRODUCT_ID r
from    PRODUCTS
order by 1
```

The number 1 used in the ORDER BY clause points back to the column in position 1 of the column list, in this case the PRODUCT_NAME column.

6. Click Create List of Values to finish the job.

Now that you have a shared list of values, you can use it in your detail form.

7. Return to the main development page for the application by clicking on the application ID in the breadcrumb list.

8. Click on the detail page, named Order Items, in the master-detail set of pages you created previously. If you have been following these exercises exactly, this page should be Page 5.

9.   Click on the item listing for PRODUCT_ID.

10.   In the top section, change the Display As to Select List, either with the dropdown list or by selecting the link below the field. Change the Label, two sections below, to Product Name, since that will be a more accurate description of what the page will be showing.

11.   Click the LOV button at the top of the page to isolate the section of LOV attributes. Set the Named LOV value to the LOV you just created, PRODUCTS_LOV.

12.   Click Apply Changes.

13.   Click on the Run icon to display your new page, as shown in Figure 3-18 for inserting a new row into the PRODUCTS table.

Figure 3-18

The resulting page is more attractive, easier to use, and prevents your user from entering incorrect data values. Nice results from just a handful of clicks. So nice, in fact, that you might want to set up the same type of relationship for other columns where you want to limit the user's choices. Fortunately, APEX gives you a quick and easy way to accomplish this, even when you don't have a related table in your database.

Try It Out   **Creating a Related Table, and Using It with an LOV**

You may have noticed that each product is assigned to a particular category. This category column is a prime candidate for invalid data entry. A user could easily enter something like TV for the category when the Video category already exists. In addition, your organization might want to add new categories from time to time, so storing those values in a related table is probably the best solution.

You can use a feature of the SQL Workshop to automatically create a related table and the foreign key constraint to support it.

   1.   Return to the main development page. Click on the SQL Workshop tab at the top of the page.

   2.   Use the cascading menus from the Object Browser to browse tables.

   3.   Select the PRODUCTS table from the left-hand panel.

   4.   On the far-right side of the buttons at the top of the main panel is a button labeled Create Lookup Table. Click on the button to bring up the page shown in Figure 3-19.

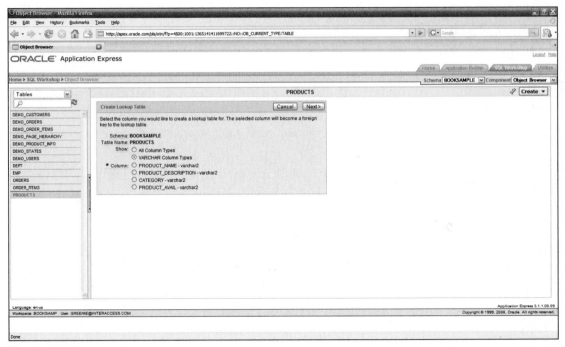

Figure 3-19

SQL Workshop knows that lookup tables are used to replace a character, or VARCHAR, column with a number that points to a lookup table. Based on that understanding, you are initially presented with a list of character columns, although you can change the selection by the Show: label to show all columns.

   5.   Select the CATEGORY column and click Next to bring up the page shown in Figure 3-20.

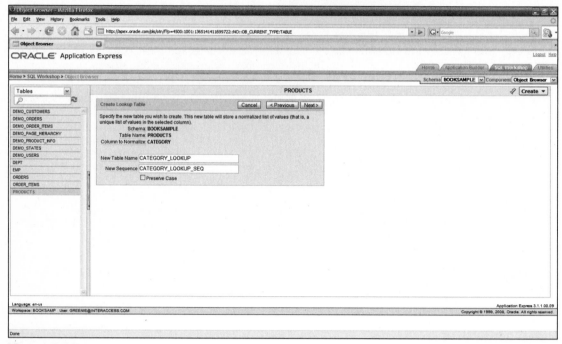

Figure 3-20

This page prompts you to name the target lookup table, and the sequence that will be used to generate the matching numbers.

6. Change the New Table Name to CATEGORIES, and the New Sequence to CATEGORIES_SEQ to preserve the naming conventions you have been using. Click Next.

7. Click Finish to create the new table and supporting objects. You will be shown the created table in the page once the creation is completed.

You created a table and a sequence, but SQL Workshop actually did a bit more.

8. Click on the PRODUCTS table in the left-hand panel. Notice that the CATEGORY character field has been replaced with the CATEGORY_ID number field.

9. Click on the Constraints button to bring up the page shown in Figure 3-21.

You can see that there is a new foreign key constraint, linking the PRODUCTS table to the newly created CATEGORIES table.

The constraint has a rather cryptic name, generated from internal values in the APEX environment. But you will normally never have to access the constraint by name, so the name itself should not matter. You could also rename the constraint to a more meaningful name.

Now you have to go back to the form for the PRODUCTS table, add the LOV for the newly created lookup table, and change the display to a select list.

1. Click on the Application Builder tab, double-click on your application, and double-click on the PRODUCTS form.

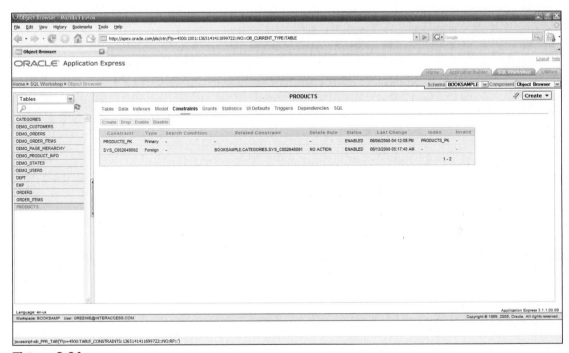

Figure 3-21

On this Products form, the CATEGORY column is represented as an item. You will have to do a few things to add the lookup functionality to this form.

2. Click on the item for the CATEGORY field. On the following page, click Source to only show attributes for the source of the field, as shown in Figure 3-22.

Remember, the action you took in the SQL Workshop changed the CATEGORY character field to the CATERGORY_ID numeric field.

3. Change the text in the Source value or expression from CATEGORY to CATEGORY_ID. Click the LOV button to bring up that section of the page, as shown in Figure 3-23.

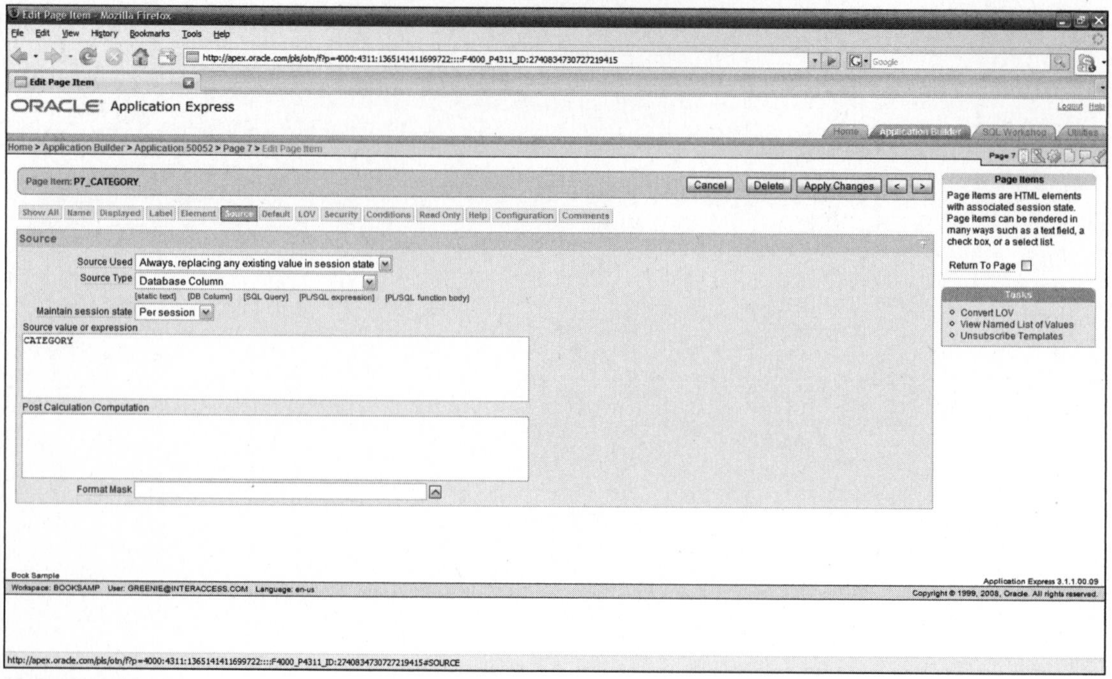

Figure 3-22

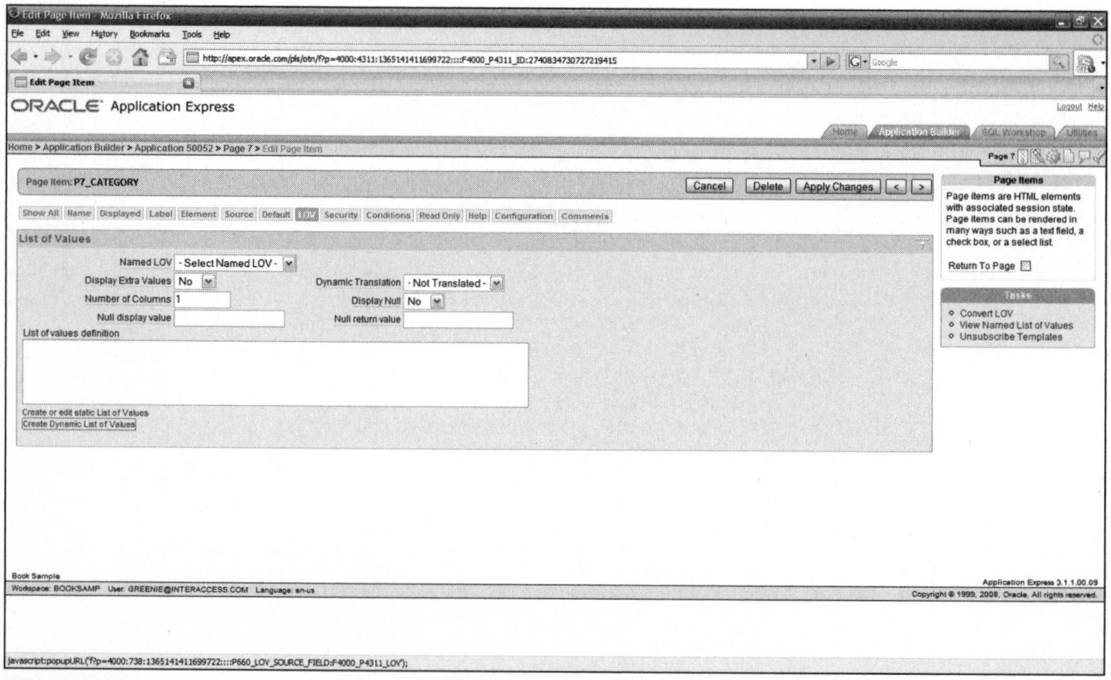

Figure 3-23

4. Click on the `Create Dynamic List of Values` link, which will bring up a new window.

5. Accept the default value for Table/View Owner, and click Next.

6. In the next page, select the `CATEGORIES` table in the Table or View select list. Click Next to bring up the page shown in Figure 3-24.

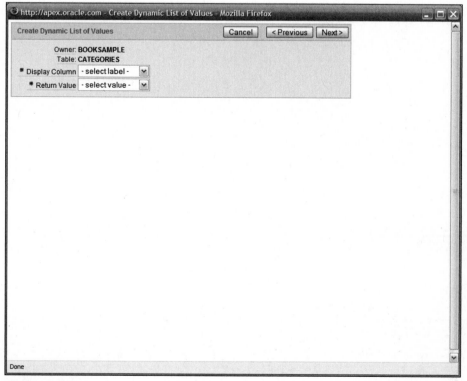

Figure 3-24

On this page, you can see that all you have to do is to indicate the `Display Column` and the `Return Value`.

7. Select `CATEGORY` as the Display Column and `CATEGORY_ID` as the Return Value. Click Next.

The final page in this wizard shows you the SQL which will create the LOV. You can see that this SQL statement has a little more in the way of documentation than your previous dynamic SQL LOV, calling out `display_value` and `return_value` as labels. All you have to do is accept this statement.

8. Click Finish, which will close this window and insert the SQL into the appropriate text field.

9. Click Show All, change the `Display As` value by clicking on the Select List choice below the field. Click Apply Changes to return you to the main development page.

10. Click Run to bring up the page, as shown in Figure 3-25.

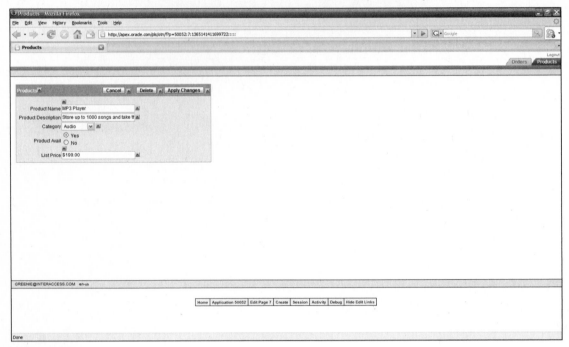

Figure 3-25

How It Works

You can see that the List of Values is now an integral part of this page. You can change the value for an item, and then click Apply Changes.

But wait — something seems amiss here. You get a mysterious looking error when you return to the report on Products. Well, of course — this report was based on the old structure of the PRODUCTS table, one that included the CATEGORY field, which is no longer present. It's easy to fix that problem though.

1. Click on the Edit Page link at the bottom of the page to return to the development page for the report on PRODUCTS.

2. Click on the Interactive Report link to bring up the attributes of the report.

Until now, this has been the only page you have seen for a report. But notice that there are tabs across the top of the page. You have been on the Report Attributes tab, which contains the most commonly changed attributes of a report. But you want to change the source of the report.

3. Click on the Region Definition tab to bring up the page shown in Figure 3-26.

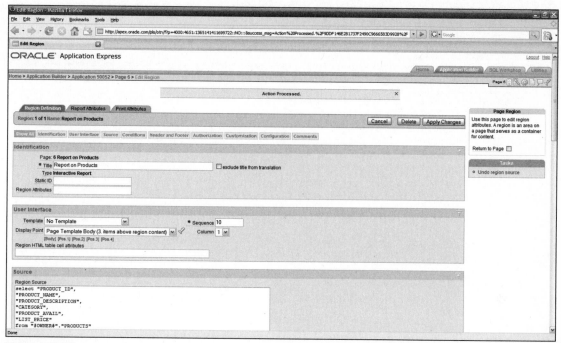

Figure 3-26

You can see that there is an SQL statement in the third section of the page. You can recognize the column and table names used in the report. All you have to do to fix the operation of this report is to correct the errant column name.

4. Change "CATEGORY" to "CATEGORY_ID" in the Region Source text field. Click Apply Changes.

5. You will be prompted to confirm that you really want to change the columns in the report source. Click Apply Changes, which will take you back to the main development page.

6. Click on the Interactive Report link in the Regions section again.

7. Look at the list of columns. You can now see that the CATEGORY column is gone, replaced by the CATEGORY_ID column. Now you understand how APEX knows what columns to put into the report — it's all based on the SQL.

For those of you readers who are familiar with SQL, this realization is probably great news. Since the report is based on an SQL statement, you can use any SQL statement as the foundation for a report. All the power of SQL is at your command. This flexibility is a source of great power.

8. Click on the Run icon to bring up the new page, as shown in Figure 3-27.

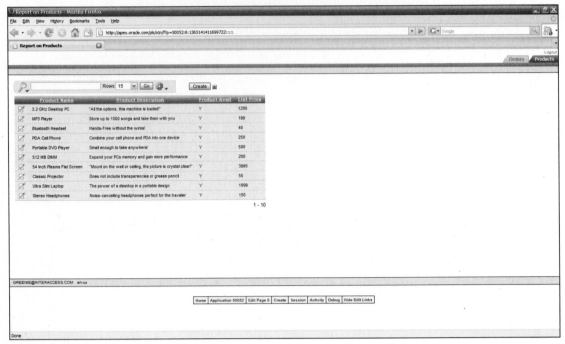

Figure 3-27

But wait again! Didn't you just add the CATEGORY_ID field to the report? Because this is an interactive report, by default, new columns are not displayed in the report. But the power of the interactive report, which you will explore more fully later in this book, makes it easy to bring that column into the report.

   9.   Click on the gear icon at the top of the page to bring up a menu. Click Select Columns to bring up the page shown in Figure 3-28.

   10.   Highlight the Category Id column from the left-hand list box, and use the right arrow to move it to the bottom of the list in the right-hand box. Use the up arrow to move it to a position between PRODUCT_DESCRIPTION and PRODUCT_AVAIL, and click Apply.

OK, that's better — a little better. You can see the value for the field, but you are displaying the ID of the category, which is rather cryptic. It would be much better if this report could show the name of the category, but that value is in another table. Since you can use any SQL statement for a report, you can retrieve information from more than one table, as long you specify how the two tables are related.

You can do this by modifying the SQL statement again. Those of you fluent in SQL could probably just modify the SQL statement. For those not as familiar with SQL, or who type badly, SQL Workshop has a way to create SQL statements with a few clicks on some lists and graphics.

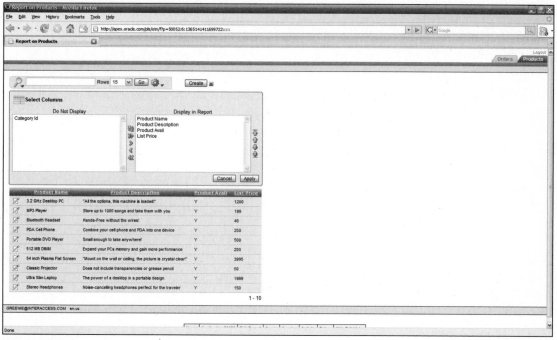

Figure 3-28

Try It Out   **Reporting on Data from More Than One Table**

Since reports are based on SQL statements, you can combine data from multiple tables by crafting the proper SQL to accomplish this task. For those of you who need, or want, help creating SQL statements, SQL Workshop has a tool to help.

1.   Return to the development area by clicking on the Edit Page link.

2.   Click on the SQL Workshop tab, and then on the Query Builder icon to bring up the page shown in Figure 3-29.

3.   Click on the PRODUCTS table in the left-hand list of tables and then on the new CATEGORIES table. This action will cause the two tables to appear in the upper-right panel.

You can see that the tables are shown, along with their columns, an icon representing the type of data the column contains, and a check box that allows you to select a column to perform a join. A join is the SQL term for linking two tables together. You will want to create a join between the two tables you have selected.

4.   Click in the box on the right of the CATEGORY_ID in the PRODUCTS table, and then click on the box on the right of the CATEGORY_ID for the CATEGORIES table. A link will appear between the two tables, as shown in Figure 3-30.

Figure 3-29

Figure 3-30

You next select the columns you want to appear in the query.

5. Click on the check box on the left for the PRODUCT_ID, PRODUCT_NAME, PRODUCT_DESCRIPTION, PRODUCT_AVAIL, and LIST_PRICE columns in the PRODUCTS table, and the CATEGORY column in the CATEGORIES table.

As you select the columns, they appear in the list below. Each column has a number of attributes that you can set to affect the rows and data returned, including sort order, conditions attached to the column, and any functions to aggregate the data for a column. There are also arrows that allow you to move a column's position in the query.

In an SQL statement, it doesn't make any difference where a column occurs in a query, but remember that the report is constructed from the query, so you should change the position of the CATEGORY column.

6. Use the arrows to move the CATEGORY column to a location between the PRODUCT_DESCRIPTION and PRODUCT_AVAIL columns.

7. Enter the number 1 in the Sort Order field for PRODUCT_ID.

This specification will sort the rows based on the value of PRODUCT_ID. You used a number to specify sort order because you could have sorting within the different groups by specifying multiple sort orders.

This query looks right, but you can easily verify that the data returned is what you want.

8. Click Run, which will run the query and return the rows, as shown in Figure 3-31.

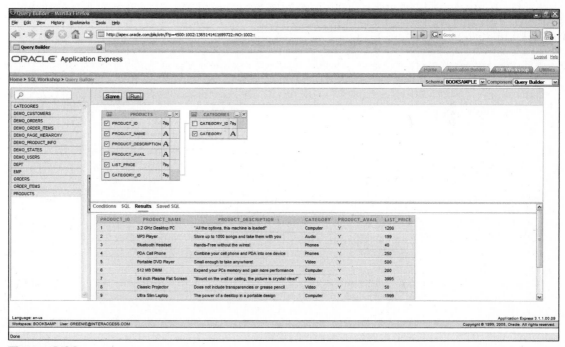

Figure 3-31

The data looks right, so now it's time to grab the SQL statement you created.

9. Click the SQL button in the lower panel. This action will bring up the following SQL statement:

```
select "PRODUCTS"."PRODUCT_ID" as "PRODUCT_ID",
"PRODUCTS"."PRODUCT_NAME" as "PRODUCT_NAME",
"PRODUCTS"."PRODUCT_DESCRIPTION" as "PRODUCT_DESCRIPTION",
"CATEGORIES"."CATEGORY" as "CATEGORY",
"PRODUCTS"."PRODUCT_AVAIL" as "PRODUCT_AVAIL",
"PRODUCTS"."LIST_PRICE" as "LIST_PRICE"
from "CATEGORIES" "CATEGORIES",
"PRODUCTS" "PRODUCTS"
where "PRODUCTS"."CATEGORY_ID"="CATEGORIES"."CATEGORY_ID"
order by "PRODUCTS"."PRODUCT_ID" asc
```

This SQL syntax uses slightly different conventions than you saw in the Region Source earlier, but this SQL statement should work just fine.

10. Highlight the SQL statement, and select the Copy option from the Edit menu of your browser.

11. Click on the Application Builder tab, your application, and select the report on PRODUCTS.

12. Click on the Interactive Report link in the Regions section and then the Region Definition tab.

13. Paste the copied SQL into the Region Source field.

14. Click Apply Changes. You will again be prompted as to whether you want to replace the columns in the previous SQL definition with the new fields. Click Apply Changes and then the Run icon to run the report.

The good news on the next page is that the report runs fine, and that you do not seem to have lost any of the functionality of the report, including the Edit link on the left of each row. The bad news is that the column you just added is not visible on the report. But, as with the last change to the interactive report, new columns do not automatically show up in the new report.

15. Click on the gear at the top of the report. Click the Select Columns option, and move the Category column into the right-hand list box, then move the column up between the Product Description column and the Product Avail column. Click Apply to bring up the page shown in Figure 3-32.

This version of the report is just what you wanted. You were able to bring data from two tables together to peacefully coexist in a single report, and you didn't even have to know SQL to accomplish this.

The power of SQL and the way that SQL statements form a foundation for data access, give you the ability to shape your reports to fit the needs of your users. There is another report that could use this type of modification — the master-detail report, which still shows the PRODUCT_ID column instead of the PRODUCT_NAME column. You could modify the SQL underlying that page yourself — as has been done in the final version of this application and will be shown in subsequent screen shots for the application.

Figure 3-32

Summary

You learned a lot more about the capabilities of your APEX environment in this chapter, including:

❑ How to format fields in APEX pages, both from the attribute page and directly from the runtime environment

❑ How to add default values for fields

❑ Using lists of values to limit user data entry, and how these LOVs can be presented to the user in different ways

❑ A brief introduction to shared components

❑ Using Query Builder to create SQL syntax

❑ Modifying a report to combine data from two different tables

You also became more familiar with the overall use of the APEX environment. You will be exploring more of the options available to you with APEX in the next chapter to extend your application even further, including providing validation, adding calculations to reports, and understanding and changing the way that users can navigate throughout your application.

Validation, Calculation, Navigation, and Lists

If you have been reading this book sequentially, you have an application that was built with a lot of default functionality, and you have modified that default application to increase ease of use and protect data integrity.

This chapter will take your application farther, in several ways. You will learn how to add logical checks on data validity before allowing the data to be added to your database. You will learn how to easily add more information to existing reports by including calculations in the reports. And you will learn all about how to specify navigation in your application and how your navigation can be used to model business processes you are supporting, increasing the productivity of your users.

Validation

At this point (and hopefully before), you should understand that the goal of your application is to collect, store, and report on data. If data is not correct — if the data lacks logical integrity — the condition will undermine the value of your entire application.

You have protected the integrity of your data in a couple of ways so far, by using data types for different columns, which limit, for instance, the data in some columns to numeric or date values. Your application contains some user interface objects that help guide your users to proper data values, including a date picker to select valid dates, radio button groups, and picklists.

Sometimes you cannot use these simple methods to ensure that the data entered is valid, often because the business rules that must be enforced are a bit more complex. For situations like this, APEX gives you the ability to specify validation rules that are applied to data before the data can be saved. If the data values do not pass the validation test, the data is not saved, protecting your all important data integrity, and an error message is displayed to let the user know why the data was rejected.

Try It Out   **Validation Rules**

The business rule you wish to enforce applies to the date of an order. Although you have already provided a default of the current date for this field, you want to check to make sure that the user has not entered a date in the future.

The basis for this rule is to prevent users from forward-dating orders. The rule is a simple example, to help you understand the basics of validation rules in APEX.

1. Go to the Application Builder area.

2. Select your application, and then select the master-detail form you created for ORDERS and ORDER_ITEMS, the first page labeled Order Items.

3. Click on the plus sign (+) on the right at the top of the Validations section of the middle Page Processing column, which will bring up the first page of the Validation Wizard, shown in Figure 4-1.

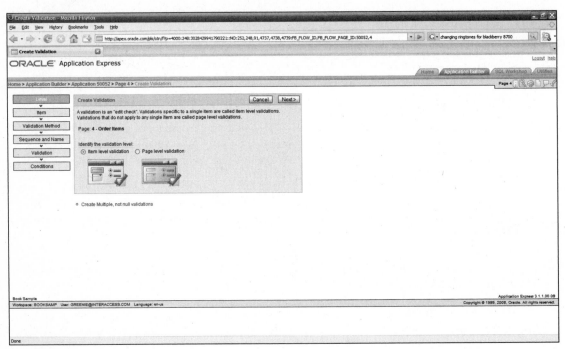

Figure 4-1

This is the first time you will be adding anything to the Page Processing area. As the name implies, this section covers actions that take place in response to events in the page. Validations are applied whenever a user attempts to save data, either by inserting a new row or updating the value of an existing row.

4. Leave the Item level validation choice selected, and click Next.

On the next page, shown in Figure 4-2, you are presented with a list of columns on the page.

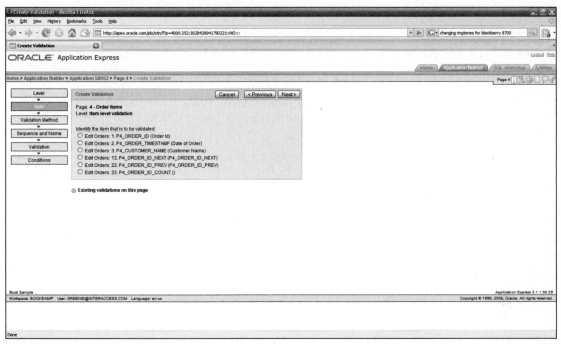

Figure 4-2

5. Click on the column for the ORDER_TIMESTAMP, which should have a prefix of the letter P and the number of the page. If you have been doing these exercises in order, the name of the field should be P4_ORDER_TIMESTAMP. Click Next.

The next page, shown in Figure 4-3, gives you choices for the type of validation you want to perform. You can use an SQL statement or PL/SQL expression, as well as doing either standard string comparisons or using regular expressions, or just designating that the item must contain a value, that is, is not null.

You may have noticed a link on the first page of this wizard that gave you the option of making multiple fields not null at the same time.

6. Select the PL/SQL option, and click on Next.

7. On the next page, accept the default option of PL/SQL Expression, and click Next.

On the next page of the Validation Wizard, shown in Figure 4-4, you have to specify a sequence for the validation as well as a name for the validation. If you are doing a simple validation, like this one, the sequence number is not that important, but for more complex scenarios, you may want to attempt one type of validation before another. The sequence number gives you control over the order that validation routines are executed, and it will also determine the order in which error messages are presented if there are multiple validation rules that fail.

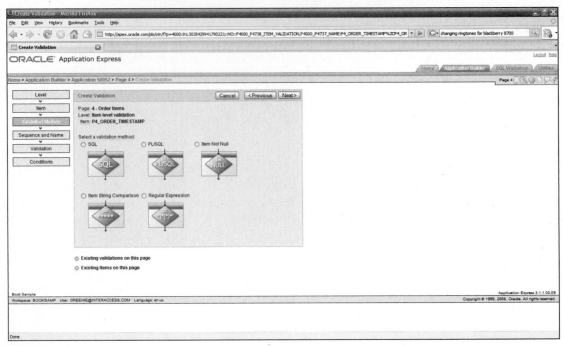

Figure 4-3

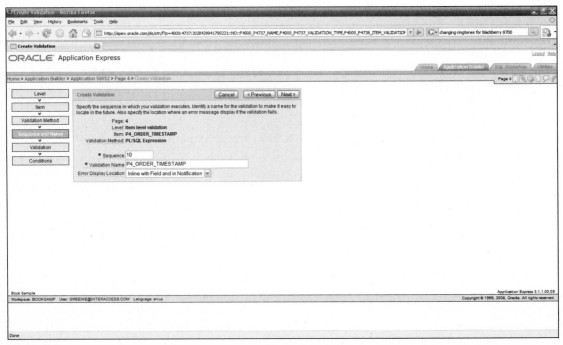

Figure 4-4

You can also choose where you want an error message to show up. For this example, you can leave the default.

8. Click Next to bring up the page shown in Figure 4-5, in its completed state.

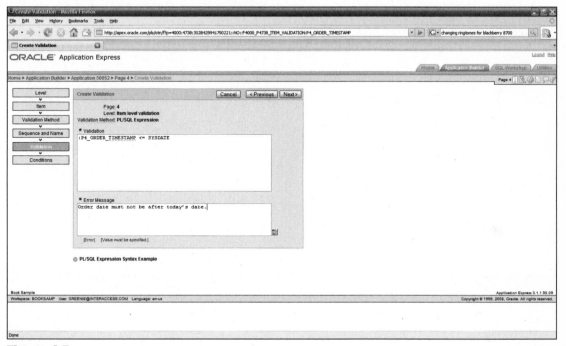

Figure 4-5

This next page is where you actually specify the validation. The syntax for the validation is pretty simple — you want to make sure that the value entered in this field is less than or equal to today's date. You already have used a PL/SQL expression that returns today's date when you specified the default for this field. You can use that expression, SYSDATE, again in the validation specification.

There is one small syntax requirement you will have to mind. Remember that you designated this validation routine as a PL/SQL expression. PL/SQL routines execute in their own environment, so the PL/SQL routine will assume that an identifier like P4_ORDER_TIMESTAMP indicates a PL/SQL variable with that name — not a field on a page. You have to connect to the field by declaring the name as a *bind variable*, which will bind the representation within PL/SQL to the field.

Bind variables are a standard part of SQL syntax, so you may be aware of how they operate. If this concept is new to you, fret not — all you have to do to indicate a bind variable is to precede the name of the field with a colon.

The specification for this PL/SQL expression is:

```
:P4_ORDER_TIMESTAMP <= SYSDATE
```

Make sure that you use <=, which is a valid PL/SQL operator; =< is not.

9. Enter the specification into the Validation text box. Enter `Order date must not be after today's date.` as the Error Message. Click Next to bring up the page shown in Figure 4-6.

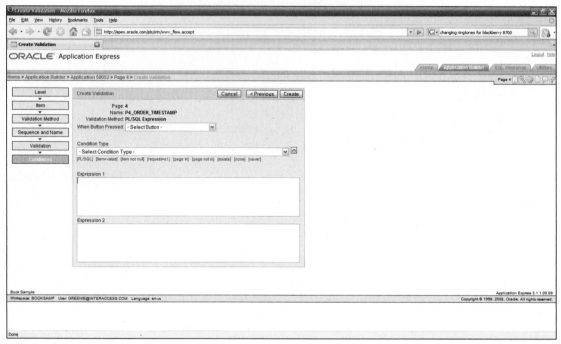

Figure 4-6

This page lets you indicate that a validation is only run when a particular button is pressed or when certain conditions are met. You could specify that you only want this validation done when a row is added or saved, but you can just leave When Button Pressed with the default choice of no button. This will cause the validation to be run every time any button is pressed.

10. Click Create to create the validation routine.

When you return to the main development page, you can see that the validation you just created is now listed in the center `Page Processing` column.

Before your work is completely finished, you will have to make one small change to the way that the date picker for the `ORDER_TIMESTAMP` field works.

1. Select the `P#_ORDER_TIMESTAMP` item in the `Items` section of the main attributes page.

2. Change the `Display As` type to `Date Picker (DD-MON-YY)`, which will allow the value in this field to be properly compared to the date format returned by the `SYSDATE` function.

3. Click Apply Changes to save the change.

You are now ready to test out your new routine.

How It Works

Now that you have added a validation rule, it's time to see it in action.

1. Click Run to bring up the page you have modified.

2. If the report is in Create mode, without values showing for an order, return to the report on ORDERS by clicking Cancel, and select the first order to edit.

3. Use the date picker (accessed by clicking on the icon to the right of the Date of Order field) to select a date after today's date.

4. Click Apply Changes, which will bring up errors caused by the failure of the validation, as shown in Figure 4-7.

Figure 4-7

There are actually three indicators of a failed validation — the red X to the left of the label for the Date of Order field, the error message in red underneath that label, and the grey message area at the top of the page. You could have eliminated either the upper error or the lower two indicators with the configuration choice.

You have learned how to validate data to protect integrity. Now it's time to create some new information out of the data already stored in the database.

Calculation

One of the guidelines for good data design is to reduce the amount of storage needed for your data. In olden times, when storage was more expensive, this guideline made economic sense, and it still makes logical sense today — why store something you can recreate at will?

In this section, you will add some information relating to Order Items that will be useful to the user but that will not require any changes in data storage.

Try It Out   **Adding a Calculation**

The columns for the ORDER_ITEMS table contain the list price of the item and the quantity of the item. The user may not want to perform the multiplication in his head to figure out the total charge for the items, but you can easily add this result to the report you have created with techniques you already know.

1. Return to the main development area for the master-detail page for ORDERS and ORDER_ITEMS, which should be Page 4 if you have been following along in the instructions.

2. Click on the Report link in the second Region of the page, and then click on the Region Definition tab. Click on the Show Source link in the Source section of the page.

The source shown is displayed as text — you don't have the ability to edit it, as you will have to so that you can accomplish your task. When this report was created, the report was designated with a type of SQL Query (Structured Query). This type of report has an additional tab for the report attributes labeled Query Definition. If you go to this tab, you will see that the query columns, join conditions, and query conditions have sections, with buttons that allow you to edit each of these areas without writing any SQL at all.

A report that uses a structured query is easier to work with for users who know nothing about SQL. But this type of structure imposes its own limitations, such as not allowing you to modify the SQL directly. This limitation makes sense, since you could modify the SQL in any way, including ways that the APEX environment could not readily convert back into a highly structured form.

You will have to change the type of the report to a standard SQL Query to directly edit the SQL. Fortunately, there is a task link readily available to accomplish this job.

3. In the Task area on the right, click Convert to SQL Query.

4. You will be prompted with a warning, explaining that you cannot convert the SQL query back to a structured query. Click OK.

5. You will be returned to the main attribute page. Click on the Report link again to return to the report attributes. You can immediately see that the Query Definition tab is gone.

6. Click on the Region Definition tab and scroll down to the Source area.

7. Change the Region Source to the following SQL by adding the screened text.

```
SELECT
    "ORDER_ITEMS"."ORDER_ITEMS_ID" "ORDER_ITEMS_ID",
    "PRODUCTS"."PRODUCT_NAME" "PRODUCT_NAME",
    "ORDER_ITEMS"."UNIT_PRICE" "UNIT_PRICE",
    "ORDER_ITEMS"."QUANTITY" "QUANTITY",
```

```
    "ORDER_ITEMS"."QUANTITY" * "ORDER_ITEMS"."UNIT_PRICE" AS "Total for Item"
FROM
    "ORDER_ITEMS", "PRODUCTS"
    WHERE "PRODUCTS"."PRODUCT_ID" = "ORDER_ITEMS"."PRODUCT_ID"
    and(("ORDER_ITEMS"."ORDER_ID" = :P4_ORDER_ID))
```

The code listed above includes the modification suggested at the end of the last chapter — adding in the use of the PRODUCTS *table and the* PRODUCT_NAME *field for improved usability. Also notice that you must add a comma after the* QUANTITY *field, since you are adding an additional field to the selection list. The code for this SQL statement is included in* Page_4_SQL.txt *in the Chapter 4 directory of files for this book.*

You haven't done very much here — just added another column to the SQL statement.

Make sure to add the comma after the QUANTITY *column on the previous line to indicate that there are additional columns in the SQL statement.*

This column is simply a multiplication of two existing columns. Note that you have given the calculated column a name, Total for Item, with the syntax AS "Total for Item". This label is called an alias, and you must have an alias for any calculated column with Oracle SQL.

8.   Click on Apply Changes, which will take you back to the main development page.

9.   Click on the Report link again, to go back and change the formatting of the new column.

10.   Click Edit for the newly created column.

11.   In the Column Definition section, change the Column Alignment to right to align properly for a number.

12.   In the Column Formatting section, click on the dropdown button to select appropriate currency formatting for the field.

13.   Click Apply Changes and then the Run icon to see the page in its new state, as shown in Figure 4-8.

Now, that wasn't very hard. You could make this information even more useful by including a total for the entire order. In this chapter, you will accomplish this simply by modifying the report. Later, you will add some procedural logic to automatically calculate the total and add it to the ORDERS table, which will make the total available to every application that uses the data.

14.   Click on the Edit Page link to return to the development environment.

15.   Click on the Report link in the Regions area.

On the Report Attributes page, you can see that there are three check boxes towards the right of each line in the Column Attributes list labeled Show, Sum, and Sort. You have already seen the Show checkbox at work, and you can probably guess what Sum and Sort can do for you.

16.   Click on the Sum checkbox for the new Total field, and then Apply Changes.

You are adding a sum to the report for all users. In the next chapter, you will explore how users can create their own totals in an Interactive Report.

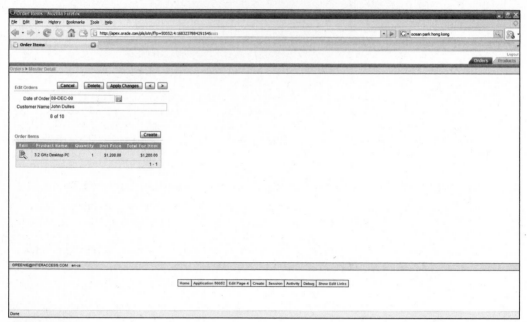

Figure 4-8

17. Click Run to see your changes at work.

Figure 4-9 shows the results of your actions. The totals for the report on ORDER_LINES provide valuable information for the user.

Figure 4-9

How It Works

Displaying the total on the page is a nice feature, but you can learn more about how the total works (and set up a problem to be solved for the next sections) by interacting with the page.

1.   On the master-detail page, click Create.

2.   Select a Product Name, and add a value for Unit Price and Quantity.

3.   Click Create to add the new order item to the order and return to the master-detail page, as shown in Figure 4-10.

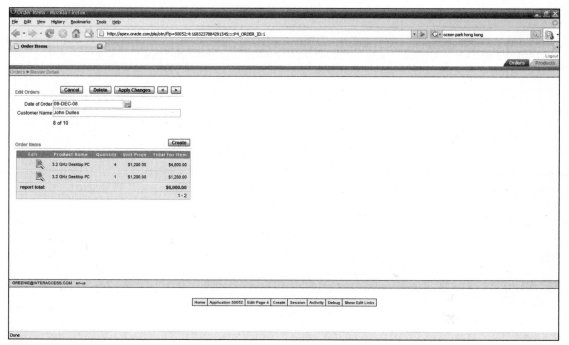

Figure 4-10

You can see that adding the new row has resulted in the total for the order being updated. You were able to add the total simply by checking a box on the report definition. This total is in the report, but users will have to access the report to see the total. Later in the book, in Chapter 8, which is on PL/SQL, you will see how to add the total information as a column on the ORDERS row.

Your next area of APEX exploration will center around the way end users get around your application.

Navigation

At this point in your exploration of APEX, you have created quite a few individual pages. Some of them work together, such as the reports and their associated editing forms, and all of the applications work in the context of the tabs at the top of the page. But you are ready for a more detailed look at how APEX specifies navigation from one page to another.

As part of this examination, you will come to understand how to change existing navigation, create conditional destinations, and modify the tab structures that control the overall application. You will also learn how to add new regions to a page and create links to other pages.

Understanding Navigation

The application you have created already has navigation capabilities built in. A good starting point to understand APEX application navigation is to examine some of the default navigation in your existing application.

How It Works

The easiest way to get an introduction to navigation is to look at a page whose navigation you might want to change.

The candidate for change is the first page you created.

1. Go to the main development area for your application and double-click on the first page you created for Orders, which should have a page number of 1.

2. Run the page by clicking Run.

You can see that this report on the ORDERS table is a nice interactive report.

3. Click Edit for an order to bring up the form associated with this page.

Now you can see that the form called up is not as functional as the master-detail page you created the second time through, which is shown in Figure 4-11. It would be great if you could combine this nice master-detail form with the nice interactive report.

You can, and you will, but before jumping right to the fix, you should understand how APEX determines how to navigate to a different page.

4. Click Cancel to return to the previous page, and then click on the Edit Page link.

5. Click on the Interactive Report link in the Region area of the page.

The navigation is done through that Edit icon, which is referred to as a *link column*.

6. Click the Link Column button at the top of the page to isolate the section shown in Figure 4-12.

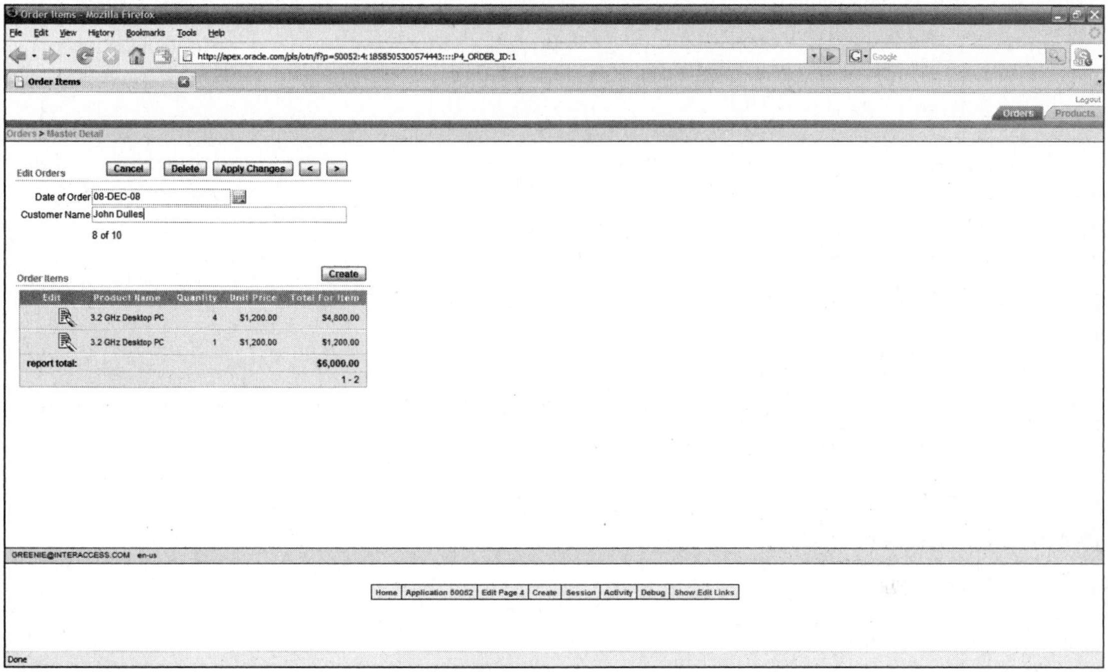

Figure 4-11

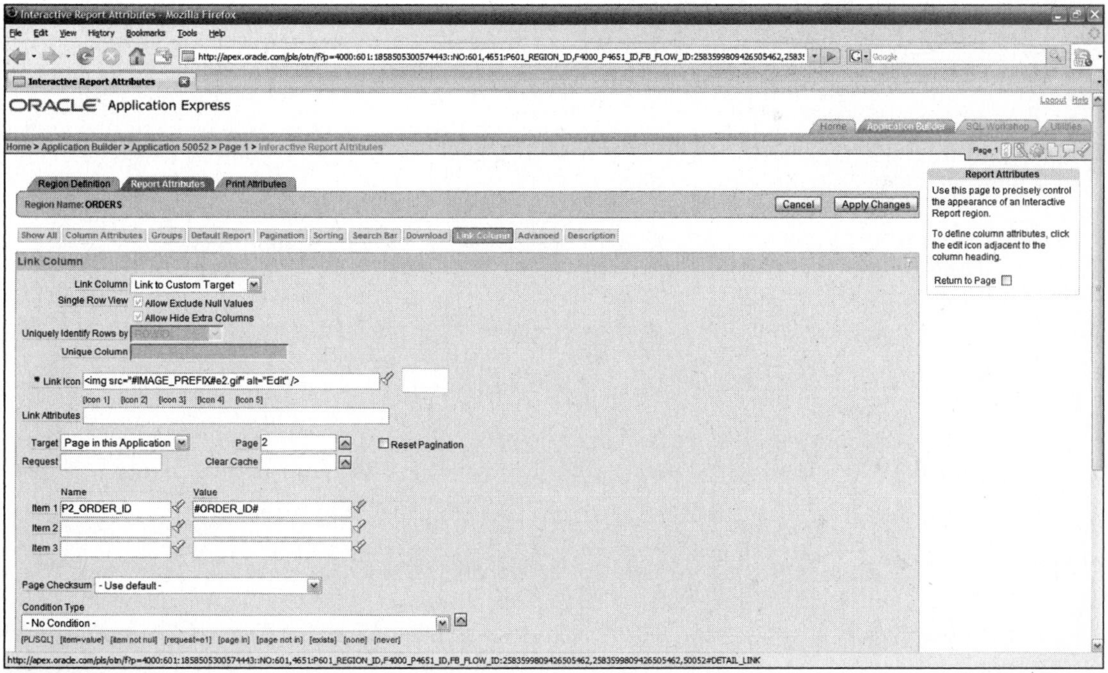

Figure 4-12

You can see that this section includes attributes that shape how the link column operates. On this page, as on so many other APEX attribute pages, you have a lot of flexibility. You should, as you have time, explore some of the options presented on the page, but for the purposes of this book, you should just focus on the attributes that directly apply to your task.

You can also see the Link Column picklist is set to Link to Custom Target. Farther down the page, you can see that the Target picklist is set to a Page in this Application. You want to link to a page in the application in the same way that this page links to the edit form.

You have seen enough — it's time to make that change.

Changing Navigation

In this section, you will change the navigation for that first report and then move on to change the navigation that is sending your users off the master-detail page before they are ready.

Try It Out **Changing Navigation**

In this exercise, you will make a couple of quick changes to the attributes for the Link Column to change the navigation for your application

1. While still on the Link Column section for the Interactive Report on your first page, click the dropdown arrow for the Page attribute, just to the right of the Target attribute.

2. You can see a list of all your pages, identified by both page number, which is held in the Page attribute, and the name of the page.

3. Click on the master-detail page, which should be Page 4 if you have been following along in the exercises.

You have changed the destination, but you have to change one more thing. The way the attributes currently stand, you will pass the ORDER_ID from this page to the P2_ORDER_ID field, which would be only meaningful if you were still linking to Page 2.

4. Click on the flashlight icon next to the Name column for Item 1 in the list of parameters, a little below the Target and Page field.

The resulting popup will give you a list of all the fields in the new target page.

5. Click on P4_ORDER_ID to set up the right connection.

When Page 4 is called by this link, the value for ORDER_ID is passed as a parameter to the page. The value of the P4_ORDER_ID is set, which causes the page to retrieve the data values for that particular Order ID.

6. Click Apply Changes, and then click on the Run icon.

7. Click on the Edit icon for an order, and watch the master-detail form appear, as desired.

You have successfully changed the navigation from the Edit link on your interactive report to go to the new destination of your master-detail page. You will have to change one more component that navigates from this page, the Create button.

8. Return to interactive report by clicking the Back button in your browser and then to the development environment for the page.

9. Click on the Create link in the Buttons section of the Page Rendering column on the left.

10. Click on URL redirect to highlight this section of the attributes.

11. Change the Page value to the master-detail page, which should be Page 4.

12. Change the value in the Clear Cache field to the number of the target page. By clearing the cache, you ensure that the master-detail page will come up without any values for the fields, which is what you want to insert a new record.

13. Click Apply Changes to save your work.

You have finished the primary task of integrating the two preferred pages by specifying navigation from the interactive report to the master-detail form. You have two more steps to complete your work for this page and specify navigation from the master-detail form back to the interactive report.

1. Go to the development page for the master-detail page.

Look at the listing for the Cancel button. The description states that the button will redirect the user to Page 3, the old report. You will want to change this to return the user to Page 1.

2. Click on the Cancel button link in the Buttons area of the left-hand Page Rendering column.

3. Click the URL Redirect button to isolate that section of the page.

4. Change the Page target to Page 1.

5. Click Apply Changes.

The final step will be to change the destination of the unconditional branch of the page to Page 1.

1. Click on the link for Got To Page 3, Unconditional in the Branches section, the bottom section in the middle Page Processing column.

2. Change the Page target in the Action section to Page 1, and click Apply Changes.

Don't worry about not understanding branching just yet. You will in a few paragraphs.

You now have the best of both worlds — an interactive report coupled with a master-detail entry form. At this point, you are done with the entry form called from the interactive report for Orders, which was Page 2, and the standard report for Orders, which was created as part of the master-detail pages you made with the Page Wizard. You should probably delete these pages if you want to clear up your application space, since you will not need them anymore.

These navigational changes have been pretty straightforward, simply a case of switching one navigation destination for another. You have simply been changing the destination for a fixed link. But APEX offers more flexible navigation, which can take the user to different destinations, depending on the conditions in the calling page. This capability is built with APEX branching.

Branching

You may have noticed a section in the Page Processing column of the main attribute page with a label of Branching – the portion of the master-detail page you just modified. Branching allows you to take conditional navigational actions in response to user interaction on your application page.

How It Works

When a user takes an action on one of your APEX pages, a message is sent back to the server handling the page. That message contains a variety of information, including an identifier for the action performed by the user. You can implement processes based on the type of action identified.

Frequently, though, you want to accept the default processing built into your APEX application, but you may want to direct the user to a different page following the default processing, based on the identifier for the user action.

This concept is easily understood when you look at some branching entries that already exist for the master-detail form.

1. Go to the development environment for the master-detail page.

Notice the Branching section in the Page Processing column, as shown in Figure 4-13.

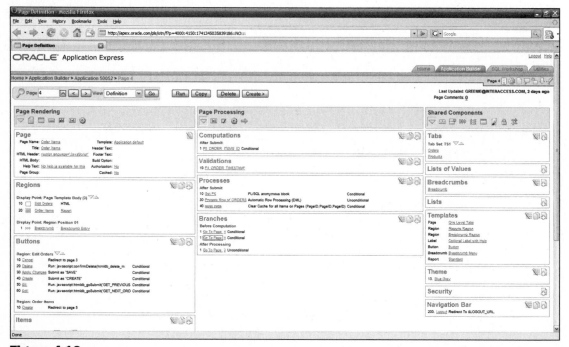

Figure 4-13

You can see that there are three branching choices already included as part of this page. As you can see from the listing of the branching choices, you can assign the branching decision to take place before or after processing.

The easiest place to start looking at the effects of branching is with the final choice. This choice is the only one listed as Unconditional. APEX treats a conditional branch like an IF statement. If the conditions specified in the branch are met, the action for the branch is taken. If the condition is not met, the next conditional branch is evaluated. The unconditional branch is used as the default branch for any actions that have not satisfied any of the conditions to that point.

Like many other items in APEX, branches are assigned a sequence number, which determines the order in which they are evaluated. If branches have the same sequence number, as the branches in this automatically generated page do, the branches are executed in the order listed for the same sequence number.

For this particular page, there is only one post-processing branch, which is listed as an unconditional branch. If there were conditional branches for this section, these branching options would have a lower sequence number, as you will see shortly.

2. Click on the branch identified as the Unconditional branch to bring up the page shown in Figure 4-14.

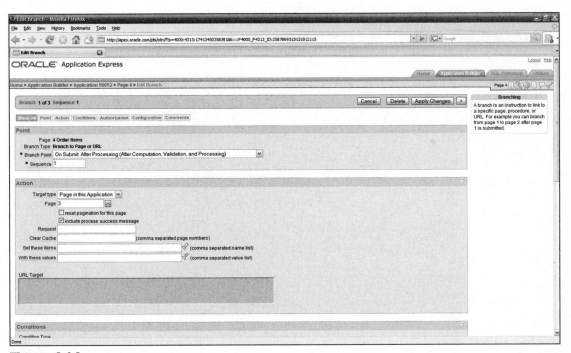

Figure 4-14

As with other attribute areas, there are a number of sections of branching attributes. For this particular branch, you should notice two attributes. The Branch Point indicates when the branch action should take place. Most branching actions take place after the page has been submitted by a user action, but you can indicate where you want the branch to be evaluated in the standard sequence of computations, validations and processing.

> *You have already created a validation, and you will learn more about processing and computation later in this book.*

The other key attribute for this branch is the Target type, which indicates what page you want to return to the user. You can send the user to another page in the APEX environment, or to a standard URL. For this attribute, you want to send the user to Page 4, the report page, after the processing of any changes in the ORDERS row.

Remember, this is the default branch that will only be used if the other branches are not used.

3. Click Cancel to return to the main attribute page. Click on the first entry for Branches. Portions of the page are shown in Figure 4-15.

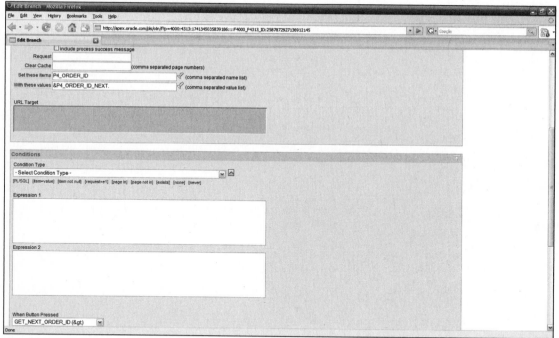

Figure 4-15

This branch has a couple of additional attributes. The first to notice is at the bottom of Figure 4-15, a picklist labeled When Button Pressed. An APEX page has a number of buttons on the page, and this picklist allows you to add a condition that limits the evaluation of this branch to those times when the user has clicked on a particular button — in this case, the GET_NEXT_ORDER_ID button. As the name implies, this is the button with a right pointing arrow.

The other attributes to notice are higher in Figure 4-15. The Set these items field accepts a comma-separated list of items on the target page, and the With these values field matches those items with values. In this case, the target item P4_ORDER_ID, which controls which row in the ORDERS table to fetch, is set to the value that holds the ID of the next order.

When the GET_NEXT_ORDER_ID button is clicked, this branch returns the same page, Page 4, but with the row from the ORDERS table with the next ORDER_ID. Now that you understand how to implement conditional branching, it's time for you to make your branching modifications.

Try It Out   Shaping Branching

You can add some functionality to the detail page for ORDER_ITEMS, which is called from the master-detail page.

As the page now stands, you can add a new ORDER_ITEMS row, click on Create, and return to the master-detail page. Your users may find this a bit unwieldy, as they typically add multiple order items at one time.

You will change the operation of this page through three simple tasks: changing the label on the existing button to clarify its purpose, adding a button to the page to allow users to save the row and add another, and then modifying the attributes of the new button to implement the exact functionality you desire.

1. Return to the main attribute page by clicking Cancel.

2. Go to the detail page for ORDER_ITEMS, which should be the next page in the application.

3. Click on the last button listed in the Buttons section of the left Page Rendering column.

4. Change the Text Label / Alt in the Name section to Create and Return. Click Apply Changes.

You want to change the label on the existing button to more properly identify its action, and to distinguish it from the button you are going to create.

5. Click on the plus (+) icon in the upper-left corner of the Buttons section to start the Button Creation Wizard.

6. On the first page, leave the default region choice of Edit Order Items and click Next.

7. On the following page, leave the default choice for Position and click Next.

The next page, shown completed in Figure 4-16, lets you name the button and assign a label. The name will be used in the branching options to identify the button, while the label is displayed to the user.

8. Set the Button Name to CREATE_ANOTHER and the Label to Create Another. Click Next.

9. On the next page, accept the default Button Template and click Next.

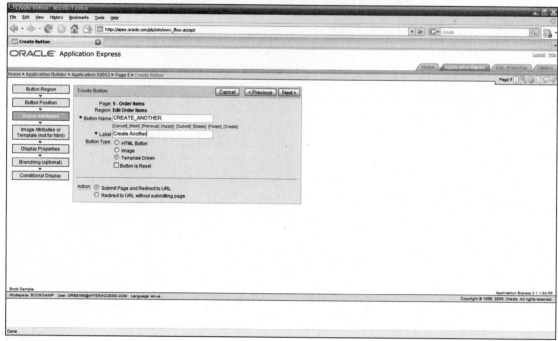

Figure 4-16

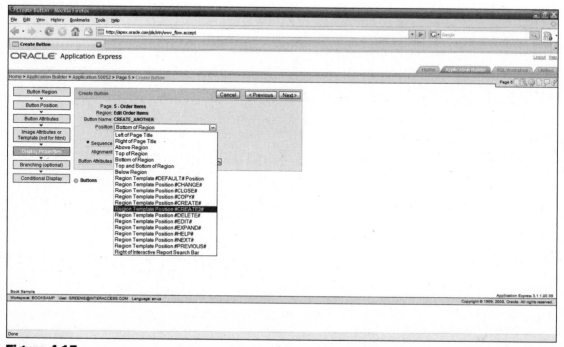

Figure 4-17

The next page, shown in expanded form in Figure 4-17, lets you assign the button to a particular position in the region. There are some positions defined for all pages, such as buttons relative to the page title, as well as positions defined in the region template.

10. Select the #CREATE2# position for the button, accept the other defaults, and click Next.

11. Select the current page as the Branch to Page, and click Create Button to return to the page attributes page, which you can see in Figure 4-18.

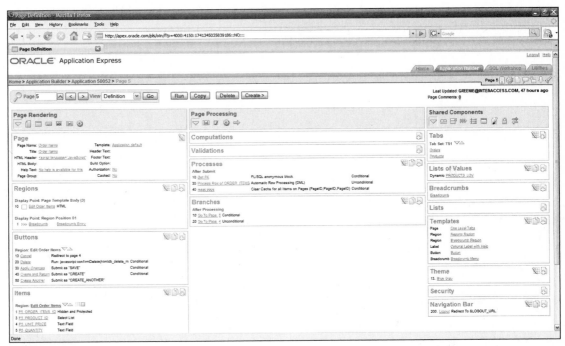

Figure 4-18

You can see that there are two new entries on this page. The first, as you would expect, is the new entry in the Buttons section. The second is a new entry in the Branches section, marked as Conditional. The APEX Button Creation Wizard was very thoughtful to create both of these entries, since your page will need both of them to properly operate. But you will have to modify these default creations just a bit.

12. Click on the Create Another button link to bring up the button attribute page.

The attribute you want to change is in the fourth section down, labeled Database Manipulation Request. Right now, the specification is for - No Database Action -, which is not correct for this button.

13. Change the Database Manipulation Request to SQL INSERT Action. Click Apply Changes.

When you look at the entries in the Branches section, you see that, by default, the new conditional branching action was assigned a sequence number after the existing unconditional branch, which means that the conditional branch will never be executed.

14. Click on the Unconditional branch, change the Sequence to 20 and click Apply Changes. Change the Sequence for the Conditional branch to 10 in the same manner.

Your newly modified form is ready to test.

Try It Out   **Adding Multiple Order Items**

Time to give your new, easily created functionality a test.

1. Go to the development page for Page 1, the initial report for Orders, and click on the Run icon.

2. Select the first order, and click on the Edit icon.

3. Click Create to bring up the new version of the page, as shown in Figure 4-19.

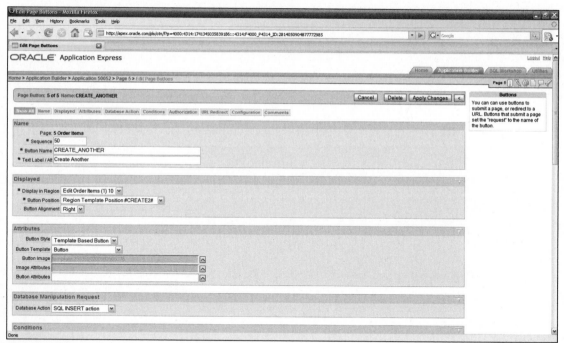

Figure 4-19

4. Add a new order item, click Create Another, and see the way the new button works.

The new version of the page includes the button you just designed, which works the way you had hoped.

Branching provides conditional navigation to move from a single page. Tabs are a way to add navigation to your overall application. You have been using tabs by default already, but the next section will look at them in more explicit detail.

Tech Talk — Client and Server Side Logic

If you looked closely at the buttons that were part of the master-detail form, you noticed that some of the buttons in the list had their actions listed as JavaScript. JavaScript is a client-side language, logic that runs in the browser, rather than on the server like all the other logic for buttons and the rest of your application.

Browser-based applications have fairly simple connections to the server code running on the back end. The browser can submit a call to the server, passing with that call a name for the request, which you have seen in the form of SAVE, CREATE, and DELETE, and parameters. In response, the server returns a page to the browser — a page which you indicated earlier in this section.

Buttons use JavaScript to perform actions on the client without server intervention or to assign values to parameters used when a request is submitted. In the master-detail application, you can see examples of both.

The Delete button uses JavaScript to bring up a dialog box to confirm that the user wants to take the delete action. The Next and Previous buttons use JavaScript to send the ORDER_ID for the next or previous order, values that are kept in hidden fields on the page.

Both of these calls use JavaScript calls that are available to all APEX pages as part of an included JavaScript library. You can find documentation on the calls available in this library in the *APEX User Guide*. You can also include JavaScript routines in the HTML header, just as you would for a standard HTML page. The attributes page for a Page has entry fields where you can specify JavaScript code. If you look at the attributes for the master-detail page, you can see another JavaScript call that indicates that the page allows the use of the Next and Previous buttons.

The server side code that creates and runs this page has logic that knows that getting a value for the ORDER_ID in a request means that the page returned should include data from the row with that ORDER_ID.

Tabs

One of the key navigation features of your APEX app, a tab set, was created by default for your application. Subsequent pages also created tabs to use for handy navigation. It's time to take a look at how APEX organizes tabs, as well as how you can create new tabs to organize the pages in your application.

How it Works

A set of tabs works across your entire application, so the attributes for tabs are accessed through the Shared Components area of your application development area.

1. Click on the Application link in your runtime environment to return to the main development page.

2. Click on the Shared Components icon.

3. In the `Navigation` section, the top section on the right-hand side, click on the `Tabs` link to bring up the page shown in Figure 4-20.

Figure 4-20

You can see a graphical representation of the tab set for this application. The tab set created by default for the application is called `TS1`, and there are two child tabs for this tab set, `Orders` and `Products`. On this page, you can add modify the attributes of a tab by clicking on the Edit icon in the tab, adding another tab to a tab set, or adding another tab set to your application. Your immediate task is to add another tab to the existing tab set, which will hold links to a number of pages that can be used for maintenance operations on some of the base tables.

<hr/>

Try It Out   Adding a Tab

You will need to define a page to associate with a new tab, so you should start the process of adding a new tab by creating a page that the tab will reference.

1. Return to the main development page for the application by clicking on the name of the application in the breadcrumb trail at the top of the page.

2. Click Create Page and accept the default selection of Blank Page in the first step of the Page Creation Wizard. Click Next.

3. Accept the default for the `Page Number` and enter `Maintenance` as the `Page Alias`. Click Next.

4. Use `Maintenance` as the page `Name` and `Title` and click Next.

The next page of the wizard, shown in Figure 4-21, prompts you to assign the page to a tab, as you did with earlier pages. You could simply add another tab to the existing tab set here, but leave the default choice of No to allow you to go back and add the page to a tab explicitly.

Figure 4-21

5. Accept the default choice, and click Next.

6. Click Finish to create your page.

Now you are ready to return to the Tab area to create a new tab and link it to your newly created blank page.

7. Click on the gear icon in the upper-right corner of the page. This icon is a shortcut to go to the Shared Components main page.

8. Click on the Tabs link.

9. In the lower bar of the tab set layout graphic, where the Orders and Products tabs are listed, click Add to bring up the page shown in Figure 4-22.

10. On this page, give the new tab a Tab Label of Maintenance, and click Next.

11. Click on the dropdown button for the Tab Current for Page, and select the Maintenance page you just created.

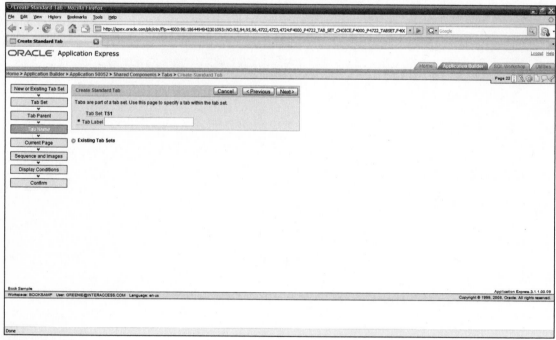

Figure 4-22

Notice that this entry allows you to specify a single page associated with this tab. Later in this section, you will see how you can assign other pages for this particular tab.

12. Click Next. You can assign a sequence number, which determines where the tab will be displayed in relation to other tabs in the tab set. Accept the default, and click Next.

13. The next page gives you the option to only display the tab when certain conditions are met. Although this option can make your user interface more flexible, you will not need it for this basic application, so click Next.

14. The final page gives you a recap of your choices. Click Create Tab to complete your work on the tab.

Another development task, another wizard to simplify the task.

How It Works

You can jump right over to the application and see your new tab in action.

1. Click on the Run icon to launch your application.

2. The tab you just created is there in the tab bar for all to see. Click on it to see the tab, as shown in Figure 4-23.

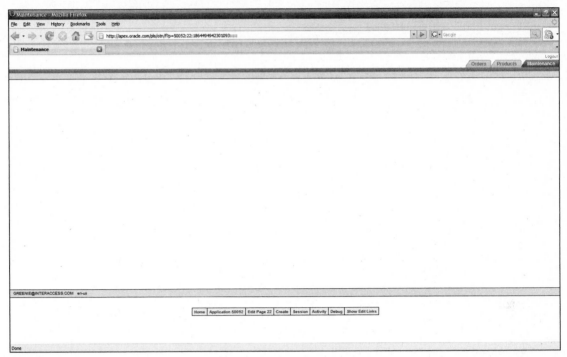

Figure 4-23

Less than exciting, right? A blank page is a blank page — seen one, seen them all. The tab won't remain blank for long. The next section will show you how to create a list of links and use that list on the blank page as well as other pages in your application.

Try It Out   **Creating Lists**

Adding the tab and assigning a blank page was just a placeholder for your real goal. For this application, as for many, there are some data tables that are not very dynamic, tables that rarely change their values. In this application, the PRODUCTS and CATEGORIES tables fit this description, since they are primarily used to ensure data integrity. Most users of this application will not need nor should have access to these tables or the pages that provide access.

You will address the issue of limiting access later in this book in Chapter 9 on security.

The Maintenance tab is a place to put the pages that handle these tables. You could create links to these pages and have those links on the now blank maintenance page. But you might want to offer access to the pages from several points in the application, and reduce maintenance by having the same list of links in all places, so you could simply modify the list in one place. This section will walk through the creation and use of this type of list.

1. Return to the development area for your application.

2. Click Create Page.

3. On the next page, select Form, and click Next.

4. On the next page, select the Form on a Table with Report option, and click Next.

5. Accept the default schema on the next page, and click Next.

6. On the next page, select the CATEGORIES table in the picklist, set the Page Name and Region Title to Categories, and click Next.

7. For the next page, accept the default, Do not use tabs, and click Next.

You will be associating this page with a tab, but you will be using a list to accomplish this task, so you do not need to assign the page to a tab now.

8. Select all of the columns and click Next.

9. Accept the default edit link image, and click Next.

10. On the next page, change the Page Name and Region Title to Categories, and click Next.

11. Once again, accept the default for Primary Key, and click Next.

12. On the next page, choose the Existing sequence option, and select the CATEGORIES_SEQ from the Sequence picklist. Click Next.

13. Select the column for the form, and click Next.

14. Accept all the buttons for the page, and click Next.

15. The final page confirms your choices. Click Finish to create the pages.

You have the report and form you will use to add, delete, and modify the data in the CATEGORIES table.

Wizard Fatigue?

Are you tired of clicking Next? (I'm certainly tired of writing it <g>) Any wizard-driven interface will use a number of pages to gather the parameters needed to create a piece of functionality. You may get a little frustrated at having to go through so many screens to create a simple default report. But wizards must always strike a balance between speed of use and flexibility. All those pages on which you simply accepted defaults give you the ability to modify those defaults when you want to add other pages which may not be quite as straightforward. Right now, those extra clicks may seem bothersome, but as your knowledge of APEX deepens and your requirements become more exacting, you will be very glad you can implement these requirements and still use the wizards.

Your next step is to create a list of links to include these pages, as well as the pages that modify the PRODUCTS table.

1. Go to the Shared Components area by clicking on the gear icon in the upper-right corner.

2. Click on the List link in the Navigation section.

3. On the main page for lists, click Create to bring up the page shown in Figure 4-24.

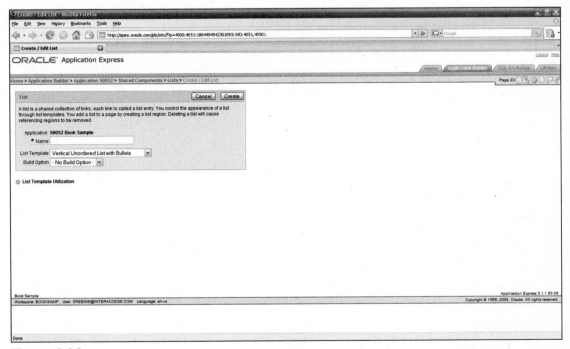

Figure 4-24

On this page, you will give your list a name and indicate the basic formatting of the list. For this list, the default of Vertical Unordered List with Bullets will be fine, but you might want to click the dropdown button on the picklist to see some of your other choices.

4. Enter Maintenance pages for the Name, and click Create, which will take you to the List Entries page for the list, shown in its completed form in Figure 4-25.

5. Click Create List Entry, which will bring up the page shown in Figure 4-26.

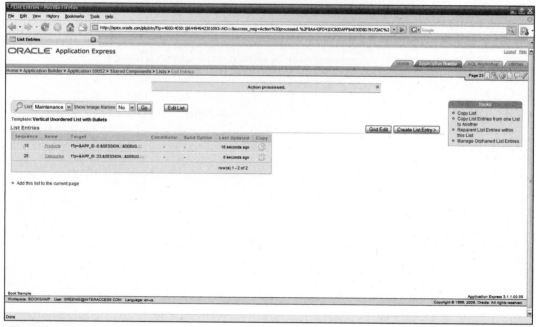

Figure 4-25

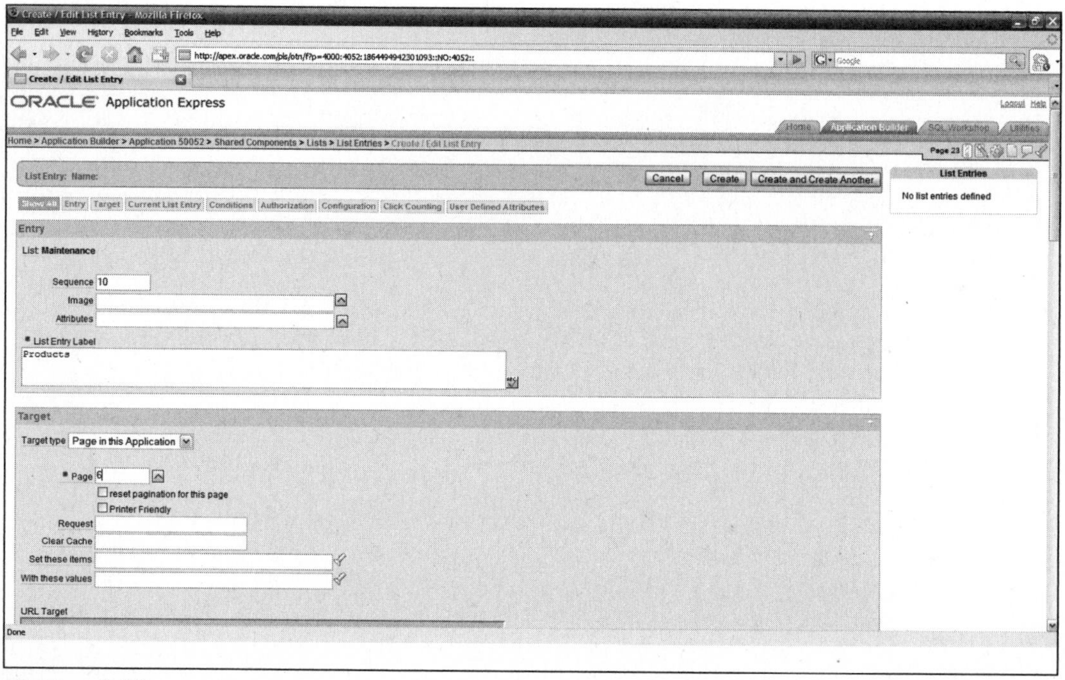

Figure 4-26

You are probably getting used to the look of attribute pages by this time. For this page, you only have to enter two values to create a link entry for the list.

6. Enter `Products` as the `List Entry Label`. Select the `Report on Products` page, which is the report on `PRODUCTS`, for the `Page`. Click on Create and Create Another to add another entry for the list.

7. For the next entry, set the `List Entry Label` as `Categories` and select the first page for `CATEGORIES` as the `Page`. Click Create, which will return you to the list of entries shown in Figure 4-25 above.

Your list is complete. You can now add the list to one or more pages in the application.

Try It Out Adding a List to a Page

Lists, like tabs, are shared objects, but lists can be used in various ways on separate pages.

1. Return to the application development page and click on the blank `Maintenance` page you created.

The main container for the contents of a page is called a region. Adding the list to your currently blank page is simply a matter of creating a region with the list.

2. Click on the plus (+) icon in the upper right corner of the `Regions` section of the `Page Rendering` column, which will bring up the page shown in Figure 4-27.

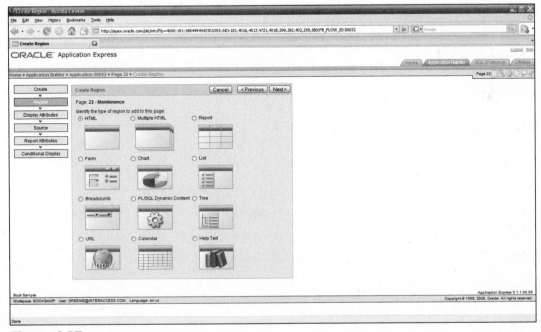

Figure 4-27

As with the creation of a page, the creation of a region starts by specifying the basic type of content that will be in the region.

3. Select the List choice, and click Next.

4. Give the region a Title of Maintenance Pages and select the Navigation Region, Alternative 1 as the Region Template. Click Next.

5. The next page has a picklist of available lists. Since you have only created one list, select the Maintenance pages list and click Create List Region.

With those few steps, you have added your navigation list to the formerly blank page.

How It Works

Time to take a look at your list in action.

1. Click on the Run icon to run the Maintenance page, which now looks like Figure 4-28.

2. Click on the Products link to bring up the Products page.

The link works just as you expected — almost. If you take a look at the tabs at the top of the page, you can see that clicking on the Products link highlights the Products tab. At this point, the Products tab shouldn't be in the tab set at all, and the Maintenance tab should be highlighted when you are on any of the pages relating to PRODUCTS or CATEGORIES.

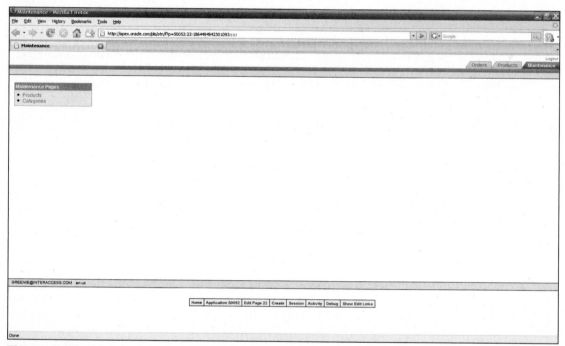

Figure 4-28

Try It Out   Modifying Tab Sets

You can easily make both these changes by editing the attributes of the tab set.

1. Return to the development environment and go to the `Shared Components` area. Once there, click on the `Tabs` link.

2. Click on the Maintenance tab link in the lower row of tabs, and then click on the Edit icon on the left of the tab to bring up the page shown in Figure 4-29.

You haven't actually seen this page before, since the tab and its attributes were created for you as part of the Tab Creation Wizard. The page has the attributes you have come to expect for an APEX object, and one attribute in particular you will want to change — the `Tab Also Current for Pages` attribute.

This attribute lets you specify more pages that should cause this tab to be selected. You want to add the four pages for the `PRODUCTS` and `CATEGORIES` pages. The field only takes page numbers, so use the dropdown button for the Tab Page picklist to determine the numbers for the desired pages. If you have been doing the exercises for this book in the specified order, those pages should be 8, 10, 12 and 13.

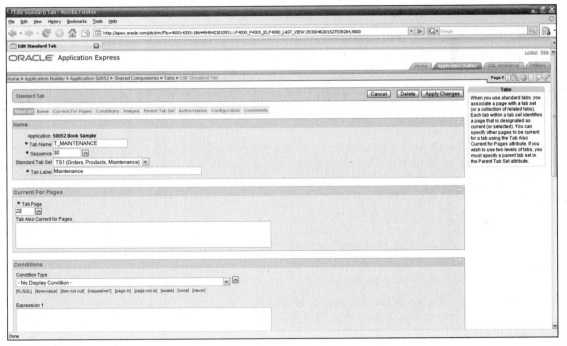

Figure 4-29

3. Add the page numbers for the four pages, separated by commas, to the `Tab Also Current for Pages` field. Click Apply Changes.

You have now associated the right pages with the maintenance tab, but you have one more change to make to adjust the new tab set.

4. Click on the Products tab in the lower tab list, and then again on the Edit icon for that tab.

5. Click Delete to remove the tab from the tab set and then confirm the deletion.

Since the pages formerly associated with the Products tab are now accessed through the Maintenance tab, you no longer need that tab.

Reusing Lists

You have already noticed that most pages in the APEX development environment have a little list of commonly used tasks on the right-hand side of the page. You could add the list you already created for maintenance to another page in your application.

1. Return to the main development area for the application, and select the master-detail page.

2. In the Regions section of the attributes page, click on the plus (+) icon to add another region to the page.

3. Select the List choice, and click Next.

4. Give the Region the title of Maintenance pages, change the Region Template to Navigation Region, Alternative 1. Accept the default Display Point of Page Template Body (3, items above region content), and click Next.

Notice that the shared list is a logical entity that can be displayed in different ways in different pages.

5. Accept the default List, since you only have one, and click on Create List Region to add the region.

If you look at the wizard progress indicator on the left of the page, you can see that you could specify more attributes for the region, including a conditional display. You didn't need to bother with those additional attributes, so by clicking on the Create List Region, you accepted the defaults for those attributes.

How It Works

Time to take a look at your newly modified page and see if the list looks right.

1. Click on the Run icon for the page to bring up the new page, as shown in Figure 4-30.

Hmmm. The Maintenance list shows up below the Orders region. You really wanted it to show up to the right of the region. Fortunately, this issue is easily addressed.

2. Return to the development environment for the current page. Click on the Maintenance Pages link in the Regions section. In the User Interface Attributes section, change the Column to 2.

The layout of the page is done, as you might have already guessed, with an HTML table component. To move the navigation list to the right of the existing regions, you have to put it in the second column of that underlying structure.

3. Click Apply Changes.

4. Click Run to see the new version of the page, as shown in Figure 4-31.

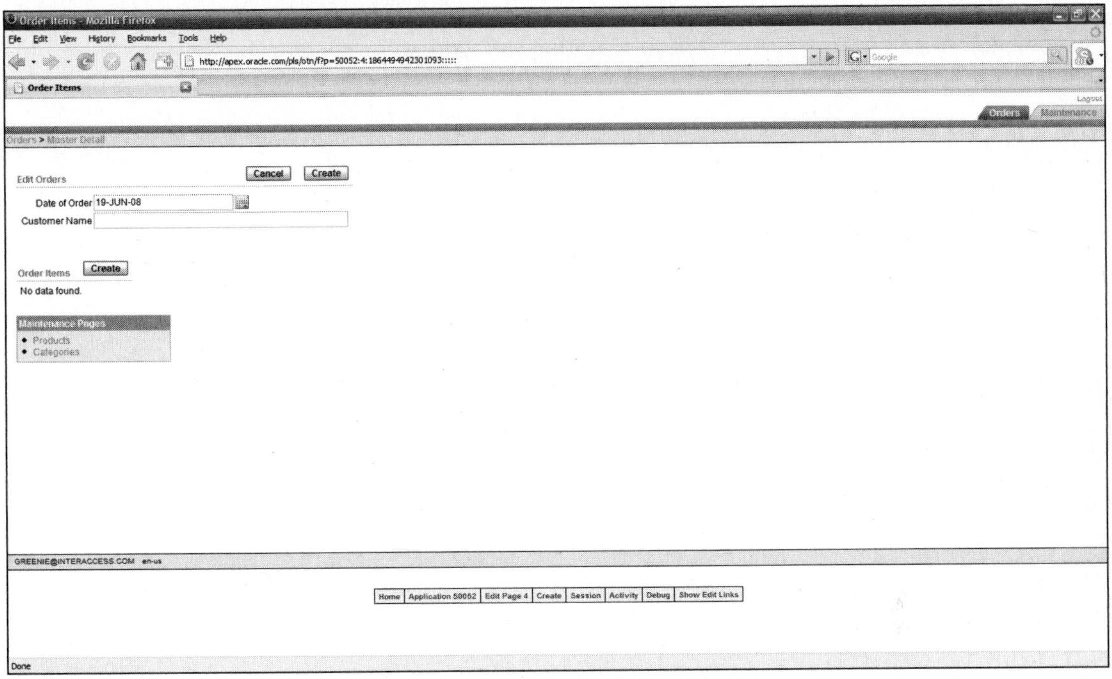

Figure 4-30

Figure 4-31

Now that's more like it. The navigation list shows up where you wanted it. You could, of course, add the list to more pages, and you could also set conditions on the display of particular list items, based on logical tests.

You have quickly seen the power of shared components — create once, use many times. This power is even more important in terms of maintenance. If your application were to grow, adding more tables would require maintenance pages, you could simply add them to the list and they would automatically appear wherever the list was used.

Summary

In this chapter, you covered a lot of ground. You:

❑   Learned how to add validation routines to your application.

❑   Learned how to add a calculation to your application.

❑   Added a navigation button.

❑   Learned about branching options for navigation.

❑   Explored the built-in navigation capabilities of your APEX application.

❑   Built a shared list to add more customized navigation to two places in your application.

With each step, you add more customized functionality to your application, through a declarative, easy-to-use interface.

The next section will explore one of the richest areas of default functionality in APEX — reporting and charts. In this chapter, you will not have to do a lot of work, since the built-in functionality of interactive reports is so rich, but you will see a whole lot of functionality that comes along with any APEX application.

Reporting and Charting

As developers, we sometimes get caught up in the fun of creating applications — applications that implement all kinds of logic, that perform cool tricks to help users enter and update data, and that are pleasing to the eye and the mouse.

But as we focus only on applications, we tend to concentrate on entering, updating, and deleting data. These processes are, in the real world, typically just precursors to unlocking the real power of collected data through reports and charts.

Oracle Application Express makes it as easy to generate powerful and flexible reports as it does to create data access pages. In this chapter, you will create some more sophisticated reports and explore the ways that users can interact with the reports.

More Data Design

The purpose of this chapter is to show you some of the wonderful things you can do with reports and charts, but the data model currently in place is less than challenging. You have one real master-detail relationship, with some other foreign keys used to implement data integrity.

Before you can really see what APEX reports and charts can do for you, you will have to add one more table to your schema. You will create the basic table for customer information using SQL Workshop, and then you will expand that table structure and use a script to load additional data.

Try It Out   **Create Another Lookup Table**

You have already created a lookup table for CATEGORIES and taken the steps required to take advantage of the table in your application. The first part of adding customer information to your schema follows the same steps:

1. Go to the SQL Workshop area of the APEX development environment.

2. Use the cascading menus from the Object Browser to browse the tables.

3. Select the ORDERS table, and click on Create Lookup Table.

On the next page, you will see that, by default, you have been presented with a list of all character columns for the table.

4.   Select CUSTOMER_NAME for the Column, and click Next.

The next page prompts you for a name for the new table and the new sequence that will be used to generate IDs for the table. You will want to change these to make the names more in keeping with the naming standards in your schema.

5.   Change New Table Name to CUSTOMERS and New Sequence to CUSTOMER_SEQ. Click Next.

6.   On the final page of the wizard, click Finish.

You have created a table containing a code and label for each customer, dropped the column that used to contain the CUSTOMER_NAME from the ORDERS table, added a column to hold the new value of CUSTOMER_NAME_ID, populated it with the right values, and created a foreign key to link the two tables together.

Accepting Defaults

You may not really like the fact that the new column in ORDERS is called CUSTOMER_NAME_ID rather than CUSTOMER_ID. You could have gone through each of these steps manually to gain full control over the naming of the new column. Of course, the best practice would be to design your data structures with these types of relationships in place from the beginning, but you may not have that option in all cases, especially when you are moving data from another source, a topic that will be covered later in this book.

You are now ready to represent the new functionality in your application.

Try It Out   Adding a Lookup Table to Your Application

You have also done the steps in this section before, so you can go through them quickly this time through.

1.   Return to your application and click on the master-detail page.

2.   Click on the item for CUSTOMER_NAME.

You will want to make three changes to the attributes of this field.

3.   In the Name section of the page, change the Display As value to Select List by clicking on the Select List link below the field.

4.   Click on Source at the top of the page to isolate the attributes of the item.

You can see that this item is bound to the CUSTOMER_NAME column in the ORDERS table. If you tried to run this page now, you would get an SQL error, since this column no longer exists in that table. You have to change the source of the item, and you could also change the name of the item to reflect the new source. For the sake of simplicity, the examples in this book will leave the name of the item as it stands.

5. Change the `Source value or expression` to CUSTOMER_NAME_ID, the name of the new column in the ORDERS table.

6. Click the LOV button to bring up the section of the attributes concerning LOVs.

7. Click on the `Create Dynamic List Of Values` link at the bottom of the section.

8. In the wizard for creating dynamic LOVs, accept the default schema and click Next.

9. Select the CUSTOMERS table in the next page, and click Next.

10. Select CUSTOMER_NAME as the `Display Column` and CUSTOMER_NAME_ID as the `Return Value`, and click Next.

11. Accept the generated SQL, and click Finish. Click Apply Changes.

You have added the LOV to the edit page for the ORDERS table. As with the use of the lookup table in the previous chapters, you will also want to add the new column to the initial report by modifying the SQL source for that report.

12. Return to the main development page for the application, and click on the initial interactive report created for the ORDERS table. If you are doing the exercises for this book in order, this page should be Page 1.

13. Click on the Region Definition tab.

14. Change the SQL in the `Source` section from:

```
select
"ORDER_ID",
"ORDER_TIMESTAMP",
"CUSTOMER_NAME_ID",
  from    "ORDERS"
```

to the following code:

```
select
"ORDER_ID",
"CUSTOMERS"."CUSTOMER_NAME",
"ORDER_TIMESTAMP"
  from    "ORDERS", "CUSTOMERS"
  where "ORDERS"."CUSTOMER_NAME_ID" = "CUSTOMERS"."CUSTOMER_NAME_ID"
```

You could, as you did before, build this code with the Query Builder if you are not familiar with SQL syntax. You are only making three small changes to the code:

❑ Deleting the reference to the CUSTOM_NAME_ID and adding the reference to the CUSTOMER_NAME field qualified with the name of the CUSTOMERS table.

Since you are adding the column to the second spot in the list, make sure to add a comma following it and remove the comma following ORDER_TIMESTAMP.

❑ Adding the CUSTOMERS table to the list of tables following the keyword FROM.

❑ Adding a WHERE clause to establish the link between the CUSTOMER_NAME_ID columns in both tables.

15. Click Apply Changes to save the changes.

You have integrated the new lookup relationship into the functionality of your application. These steps were necessary to create the new CUSTOMERS table and relate it to the existing ORDERS table. But you want to have access to more information about your customers than simply their name. You will expand the CUSTOMERS table and learn how to use SQL scripts to add data to the expanded table in the next section.

Extending Existing Tables

There are three steps to go through to extend the data in a table. First, you have to expand the structure of the table. Next, you will have to get the customer data into the newly expanded table with an SQL script. The final step will be to quickly create some pages to maintain this data and add it to the list of maintenance pages you created in the last chapter.

Try It Out   Adding Columns to an Existing Table

You begin the process by adding more columns to the CUSTOMERS table.

1. Go to the SQL Workshop, and select Object Browser > Browse > Tables from the cascading menus.

2. Click on the CUSTOMERS table.

You can see that the CUSTOMERS table you created has just two columns. You have to add more columns to hold additional information about your customers.

3. Click on Add Column to bring up the page shown in Figure 5-1.

On this page, you have to add a name for your new column, and make sure that the Type is appropriate for the data you will be storing in the column. You can also indicate that the column may or may not contain data by leaving the Nullable value to NULL.

You must allow NULL values for all new columns in this table, since rows already exist in the table, but the columns you will be adding to those rows will not have a value when first created.

4. Set Add Column to CUST_STREET_ADDRESS, the Type to VARCHAR2 and the length to 200.

The Oracle database always stores VARCHAR2 columns as variable length columns, so the Length specification does not really affect storage requirements, only the maximum length for the data in the column.

5. Click Next to bring up the verification page, where you can click Finish to add the column to the table.

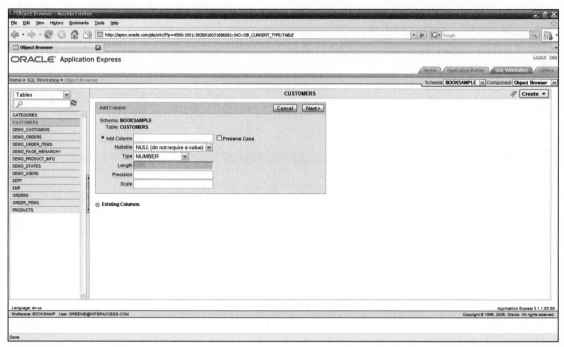

Figure 5-1

You will take the same approach to add more columns to the table. Table 5-1 lists the column names, types, and storage specifications for the additional columns for the CUSTOMERS table.

Table 5-1

Column Name	Type	Storage Specification
CUST_CITY	VARCHAR2	40
CUST_STATE	VARCHAR2	2
CUST_POSTAL_CODE	VARCHAR2	10
CUST_PHONE	VARCHAR2	15
CUST_CREDIT_LIMIT	Number	Precision: 7 Scale: 0
CUST_EMAIL	VARCHAR2	40

Normally, you could name the columns in a table anything you want. But you will be using an already written script to update the columns in this table, so the names of your column will have to be exactly the same as those listed in Table 5-1.

When you are done adding all the columns to the CUSTOMERS table, your table structure should look like Figure 5-2.

Figure 5-2

The next step is to add data to your new columns.

Try It Out   Using Scripts to Update Rows

As you know by now, the data for your APEX applications, as well as the code for the application, is stored in an Oracle database. This architecture means that you can use all standard SQL functionality to interact with that data.

You have just added columns to the CUSTOMERS table, a table that already contains a primary key, CUSTOMER_NAME_ID, and the CUSTOMER_NAME data. It just so happens that data for these customers exists, and you would like to add it to the newly modified table.

You can accomplish this by running an SQL script. A script is nothing more than a text file that contains SQL commands. In this case, the command you will want to use is the UPDATE command.

An UPDATE statement is used to set the value of columns in one or more rows in the table. If you only want to update a subset of all the rows in the table, use a WHERE clause to limit the rows affected.

The script that you will use contains two flavors of UPDATE statements — a series of statements to update columns in specific rows, and one statement to set a value for all the rows.

SQL Workshop has a handy utility to help you store and run scripts.

1. Return to the SQL Workshop main page.

2. Click on the SQL Scripts icon to bring up the page shown in Figure 5-3.

Figure 5-3

You can see that you can either create a script from scratch or upload a script file.

3. Click Upload to bring up the page shown in Figure 5-4.

4. Use Browse to bring up a file browser. Navigate to the sample code for this book and select the update_customers.txt file.

5. Set the Script Name to Update Customers, and click Upload. This action will store the script in the APEX environment, so you can easily retrieve it and run it.

When you return to the main SQL Scripts page, you can see your new script.

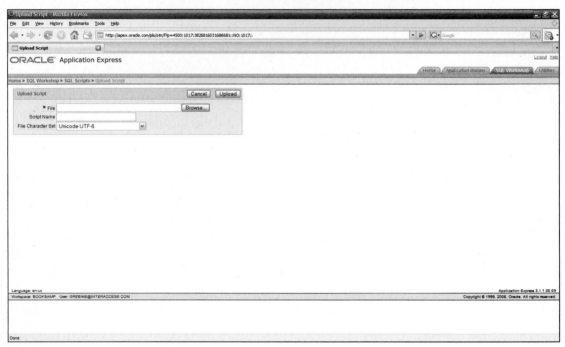

Figure 5-4

6. Click on the Update Customers script to bring up the page shown in Figure 5-5.

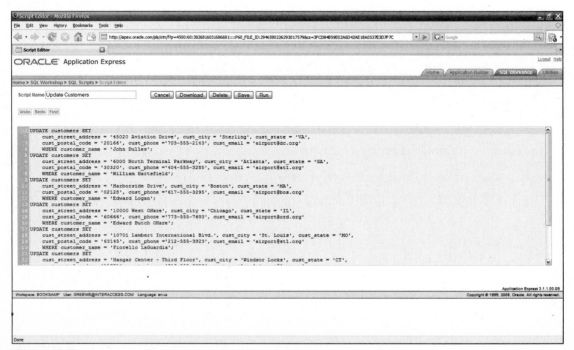

Figure 5-5

```
UPDATE customers SET
    cust_street_address = '45020 Aviation Drive', cust_city = 'Sterling', cust_state = 'VA',
    cust_postal_code = '20166', cust_phone ='703-555-2143', cust_email = 'airport@dc.org'
    WHERE customer_name = 'John Dulles';
UPDATE customers SET
    cust_street_address = '6000 North Terminal Parkway', cust_city = 'Atlanta', cust_
        state = 'GA',
    cust_postal_code = '30320', cust_phone ='404-555-3285', cust_email = 'airport@atl.org'
    WHERE customer_name = 'William Hartsfield';
UPDATE customers SET
    cust_street_address = 'Harborside Drive', cust_city = 'Boston', cust_state = 'MA',
    cust_postal_code = '02128', cust_phone ='617-555-3295', cust_email = 'airport@bos.org'
    WHERE customer_name = 'Edward Logan';
UPDATE customers SET
    cust_street_address = '10000 West OHare', cust_city = 'Chicago', cust_state = 'IL',
    cust_postal_code = '60666', cust_phone ='773-555-7693', cust_email = 'airport@ord.org'
    WHERE customer_name = 'Edward Butch OHare';
UPDATE customers SET
    cust_street_address = '10701 Lambert International Blvd.', cust_city = 'St. Louis',
        cust_state = 'MO',
    cust_postal_code = '63145', cust_phone ='212-555-3923', cust_email = 'airport@stl.org'
    WHERE customer_name = 'Fiorello LaGuardia';
UPDATE customers SET
    cust_street_address = 'Hangar Center - Third Floor', cust_city = 'Windsor Locks',
        cust_state = 'CT',
    cust_postal_code = '11371', cust_phone ='212-555-3923', cust_email = 'airport@lga.org'
    WHERE customer_name = 'Albert Lambert';
UPDATE customers SET
    cust_street_address = 'Schoephoester Road', cust_city = 'Flushing', cust_state = 'NY',
    cust_postal_code = '06096', cust_phone ='860-555-1835', cust_email = 'airport@hfd.org'
    WHERE customer_name = 'Eugene Bradley';
UPDATE customers SET cust_credit_limit = 1000;
```

The script is pretty direct. Each row in the customer table has a corresponding UPDATE statement that will set the values of most of the columns in the row. The final statement in the script updates the value of the CUST_CREDIT_LIMIT for all the rows in the table, which is fine since all customers will start out with the same credit limit.

7. Click Run, which will bring up a confirmation page. Click Run again to bring up the page shown in Figure 5-6.

This page displays information about all the scripts that have been run in this session. If you are working with scripts a lot, you will find this page very handy, since it contains links for each script, which can take you right back to the script page itself. You can also see a Status field, which initially displays Submitted.

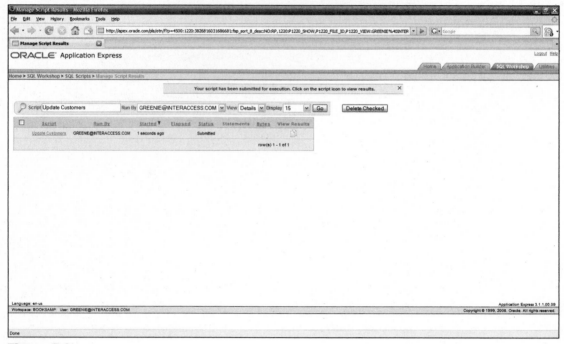

Figure 5-6

8. Refresh the page in your browser.

Unless the server is exceptionally busy, you should see that the script status has changed to Completed. Once the script is complete, you can see how many of the statements in the script have been executed.

9. To get a little more detail on the results of the script, click View Results for the script, to bring up the page shown in Figure 5-7.

If any of the statements in the script resulted in errors, this page would let you see those results. This script, though, should have run perfectly without any errors.

10. Return to the SQL Workshop, and use the cascading menus to browse the tables.

11. Select the CUSTOMERS table, and click on the data link to bring up the page shown in Figure 5-8.

You should see your CUSTOMERS table populated with data.

If you are used to using SQL, you are probably very happy to see this scripting facility. If SQL is still unfamiliar to you, you may feel yourself shying away from using this capability. But those of you in this camp should still be aware that SQL is a very, very powerful language, and you should think about using this power to help you accomplish your data-centric tasks. And you can use the Query Browser to build queries with a point-and-click interface and then examine the generated SQL as a way of becoming more familiar with its syntax.

Figure 5-7

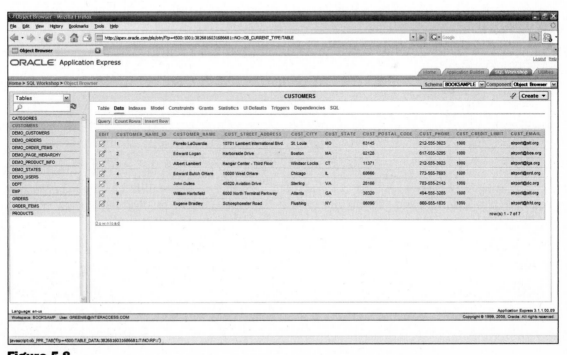

Figure 5-8

The last thing to do before moving on to reports is to quickly create and integrate pages for maintaining your customer data.

Try It Out   Adding Additional Maintenance Pages to Your Application

Now that you have your CUSTOMERS table, you will have to give your users a way to maintain the data in the table.

1. Return to the Application Builder, and click on your application.

2. Click Create Page, and then select the Form option and click Next.

3. Select the Form on a Table with Report option, and click Next.

4. Accept the default schema by clicking Next.

5. In the next page, select the CUSTOMERS table from the picklist, and click Next.

6. On the next page, you can change the Page Name and Region Title, if you want to make them more descriptive and click Next.

7. On the next page, leave the default of Do not use tabs, since you will be adding this page to your navigation list, and click Next.

8. On the next page, select all the columns except the CUSTOMER_NAME_ID and click Next. Accept the default edit icon on the next page, and click Next again.

9. You can change the Page Name and Region Title on the next page, if you want to give more descriptive names to the form, and then click Next.

10. Accept the primary key on the next page.

11. Change the source for the primary key to Existing sequence, and select the CUSTOMERS_SEQ in the picklist below. Click Next.

12. Select all the columns on the next page, and click Next. Accept all the default buttons on the next page, and click Next again. Click Finish to create the form and report pages.

You have created the appropriate pages to handle basic maintenance on the CUSTOMERS table. Now all you have to do is to add a link to the report to your navigation list to integrate these pages into your application.

13. Click on the Shared Components icon (the gear) in the upper right of the page.

14. Click on the Lists link in the Navigation section of the page to access the list you created.

15. Click on the list you created to bring up the table of list entries. Click Create List Entry.

16. Set the `List Entry Label` to `Customers`, and select the report page you just created for the `Page` in the `Target` section. Click Create.

Before seeing how the new list entry looks in your application, you want to make sure that the right tab is selected when your two new pages are in use.

17. Click on the Shared Components icon, and then the `Tabs` link in the `Navigation` section.

18. Click on the Maintenance tab to select it, and then the Edit icon to edit the values.

19. In the `Tab Also Current for Pages` text box in the `Current For Pages` section, add the page numbers for the two pages you just created. If you are not sure of the page numbers, you can use the picklist for the `Tab Pages` field above to find them.

20. Click on Apply Changes to save the changes, and then click on Run in the upper-right corner, which will launch the application.

21. Click on the Orders tab, and then click on Edit for one of the orders. The `Edit` form for the `ORDERS` table now looks like Figure 5-9.

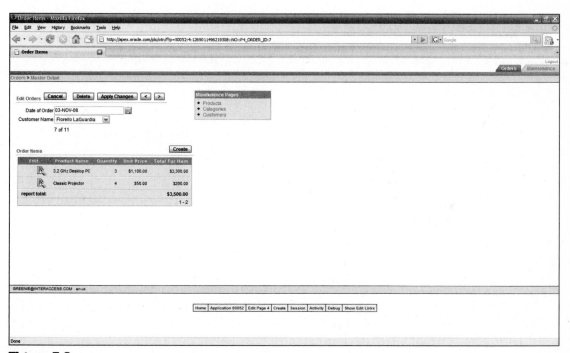

Figure 5-9

22. You can see the new link for the maintenance page for CUSTOMERS. Click on the link to go there and see how the proper tab is selected.

You have now increased the scope of the data your application is built on. The rest of this chapter will be about creating and using reports and charts on that data.

Report Creation

Your data schema is set and populated. You have pages in place to look at small amounts of data, such as a list of customers or the order items in a particular order. But the value of data expands as you create reports on larger amounts of information. Reports give your users the ability to move from a view of a single entity, such as an order, to a larger universe, such as overall sales.

You unlock this value through the use of reports and charts, and APEX gives you some very nice options to easily deliver that increased value.

Try It Out   **Creating a Standard Report**

You have already created reports as part of the page creation process. It's time for you to design some reports that provide a wider view of data by accessing more than two tables.

The first report you will create is a standard APEX report.

1. Return to the APEX development environment, and click Create Page.

2. Select the Report choice, and click Next.

You can use a Report Creation Wizard to create a report quickly.

3. Select the Wizard Report, and click Next, which will bring up the page shown in Figure 5-10.

4. Change the Page Title to Orders Report and the Region Title to Orders. Click Next.

5. On the next page, accept the default, Do not use tabs, and click Next.

The next page, shown in its complete state in Figure 5-11, is the core page in the wizard. In this page, you can select one or more tables to use in your report.

6. Select the ORDERS table in the Table/View selection list. This action will cause the columns for that table to appear in the left-hand Available Columns list box.

7. Select ORDER_TIMESTAMP, and click the > to move it to the Displayed Columns list box.

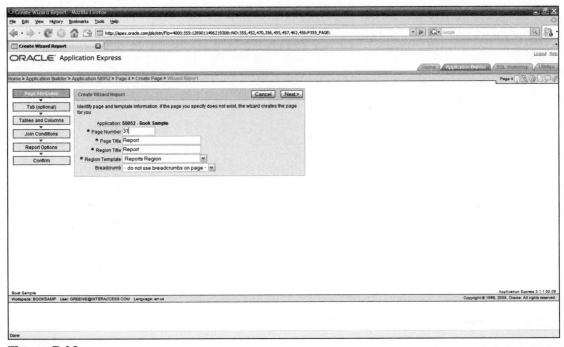

Figure 5-10

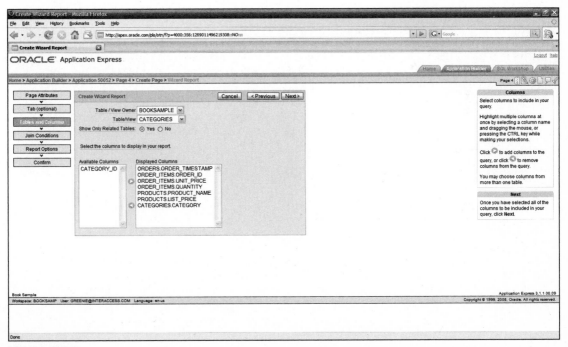

Figure 5-11

This action has two effects. The select column(s) move to the right-hand box, but the column name is preceded by the table name. Also, when you select a column from the first table, a pair of radio buttons appears just below the Table/View picklist, relating to whether that picklist should now Show Only Related Tables to the ones that have been included in the report.

8. Leave Show Only Related Tables set to the default of Yes, and click on the dropdown button for the Table/View picklist.

This time, you see that the picklist only contains CUSTOMERS, the target of a foreign key relationship from ORDERS, and ORDER_ITEMS, which has a foreign key pointing to ORDERS.

9. Select the ORDER_ITEMS table, and then select the ORDER_ID, UNIT_PRICE, and QUANTITY columns and move them to the Displayed Columns list box.

Now that you have included ORDER_ITEMS in the report, the PRODUCTS table will appear as a related table.

10. Select the PRODUCTS table, and then the PRODUCT_NAME and LIST_PRICE to include in the report.

11. Select the CATEGORIES table and the CATEGORY column for inclusion in the report and to show the page as displayed in Figure 5-11. Click Next.

Previously, when you used the Query Builder, the generated SQL produced when you linked tables included a WHERE clause that described the logical basis of the link, which is referred to as a *join condition*. On this page, the Report Wizard has automatically created the most likely join conditions based on the defined foreign key relationships.

12. The join relationships shown in this page are appropriate, so click Next.

The next page, shown in Figure 5-12, gives you the option of changing some of the basic user interface options for the report, including the template, which provides a look and feel, how many rows per page, and whether you want to allow the user to sort the report based on a particular column.

13. You will see the report soon enough, so click Next to accept the defaults.

14. The final page contains a recap of your choices. Click Create Report Page to put the choices into your page.

Your report is complete — time to see it in action.

How It Works

Creating a report with the Report Wizard was pretty quick and easy. The wizard helped you, or any developer, to understand the relationships between tables, select columns, and only asked you for some simple user defaults.

1. Click the Run Page icon to see the report itself, as shown in Figure 5-13.

Figure 5-12

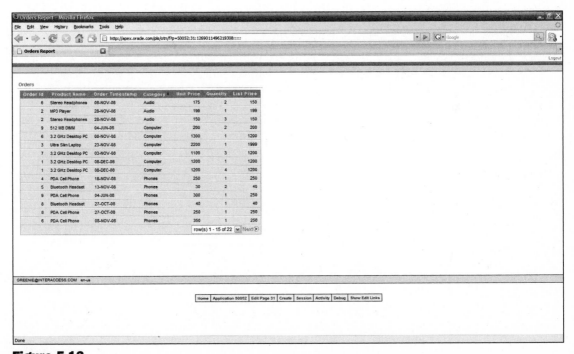

Figure 5-13

The report includes all the columns you specified. The columns are ordered in a slightly different order than you initially specified, but you can go to the report attributes for the page to change that order.

2. Click on the Product Name heading to change the report to the one shown in Figure 5-14.

Clicking on any column heading causes the rows in the report to be resorted, based on the selected column, in ascending order. The source and type of sorting is indicated by a little arrow in the column heading.

3. Click on the Product Name heading again to sort the rows in descending order.

Giving the end user the ability to sort the data in the report is a nice feature. The more you can empower the end user to shape their reports, the easier your development task will be, and the happier the end user will be. According to this principle, interactive reports is a major step forward for empowering end users, and reducing development effort, for APEX.

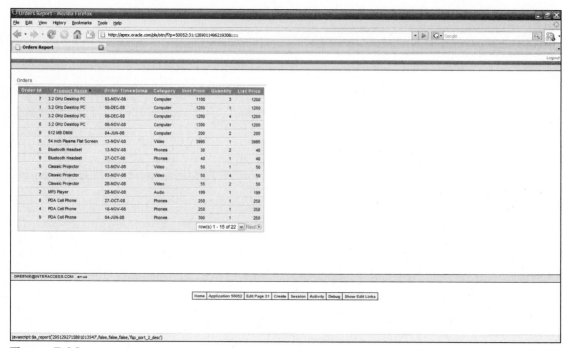

Figure 5-14

Try It Out   **Creating an Interactive Report**

Creating an interactive report is slightly different from creating a report with a wizard, but the process is not really any harder. In this section, you will create an interactive report that includes all the tables used for the previous report, along with the CUSTOMERS table for some additional analysis possibilities.

1. Return to the application development page, click Create Page, and then click on the Report choice.

2. On the next page, select Interactive Report, and click Next.

3. You should change the Page Name to Customer Orders Report and the Region Name to Customer Orders. Select the Breadcrumb choice for Breadcrumb, and leave the default. Click Next.

4. On the next page, choose to use an existing tab set and create a new tab. Give the new tab the name of Reports, and click Next.

The next page gives you the option of entering an SQL statement directly or using the Query Builder to create your SQL.

5. Click Query Builder to bring up the page shown in its completed form in Figure 5-15.

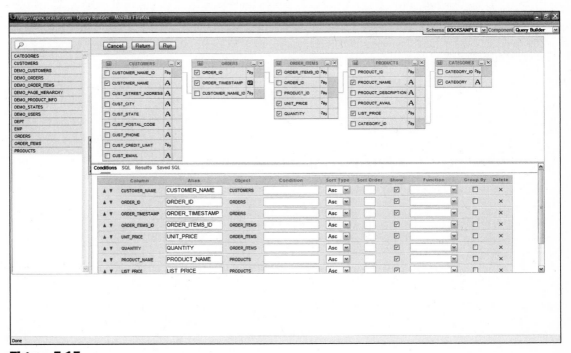

Figure 5-15

You used the Query Builder in an earlier exercise, so you can quickly design the data source for this interactive report.

6. In the left-hand panel of the Query Builder page for interactive reports, click on the CUSTOMERS, ORDERS, ORDER_ITEMS, and PRODUCTS tables, in that order.

7. Create connections between the related tables by clicking on the fields in the defined foreign key relationships for each table. In other words, click on:

    a. The CUSTOMER_NAME_ID in the CUSTOMERS table and the CUSTOMER_NAME_ID in the ORDERS table to create a link.

    b. The ORDER_ID in the ORDERS table and the ORDER_ID in the ORDER_ITEMS table.

    c. The PRODUCT_ID in the ORDER_ITEMS table and the PRODUCT_ID in the PRODUCTS table.

8. Once you have these links created, click on the Table Actions icon in the upper-left corner of the PRODUCTS table heading. Use the Add Parent selection list to add CATEGORIES to the Query Builder window, which will automatically also include the link for the table.

You can also use this shortcut to list and include child tables or to select all columns in a table with a single click.

9. Select the following columns for inclusion in the report by clicking on the check boxes to the left of each column:

    a. For the CUSTOMERS table, the CUSTOMER_NAME column.

    b. For the ORDERS table, the ORDER_ID and the ORDER_TIMESTAMP columns.

    c. For the ORDER_ITEMS table, the ORDER_ITEMS_ID, UNIT_PRICE, and QUANTITY columns.

    d. For the PRODUCTS table, the PRODUCT_NAME and LIST_PRICE columns.

    e. For the CATEGORIES table, the CATEGORY column.

When you check each column, the column appears in the column list at the bottom of the page. You could include selection conditions for any of these columns, but for this particular report, you can leave the selection conditions to the user.

The bottom panel of the Query Builder also lets you take a quick look at the results of the query, or move the order of the columns. You will see the results of the query soon enough, and you will leave the column order to the users.

10. Click on Return to copy the SQL from the query you just built to the text box in the Interactive Report Wizard, as shown in Figure 5-16, and then click Next.

There is one powerful option enabled by default just below the SQL text box. You can leave the default of Yes for Link To Single Row View, which will automatically include a link to display the entire row for entries in the report.

11. Click Finish on the final page of the wizard to create the page.

Interactive reports put loads of flexibility in the direct control of your users. You will have to understand what they will be able to do for themselves in order to understand how little you will have to do to provide all of this for them. The next section is all about the capabilities of APEX interactive reports.

Figure 5-16

Report Manipulation

The interactive report you have just created with a few pages of specifying attributes can change in many ways. This section will go through many of the ways your users can shape their interactive reports.

1. Click the Run Page icon to run the interactive report you just created. The report will initially look like Figure 5-17.

You have already seen, and played with, an interactive report in an earlier chapter. You can now poke around and explore much more of the functionality inherent in these reports. In the following steps, you will look at most of the choices available to you on the Action menu for the interactive report. Your first task is to revisit the choices available through the column headings and to change the formatting of your currency fields.

2. Make sure that the Edit Links are showing for the report page, and click on the column heading List Price to bring up the menu shown in Figure 5-18.

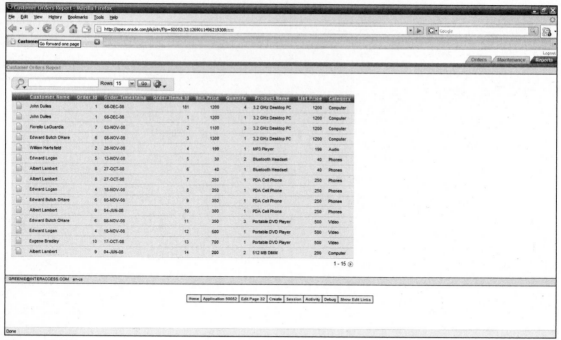

Figure 5-17

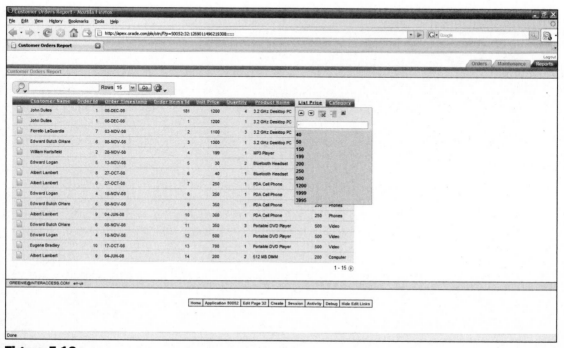

Figure 5-18

3. Click on the yellow arrow on the far right of the icons to edit the properties of the report.

4. Select the LIST_PRICE edit icon in the attribute page and change the Number/Date Format to represent currency formatting.

5. Click Apply Changes, and take the same actions for the UNIT_PRICE column. Once you have finished, click Run to return to the runtime environment.

You probably don't need to see the Order_Items_Id column in this report.

6. Click on the gear in the top bar of the report to bring up the Actions menu.

7. Click Select Columns in the Actions menu to bring up the page shown in Figure 5-19, and move the Order Items Id column into the left Do Not Display list box by selecting the column and clicking on the corresponding arrow between the list boxes. Click Apply.

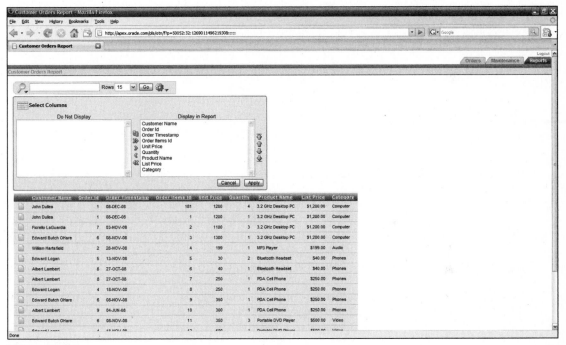

Figure 5-19

8. Select the Actions menu, and click Filter to bring up the page shown in Figure 5-20.

In Chapter 2, you added filtering conditions to your interactive report through the Search box at the top of the report. Your users can still add conditions with this method, but they can also add conditions in this dialog, with a little more flexibility.

9. Select the Product_Name column, the contains operator, and the value 3 as the expression, and click Apply to limit the rows displayed.

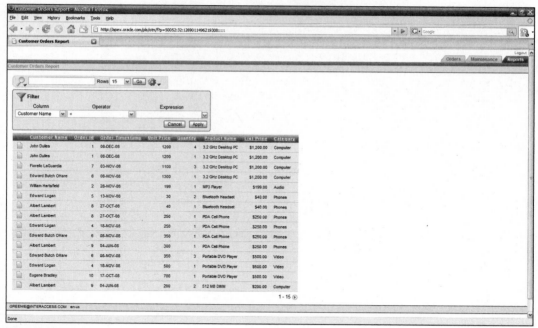

Figure 5-20

10. Return to `Filter` for interactive reports, and select the `Order_Timestamp` column. Click on the dropdown list for `Operator`, and you can see that `between` is listed for this date field.

The `between` operator makes sense for date fields and is more flexible than the choices offered in the column heading, which you used in Chapter 2. You can also see that both of the `Expression` fields for this operator include a date picker.

11. Click Cancel to return to the report without imposing a date condition.

Because of the test data, it may be difficult to assign a date range for your report. But once you get to the end of this section and see all the things you can do with your interactive reports, you will be able to see how the ability to specify a date range will be very useful.

12. Click Sort in the Actions menu to bring up the section shown in Figure 5-21.

13. Select the `Order_Id` for the first sort column, and then the `Order_Item_Id` for the second sort column. Click Apply to add the sort conditions to your report.

You saw that the `Order_Item_Id` is in a separate part of the column list, under the heading of `Other`, because the column is no longer shown on the page. You can sort on any column that is a part of the results for the report, whether it is visible or not. You can also see that the sort conditions for the report are not displayed at the top of the report, so you will have to go to the menu to see or change the sort order.

It's time to start exploring some of the more advanced features in your interactive report.

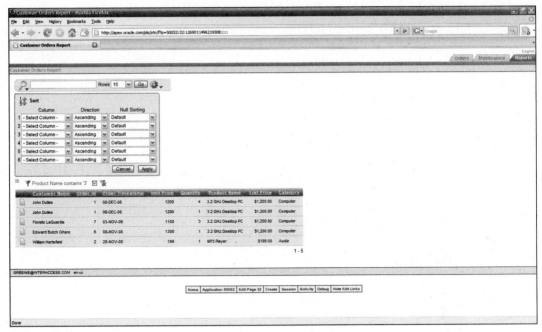

Figure 5-21

14. Click Control Break in the Actions menu to bring up the page shown in Figure 5-22.

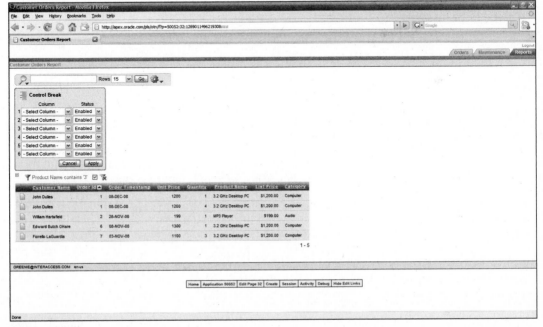

Figure 5-22

Specifying a control break has a few effects. The data in the report will be sorted on any control breaks specified. The rows for each value in any of your control breaks will be grouped together, with a header and footer. Finally, the column value and its column heading will be moved to the heading of the control break group.

15. Select the `Customer_Name` field for the first control break and click Apply to display the report as shown in Figure 5-23.

16. Add another control break for the `Order_Id` field, and click Apply to change the appearance of your interactive report, as shown in Figure 5-24.

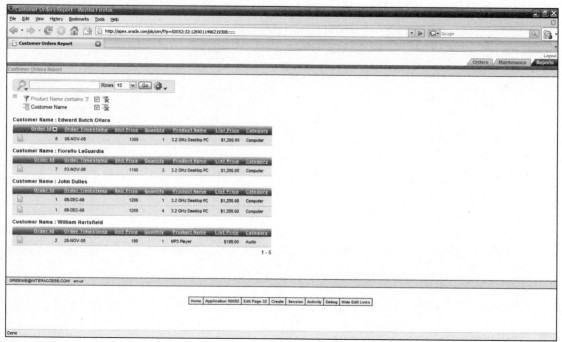

Figure 5-23

Notice that the interactive report does not add separate headings for multiple control breaks if they occur with the same row. Although both the `Customer_Name` and `Order_Id` changed with the last two customers, the interactive report only has a single heading for both of the changes.

As you saw when you added selection conditions earlier, each time you add conditions, or control breaks, to your report, an entry for the attribute is shown at the top of the report. Users can easily turn each of these attributes on or off with the check box in front of the listing, or remove the attribute entirely.

17. Uncheck the `Customer_Name` control break to show that column moving back into the report lines. Reselect the `Customer_Name` control break.

On to the next item to explore in the Actions menu.

18. Click Compute in the Actions menu to bring up the page shown in Figure 5-25.

Figure 5-24

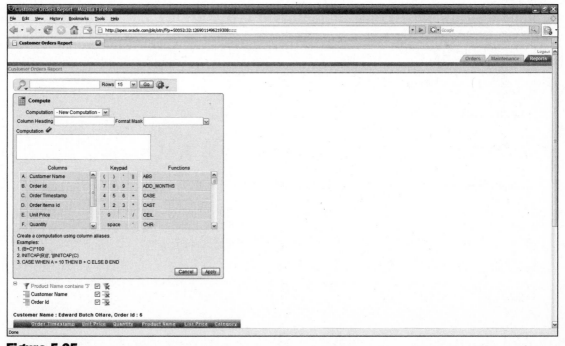

Figure 5-25

End users can increase the value of an interactive report by adding computations that derive additional information from the existing data. The Compute section gives you helper tools to build computations. The columns on the left are represented by letters that are added to the computation, along with operators and numbers selected from the keypad.

The examples at the bottom of the section point out that you can create "computations" that are not necessarily numbers. For instance, you could use the concatenation operator (||) to join two strings into a single column.

You can see that you also have access to many functions that are implemented as part of the Oracle database. You can review the syntax and operation of these functions in the Oracle documentation.

19. Give the computation the Column Heading of Total Price and a Format Mask for a currency field.

20. Click on the Unit_Price field in the Columns list, the multiplication operator (*) in the keypad, and then on the Quantity column.

The formula added to the Computation text box will look something like E * F, although the actual letters may be different if the columns in your interactive report are in a different order.

21. Click Apply to bring up the report as shown in Figure 5-26.

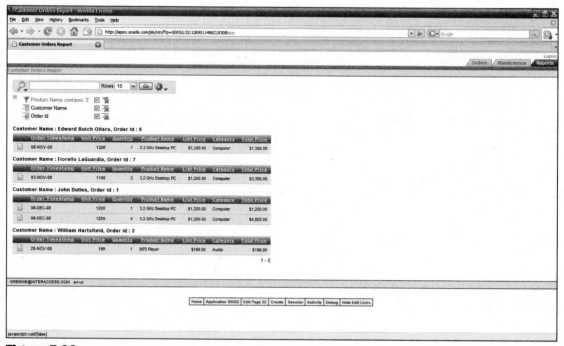

Figure 5-26

Now things are getting interesting. Your users can see very relevant information derived from the core data in your database. To make the examples in the rest of this chapter more interesting, you can add another computation.

For the purposes of the examples in this book, the Unit_Price represents the actual price the customer paid for some units, while the List_Price is the price listed in the price book. The sample data you loaded contains instances where the actual price is both greater than and less than the list price — a scenario that could occur when a product is in high demand and low supply to create a premium on the price, or overstocked items where the actual price is lower than the list price, respectively.

22. Click Compute in the Actions menu. Give the new computation a Column Heading of Savings and a currency format. Create the computation with the Columns list and the keypad to represent the following description:

```
(List_Price * Quantity) - (Unit_Price * Quantity).
```

In your actual computation, the columns will be replaced by letters representing those columns.

23. Click Apply to bring up the new page, as shown in Figure 5-27.

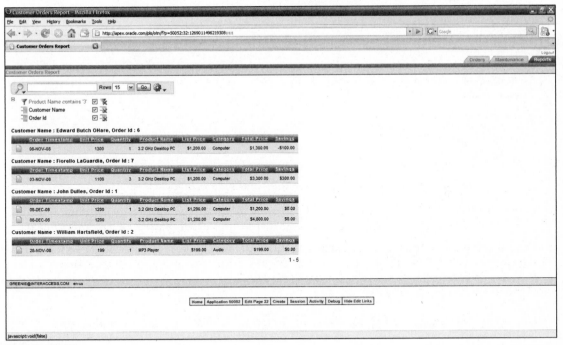

Figure 5-27

The next logical step would be to find a way to combine the price and savings for the entire order, which is easily accomplished with another Actions menu choice.

24. Click Aggregate in the Actions menu to bring up the page shown in Figure 5-28.

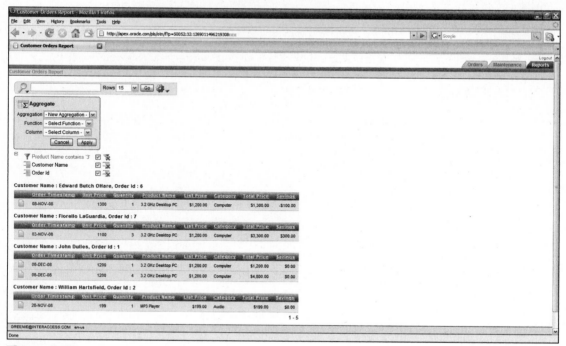

Figure 5-28

Defining an aggregate value is quite easy. You just select the aggregate function and the column on which to apply the function.

25. Select the Sum function and the `Total Price` column, and click Apply.

26. Add another aggregate value to the report by selecting Aggregate in the Actions menu, the Sum function, and the `Savings` column. Click Apply to display that page shown in Figure 5-29.

You can see that, as with sort specifications, you cannot change the aggregate columns shown in your interactive report through a list choice at the top of the report. You can take an aggregate out of your report from the Actions menu by selecting the name of the Aggregate and then clicking on the now visible Delete button.

One of the great things about using aggregates and control breaks in the same report is how they work together so well.

27. Click on the `Order_Id` control break check box to change the display of the report to the page shown in Figure 5-30.

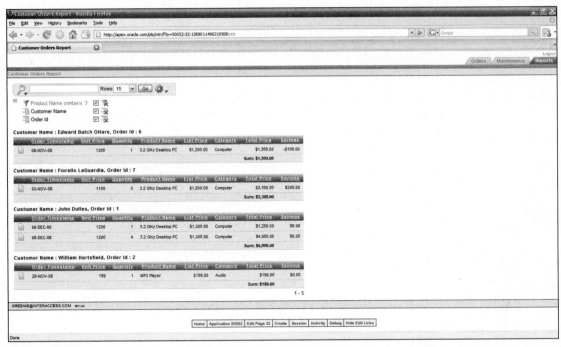

Figure 5-29

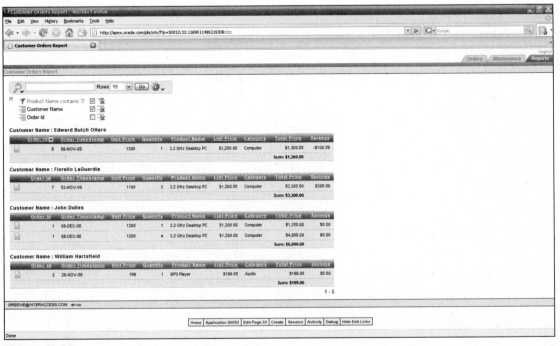

Figure 5-30

Aggregate values are only applied at the end of control breaks, so by simply changing the control breaks included in the report, your user can display different calculations. This flexibility makes your interactive reports even more popular with the user crowd.

But wait, there's more — the most visual aspect of interactive reports.

As mentioned earlier, the sample data for this book includes ORDER_ITEMS where the price paid by the customer is both greater than and less than the list price of the item. You can use the Highlight feature to bring each of these situations into focus.

28.   Click Highlight in the Actions menu to bring up the page shown in completed form in Figure 5-31.

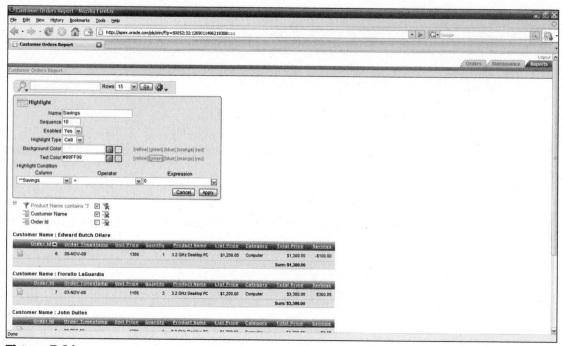

Figure 5-31

29.   Give the highlight a Name of Savings and a Highlight Type of Cell.

You can either highlight a cell or a row, based on the conditions you will enter next.

30.   Select the Savings column, the greater than operation (>) and enter 0 as the Expression.

31.   Select the green choice to the right of Background Color.

You could also use the color palette to the right of the Background Color text field. Once you have selected a color, the code for the color shows up in the text field and the color itself is displayed in the second box to the right of the field.

32. Click Apply to see your newly colorful report, as shown in Figure 5-32.

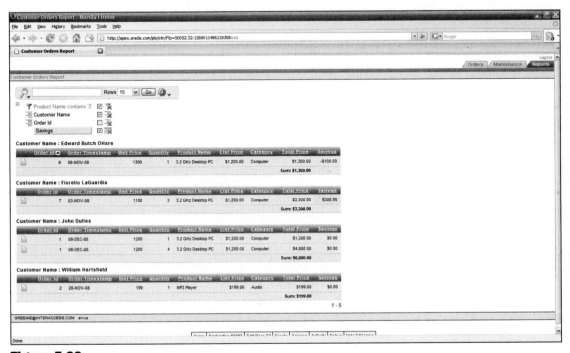

Figure 5-32

It's only fair to highlight the bad news for the user as well as the good.

33. Select `Highlight` from the Actions menu, and create a new highlight named `Overcharge`, which will display a cell in `red` if the `Savings` column is less than 0. Click Apply to produce the even more colorful report shown in Figure 5-33.

The highlights, like the selection conditions and the control breaks, are shown at the top of the page, and can be turned on and off simply by changing the check box.

You are now, hopefully, pretty excited with the flexibility of interactive reports. Interactive reports have so much flexibility that a single report could be used for many different presentations. The next section will cover some of the different ways that users can freeze the output of an interactive report.

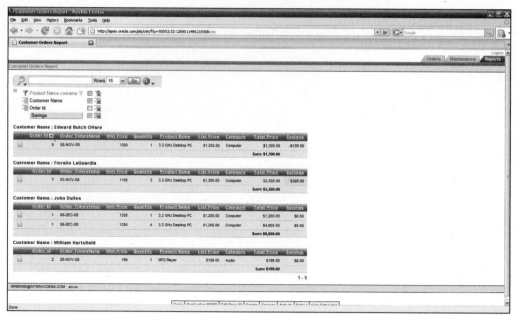

Figure 5-33

Too Much Power?

Some readers may be starting to feel a bit uneasy about now. Interactive reports seems to offer almost too much power to end users. Can this awesome power be limited somehow?

The answer is yes, in several ways. First of all, remember that all data access through Application Express is built on the Oracle database, and that you, or your database administrator, can impose security on that data. If a user does not have access to the data directly, he or she will not have access through APEX.

At the same time, remember that reports only read data. The one thing you cannot allow is for users to mess up the integrity of the data, either unintentionally or on purpose. You spent a fair amount of time in earlier chapters preventing this type of potential problem. But since a report only presents information for reading, no harm can come from any amount of flexibility in interactive reports.

But you can also limit the areas of flexibility offered by any single interactive report. The properties for an interactive report include the ability to dictate what choices are available in the Actions menu in the `Search Bar` section of the attributes, as shown in Figure 5-34. If you don't want your users to have access to the search box, any particular Actions menu choice, or the entire menu, you can just disable the display of those features. The options available for the column drop-down lists can also be controlled for each column.

You could also create a middle ground by creating and saving an interactive report with a number of selection, control break, and highlight features, but without access to the Actions menu, so that the users could select any of the choices you gave them but not add their own.

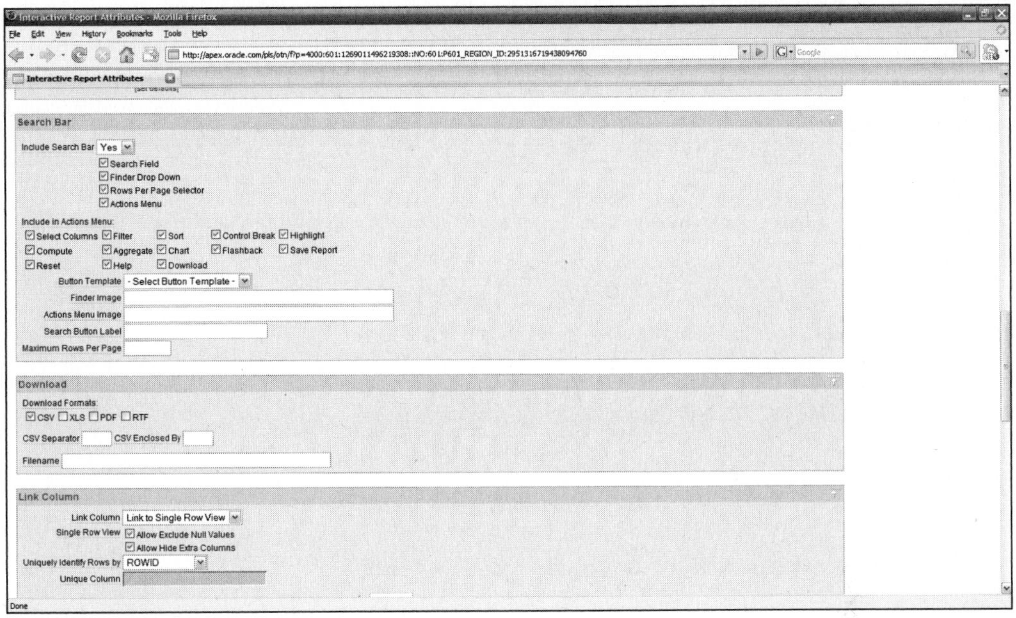

Figure 5-34

Freezing Interactive Report Output

You are probably starting to realize that creating an interactive report, on your part, is just the first step towards the use of that report. All you have to do is to specify the way that different tables are joined and the complete set of columns a user may want to include in the report. Your users can take the report the rest of the way to produce the output they really want.

But what if they want to save one, or more, of the possible versions of an interactive report? This section will cover how users can save multiple versions of reports, the data that those reports capture, and even the data at different points in time!

Try It Out   **Saving a Report**

You can probably already imagine the following scenario — a user painstakingly modifies an interactive report to just the way he likes it. He goes to lunch, and on the way back to his desk, he thinks of an even better option for the report. Can he get there without losing the beautiful configuration he has now?

1.   If you are not in the interactive report, open it, and select Save Report on the Actions menu to bring up the page shown in Figure 5-35.

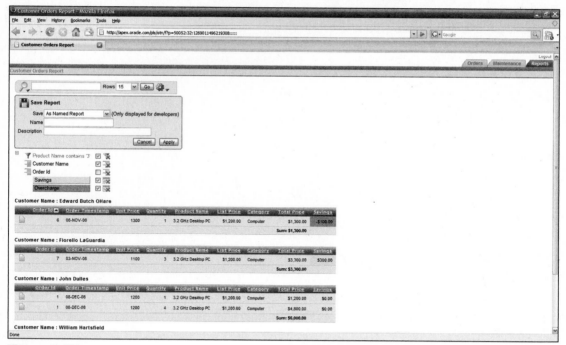

Figure 5-35

You can see that you have two basic choices as a developer. You could save the current configuration of the interactive report as the default view for all users. This option, only available to developers, allows you to create a version of the report to serve the needs of most users and act as a starting point for further modifications. The other choice, to save the configuration as a named report, is primarily for end users to save multiple personalized versions of the information in the report.

2. Give the report a name, such as `Good Report`, and a description, and click Apply to return to the page shown in Figure 5-36.

You can see that you now have a tabbed interface to the interactive report, with tabs for the report you just saved and what is called `Working Report`, a title that refers to the unsaved version of the report. If you move your mouse over the tab of this or any saved report, the description you entered will appear in a tip box.

You could make further changes to the working report and save the new versions as another saved report. Once you save a report, the configuration options become the defaults for that report.

3. Go to the saved report and change the report by unchecking the control break.

4. On the Actions menu, select Reset.

You will be prompted as to whether you really want to reset the report options to the default configuration.

5. Click Apply to bring the saved report back to its original state.

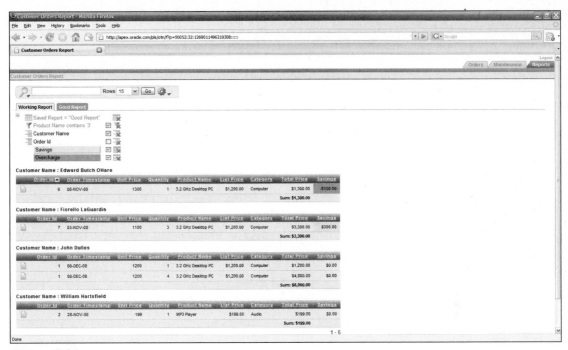

Figure 5-36

The saved reports for an interactive report are associated with the individual user, so when that user returns to the report, the saved reports will still be there. Later in this book you will learn about creating users. You can have APEX applications that do not differentiate between users — they do not have any method to log in and authenticate users. In these applications, the ability to save versions of interactive reports is automatically disabled, as you would expect.

Saving report versions is a great feature. But what about if you wanted to share the data used in a report with applications and users outside the scope of your APEX application?

Try It Out   **Saving Data**

Whenever you have a report, you can give your users the option to save the data shown in the report. There are a variety of reasons why your users would want to do this. They might want to include it in a Word document or email message. They might want to import the data into another database or application, or they might just want to create a read-only version of the report in a portable format.

Your users can do any of these things with another feature of interactive reports.

   1.   On the Actions menu, select Download to bring up the section shown in Figure 5-37.

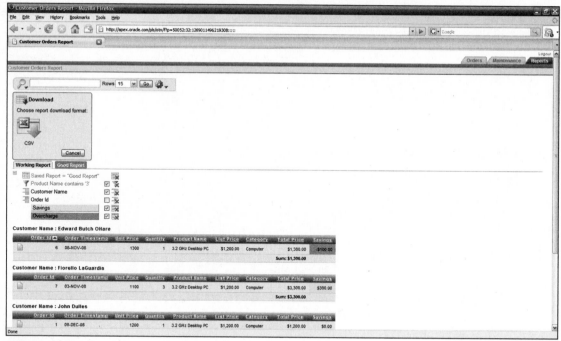

Figure 5-37

You can see that you have one option to save the data, but weren't you promised more than one? There's a simple explanation.

2. Click Cancel, and then click Edit Page and the `Interactive Report` entry in the `Regions` section to take you to the attributes page for the report. Click Download to bring up the section shown in Figure 5-38.

There they are — the additional download formats.

3. Select all of the formats and click Apply Changes, then run the page and select the Download option from the Actions menu. The new set of download options looks like Figure 5-39.

4. Select the PDF format and, when prompted, open the report in the Adobe PDF Reader.

Well, it's not the most beautiful report in the world, but the results are now in PDF format, which can be used across many platforms. You could modify the appearance of the PDF report by using the Print Attributes page for the report, where you can add information and graphics to the header and footer of the report or change the display fonts for column headings and columns. Of course, you could also modify the column headings by changing the `Column Heading` attribute for the column.

You should be aware that you can create very robust report templates for Word documents with Oracle BI Publisher, and that you can use these templates with the report data from your interactive reports.

You have saved reports and data. Can you also save time, in the form of running a report on data from the past?

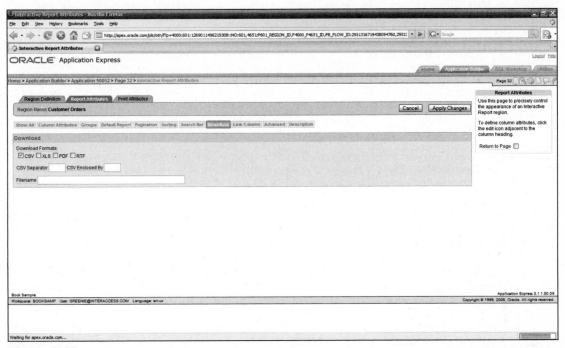

Figure 5-38

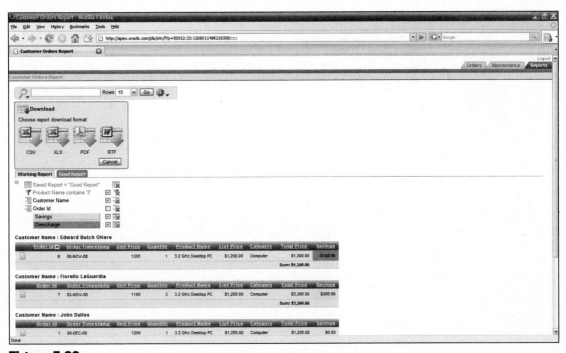

Figure 5-39

Try It Out   **Save the Past**

You may have noticed a choice in the Actions menu named Flashback. This choice allows you to query data as it existed in the recent past.

The Oracle database has included, since the late 1980s, the ability to maintain multiple versions of a data row. If someone changes data in a row, Oracle maintains the previous image of the row and automatically provides this version when a query against this row has started before the row has been changed. This feature was designed to eliminate the need to protect data being read with locks to preserve data integrity.

> *If you feel a bit lost with this brief explanation, don't worry — you don't have to understand it to take advantage of flashback. But if you want to learn more about it, check out the Concepts guide in the Oracle documentation, or Oracle Essentials by this author.*

Many years later, the development team at Oracle realized they could use these same multiple versions to support a view of data from the past, and flashback was born. The easiest way to appreciate flashback is to see it in action.

1. Return to your interactive report. Add a new `Control Break` on `Category` and disable the `Control Break` for `Customer_Name` to reduce the complexity of the report and make the individual rows easier to see.

2. Take note of the value for the `Order_Id` and the `Quantity` for the first row for the `Audio` group, which should refer to an MP3 player.

3. Click on the Orders tab and select the order with the `Order ID` you noted previously.

4. Find the `Order` with the `Order_Id` previously noted for that first row. Edit the order line for the MP3 player, changing the `Quantity`, and click Apply Changes.

5. Click on the Reports tab. You should see a changed value in the first row, since the report, by default, operates on the most recent version of the data.

6. Click Flashback in the Actions menu, which will bring up a section as shown in Figure 5-40.

7. Enter `10` into the text box and click Apply. The new report should show the old value.

8. Just to prove there is no trickery here, deselect the flashback specification. The report should refresh with the most current values.

Magic, right?

The documentation for the flashback capability of APEX states that you can go back up to 3 hours in time. In fact, the amount of time you can flashback is dependent on the space reserved for multiple versions of the data, and this space is used up in different amounts of time, depending on the allotment and the amount of updates to the data. If you try to flashback past the time when the Oracle database can give you a consistent view of your data, you will simply receive an error from the Oracle database.

The best part about the flashback capability is that you get it for free — it's a feature of the Oracle database that is simply exposed in your APEX interactive reports.

In the next section, you will learn about using charts from an APEX application.

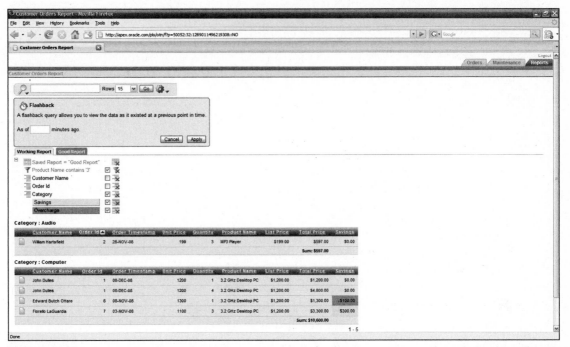

Figure 5-40

Charts

Up until now, you have been looking at reports, which present detailed information along with some aggregate summary data. Sometimes your users will want a higher-level view of their data, which can provide some telling information across a greater number of rows. For this type of examination, charts are an excellent choice.

You have no doubt noticed that one of the choices in the Page Wizard is a chart and that there is a Chart choice in the Actions menu of an interactive report. When you create a chart on a page, you have a very broad range of customization options, which you will explore in the next chapter. But for the purposes of this quick fly-by of the main APEX functionality, you can just as easily create charts based on your interactive report.

   1.   Select Chart from the Actions menu, which will bring up the section shown in Figure 5-41.

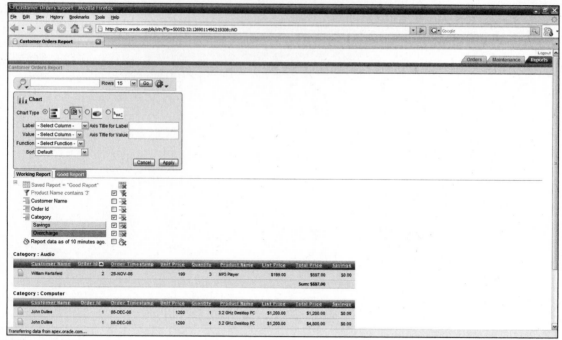

Figure 5-41

2. Select the pie chart option, the third from the left.

Once you select the pie chart, the fields for the axis labels disappear. All you have to do is to designate a column to supply the value used for the chart, a function to aggregate the values, and a sort order, if relevant.

3. Select the `Product_Name` column as the `Label`, the `Total Price` column as the `Value`, and `Sum` as the `Function`.

4. Click Apply to bring up the chart, as shown in Figure 5-42.

Your chart doesn't look too bad, especially considering how easy it was to make. If you hold the mouse over either section of the chart, the label and value will appear in a tip window.

The only real problem with the chart is that the information displayed is not really that interesting. The reason for this lack of interest has to do with the fact that the selection conditions were applied to the report to limit the number of detail rows shown. Since the purpose of a chart is to aggregate data, the chart would be a lot more interesting if it showed the total amount of sales for all the products.

With an interactive report, you can make this change with a single mouse click.

5. Click on the filter condition check box to remove the condition. The new version of the chart will look like Figure 5-43.

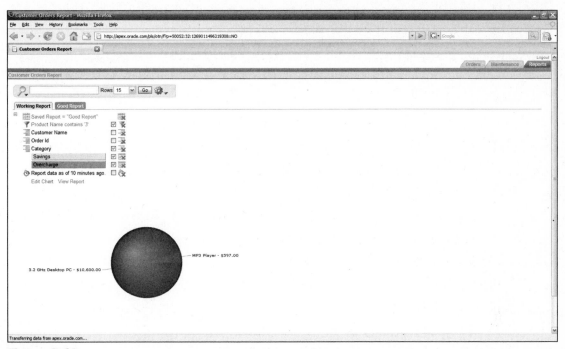

Figure 5-42

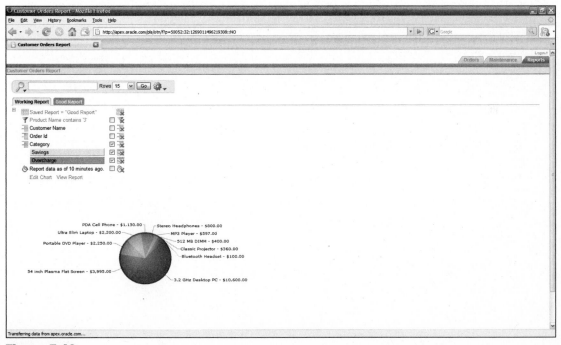

Figure 5-43

This new version of the chart presents aggregates based on more data, resulting in a more informative chart for your users.

This brief look at the charting capabilities of your interactive report has just scratched the surface of the charting possibilities in APEX, but you are probably already imagining some of the ways you can use charts in your own applications.

Summary

In this chapter, you delved into the world of APEX reports and charts. The chapter focused on the capabilities of the reports, including:

❏   Standard reports

❏   Using Query Builder to create reports based on multiple tables

❏   Interactive reports and modification of reports through the Actions menu

❏   Flashback reports

❏   Creation of standalone charts

As part of the preparation for the chapter, you also worked a bit more with SQL Workshop to both add columns to an existing table and to use the SQL script utility in the Workshop.

In the next chapter, you will learn how to combine multiple views of data to give your users a richer application experience by providing them with the option to drill down from the higher-level view of data provided by a chart, as well as the display of data within a calendar.

Components Working Together

Although you have learned a lot about the different options available in your APEX applications, and you learned how to provide access to individual pages through navigation, it might feel like your application is still nothing more than a collection of single pages. In this chapter, you will learn now to link different pages together to provide a richer application experience for your users.

In addition, you will learn about another standard page type, the calendar, which is handy for displaying information whenever that information includes dates.

Drill-Down Charts

As discussed in the last chapter, a chart is a great way to give a high-level overview of your data. But users, curious types that they are, may be enticed by those high level charts to learn more about the underlying detail data.

Wouldn't it be great if a user could simply click on one of the sections of the chart to bring up a detailed report for the data represented by that section? Wouldn't you know it? APEX makes this easy to do.

Your first step is to create the detailed report that will be called from the chart. As you remember, the chart you created from the interactive report in the last chapter showed the sum of purchases of different products. In this chapter, you will create a chart that will aggregate the value of purchases by product category.

A detailed report would have information about the ORDER_ITEMS displayed, by category. You will have to link together multiple tables to get just the information you want, but with the help of the Query Builder, even this mildly complicated task is easy.

1.   Return to the main development area for your application, and click Create Page.

2.   Select the Report option, and click Next.

3.   On the next page, select Interactive Report, and click Next, or click on the icon directly.

4.   On the next page, set the Page Name to Orders and the Region Name to Order Report, and click Next.

5. Change the `Tab Options` to `Use Existing tab set and create a new tab` and give the new tab the name of `Purchases by Category`. Remember that this page will act as the detail page for a report on purchases.

You leave the default choice of no breadcrumbs, but you will be adding breadcrumbs for this page and the chart that will call it once you create that chart later in this chapter.

6. Click Next to bring up the SQL definition page.

On this page, you will define the SQL used as the basis of the report. You will be pulling data from a lot of different tables in this report, so it is probably best to use the Query Builder to avoid the complications that can occur whenever you start writing code.

7. Click the Query Builder button to bring up the page shown in Figure 6-1 in its completed form.

You used the Query Builder to create an SQL statement in the previous chapter. The query you will build here is similar to that query, so if you are familiar with SQL, you could simply copy that query and modify it for use in this report.

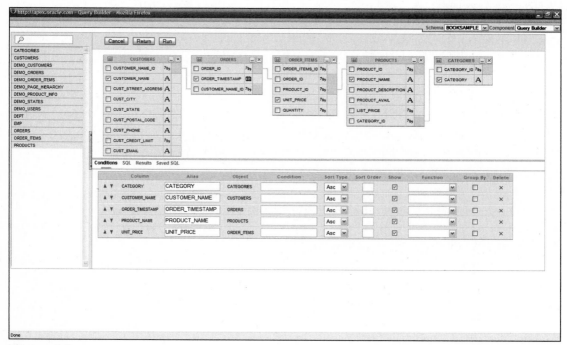

Figure 6-1

8. Select the following tables from the left-hand panel by clicking on each of them once:

   a. CUSTOMERS

   b. ORDERS

   c. ORDER_ITEMS

    d.   PRODUCTS

    e.   CATEGORIES

9.   Link these tables together by clicking on the following sets of columns, which make up the foreign keys between the tables:

    a.   CUSTOMERS.CUSTOMER_NAME_ID and ORDERS.CUSTOMER_NAME_ID

    b.   ORDERS.ORDER_ID and ORDER_ITEMS.ORDER_ID

    c.   ORDER_ITEMS.PRODUCT_ID and PRODUCTS.PRODUCT_ID

    d.   PRODUCTS.CATEGORY_ID and CATEGORIES.CATEGORY_ID

10.   Select the following columns for inclusion in the report:

    a.   CUSTOMER_NAME from the CUSTOMERS table

    b.   ORDER_TIMESTAMP from the ORDERS table

    c.   UNIT_PRICE from the ORDER_ITEMS table

    d.   PRODUCT_NAME from the PRODUCTS table and

    e.   CATEGORY from the CATEGORIES table

11.   Use the arrows to move the columns so that they end up in the following order:

    a.   CATEGORY

    b.   CUSTOMER_NAME

    c.   ORDER_TIMESTAMP

    d.   PRODUCT_NAME

    e.   UNIT_PRICE

You should end up with the page looking like Figure 6-1. The SQL that this will generate will not be the exact SQL used for the report, but you will modify it on the report when it is saved.

12.   Click Return to return to the Interactive Report Wizard to add the newly created SQL to the report definition.

You have created an interactive report to take advantage of the control break formatting for the report, but the final result will not allow users to modify the report, since the report is meant to address the single purpose of providing more detail from a chart.

Because of this, you will want to do a few things to implement some of the features of the interactive report directly in the SQL code.

The SQL in the text box look like this:

```
select "CATEGORIES"."CATEGORY" as "CATEGORY",
  "CUSTOMERS"."CUSTOMER_NAME" as "CUSTOMER_NAME",
  "ORDERS"."ORDER_TIMESTAMP" as "ORDER_TIMESTAMP",
  "PRODUCTS"."PRODUCT_NAME" as "PRODUCT_NAME",
  "ORDER_ITEMS"."UNIT_PRICE" as "UNIT_PRICE"
  from "CATEGORIES" "CATEGORIES",
  "PRODUCTS" "PRODUCTS",
  "ORDER_ITEMS" "ORDER_ITEMS",
  "ORDERS" "ORDERS",
  "CUSTOMERS" "CUSTOMERS"
```

```
where    "PRODUCTS"."CATEGORY_ID"="CATEGORIES"."CATEGORY_ID"
and "PRODUCTS"."PRODUCT_ID"="ORDER_ITEMS"."PRODUCT_ID"
and "ORDER_ITEMS"."ORDER_ID"="ORDERS"."ORDER_ID"
and "ORDERS"."CUSTOMER_NAME_ID"="CUSTOMERS"."CUSTOMER_NAME_ID"
```

You want to add a calculation and sort order to this SQL.

13. Change the SQL by modifying the Source statement by changing the UNIT_PRICE spot in the SQL statement to a calculation, as shown in the screen below.

```
select "CATEGORIES"."CATEGORY" as "CATEGORY",
"CUSTOMERS"."CUSTOMER_NAME" as "CUSTOMER_NAME",
"ORDERS"."ORDER_TIMESTAMP" as "ORDER_TIMESTAMP",
"PRODUCTS"."PRODUCT_NAME" as "PRODUCT_NAME",
("ORDER_ITEMS"."UNIT_PRICE" * "ORDER_ITEMS"."QUANTITY") as "Total Cost"
from "CATEGORIES" "CATEGORIES",
"PRODUCTS" "PRODUCTS",
"ORDER_ITEMS" "ORDER_ITEMS",
"ORDERS" "ORDERS",
"CUSTOMERS" "CUSTOMERS"
where    "PRODUCTS"."CATEGORY_ID"="CATEGORIES"."CATEGORY_ID"
and "PRODUCTS"."PRODUCT_ID"="ORDER_ITEMS"."PRODUCT_ID"
and "ORDER_ITEMS"."ORDER_ID"="ORDERS"."ORDER_ID"
and "ORDERS"."CUSTOMER_NAME_ID"="CUSTOMERS"."CUSTOMER_NAME_ID"
```

In an interactive report, as you learned in the last chapter, users could have created a calculation and added it to the report themselves. In this scenario, though, you want to include a calculation in the report and, as you will soon see, also prevent the user from modifying the report with the interactive menu.

You will want to make one more change to the SQL, for a similar reason. You want to specify the sort order of the rows in this report as part of that SQL.

14. Add the following line of code to the end of your SQL statement in the Source section:

```
order by "CATEGORIES"."CATEGORY", "CUSTOMERS"."CUSTOMER_NAME"
```

As with your previous change, you are adding in a sort order which the user could have specified themselves.

15. Click Next and then Finish to generate the interactive report.

16. Click on the Run icon to run your newly modified report, as shown in Figure 6-2.

17. Use the interactive menu to specify a control break on the Category column, and click on Apply to modify the report to look like Figure 6-3.

18. Use the interactive report menu to save the report, and specify that this version of the report will be the default version for all users.

Now that you have saved the interactive report just the way it should be when acting as a detailed report from a chart, you can remove the interactive menu from the report.

19. Return to the development environment by clicking on the Edit Page link, and select the Interactive Report attributes page link.

20. In the Search Bar section, change the Include Search Bar select list to No, click Apply Changes, and run the report again, which should now look like Figure 6-4.

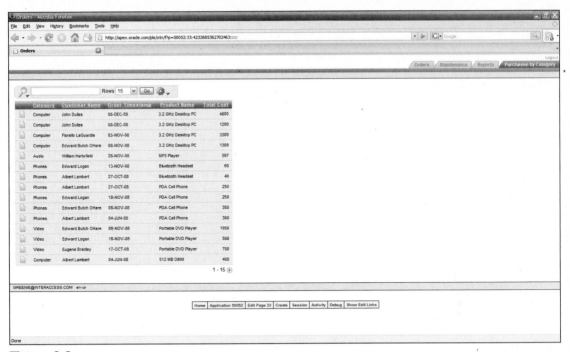

Figure 6-2

Figure 6-3

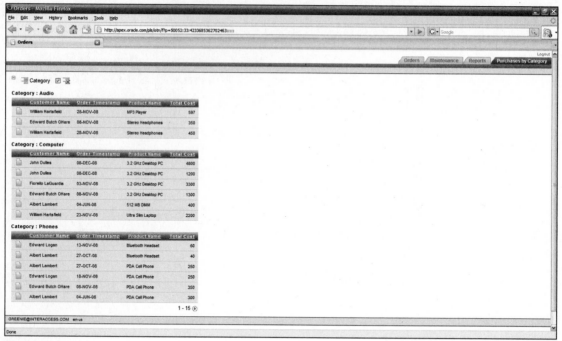

Figure 6-4

There you have it — a detail report just waiting to be called from a chart. Creating that chart will be your next task, but before you leave, you should take the SQL you used for this report, since you will want to get the same data to use as the basis of that chart.

21. Return to the development environment, go to the `Interactive Reports` attribute area and select the `Region Definition` for the report. Select the SQL statement and copy it. Click Cancel to return to the development area.

You might want to save the SQL to a Notepad page, or you could just leave it on the clipboard. In either event, you can now quickly create the chart that will link to this report.

Try It Out   **Create a Flash Chart**

You created a chart from an interactive report in the last section. This time, you will create a chart page from scratch, while learning about the additional options you have for the configuration of that report.

1. Click Create to start a new page.

2. Select the `New page` and click Next.

3. Select the Chart option ,and click Next to bring up the page shown in Figure 6-5.

You can see three choices. When you created a chart from an interactive report in the previous section, APEX used a Flash chart. For this chart, you will also create a Flash chart, which will work as long as you have an Adobe Flash viewer installed on your machine, as most people do.

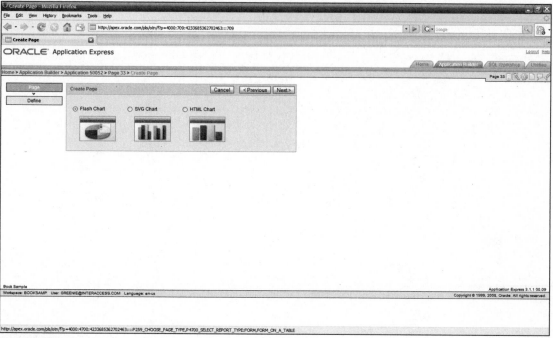

Figure 6-5

The SVG chart also used a browser plug-in. The HTML chart choice can be selected if your user community will not have either of these plug-ins on their computers.

4. Click Next, where you should set the Page Name to Purchases by Category and the Region Name to Purchases.

Since this page will be the parent for the breadcrumb display mentioned earlier, you should start the creation of your breadcrumb trail on this page.

5. Change the selection for Breadcrumb to Breadcrumb, which will change the appearance of the page to that shown in Figure 6-6.

6. Leave the default breadcrumb Entry Name of Purchases by Category and click Next.

This time, you should select the third choice on the Tab page of Use an existing tab set and reuse an existing tab, since you have already created a tab for this set of pages.

7. Click Next and select the Purchases by category tab you already created. Click Next.

The next page, as shown in Figure 6-7, is where you will define the characteristics of your Flash chart.

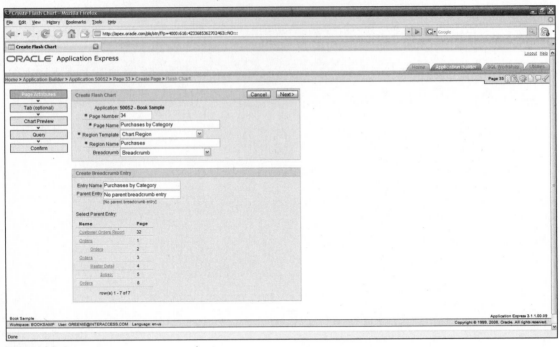

Figure 6-6

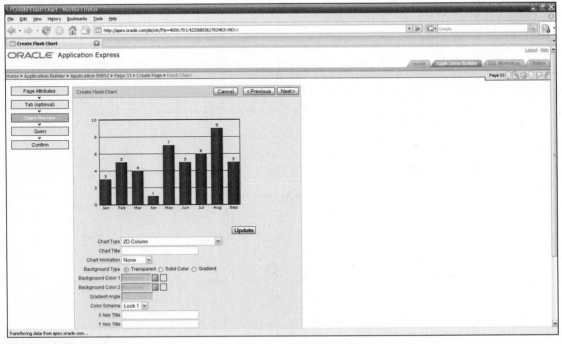

Figure 6-7

8. Select 3D Pie as the Chart Type, set the Chart Title to Product Sales, and select Dissolve as the Chart Animation, if you like. Click Update to see the results of your changes.

9. Uncheck the Show Values check box, and change Show Legend to Left. Click Next to bring up the query attributes page.

As in the previous section, you will use a wizard to build the initial query and then modify it after it is generated.

10. Click the Build Query button to bring up the Chart Query Wizard.

11. Accept the default Table/View Owner choice, and click Next.

12. Select the ORDER_ITEMS table, since this table is the source of the total cost calculation you will be using, and click Next.

The next page, shown in Figure 6-8, is where the core work of the chart is defined.

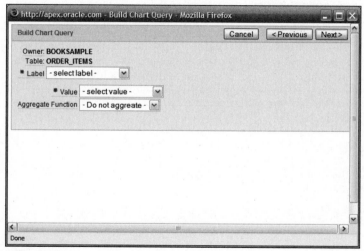

Figure 6-8

13. Select PRODUCT_ID for the Label, QUANTITY for the Value, and SUM for the Aggregate function.

You will not be using either of these columns in your actual report, but select them to act as placeholders in the SQL query that will be generated.

14. Click Next to bring you to the page shown, as it will be when completed, in Figure 6-9.

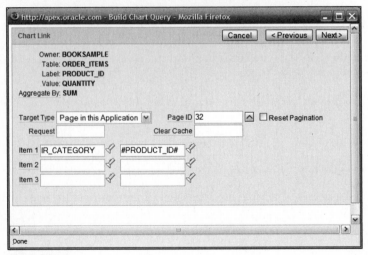

Figure 6-9

The remainder of the chart functionality is described in the attributes on this page, the functionality which will use the report you just created. APEX charts have the built-in ability to link to a detail chart, passing a value from the chart to the report, which is used to limit the data shown in the detailed report.

15. Change the `Target Type` to `Page in this Application`. Select the `Page ID` for the interactive report you just defined.

The next step is to establish what value will be passed from this chart to the linked page.

16. Click on the flashlight icon for the right-hand text box in the `Item 1` row, which will bring up the page shown in Figure 6-10.

The link columns shown are the columns that are available in the `ORDER_ITEMS` table you selected as the basis for the chart. Notice that each of the columns has a number sign (#) before and after the column name. Once again, you will select a column from this list that you will replace later.

17. Select the `#PRODUCT_ID#` choice, which you will also be changing, to return to the wizard page.

You now have to select the item in the target page that will use the passed value.

18. Click on the flashlight icon for the left-hand text box in the `Item 1` row.

In the selection dialog that appears, you can pick from a list of items for all pages in your application.

19. Use the Page selection list to select the interactive report you just created, which will bring up the results shown in Figure 6-11.

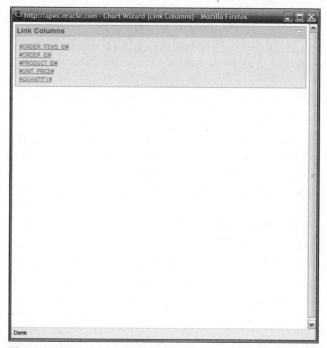

Figure 6-10

Figure 6-11

Hey, wait a second — there's nothing there! This result is actually correct. Remember that this page is looking for items, and the interactive report page doesn't have any items, just the interactive report.

The URL that will be generated to implement to link to your interactive report page can, in most situations, only pass to an actual item on the page. If you were using a classic report, you would have to define an item for the report page, which would probably be a hidden item, and then use that item in the selection condition for the report, with code something like this:

```
where CATEGORY = :P10_CATEGORY
```

The colon (:) in front of the item name is necessary to indicate the item is a *bind variable*, which means that the value will be coming from outside the SQL statement. You could use any item on any page in an SQL statement for an application.

Fortunately, interactive reports have a method that allows you to directly pass a value to the interactive report. For a value to be used with the equality (=) operation, you simply precede the name of the column in the report with the characters IR_.

There are other characters that you can use to set up different comparison conditions. Please refer to the APEX online documentation set for further details.

20. Close the selection dialog and enter IR_CATEGORY into the left-hand text box, then click Next to display the SQL for the chart query, as shown in Figure 6-12.

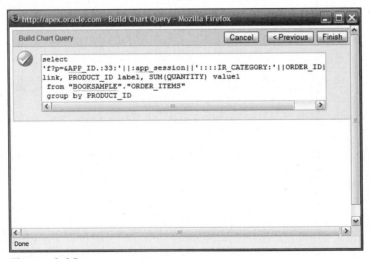

Figure 6-12

The chart query currently consists of the following code:

```
select 'f?p=&APP_ID.:10:'||:app_session||':::::IR_CATEGORY:'||PRODUCT_ID||':' link,
PRODUCT_ID label, SUM(QUANTITY) value1
  from "BOOKSAMP"."ORDER_ITEMS"
  group by PRODUCT_ID
```

where the number following the APP_ID is the page number of the chart you are creating.

You will be modifying this code significantly, in the larger display window presented for the chart source. For now, you should take a minute to consider what is represented by the query.

The first column in the query is a concatenation, which will create the link to the other page in the application. The string shown here is concatenated (using several instances of the concatenation operator [||]) onto the URL for the APEX server process on the Oracle database server.

The string is somewhat long and complicated, but there are five main parts to understand.

❑ The APP_ID token is replaced with a number that identifies this particular application. This ID is the same number you see on the icon for your application in the development page.

❑ The number following the APP_ID bind variable is the number of the target page.

❑ The :app_session is a bind variable that is replaced with the current session ID. The current session carries information about the current user of the application, such as their identity. This session ID is unique to each user session and changes each time they log in to the application. For security purposes, the session ID sent as part of the URL is checked against the database credentials to ensure that the user is authorized to access the application.

❑ The IR_CATEGORY is the "item," which will receive the value.

❑ The PRODUCT_ID is replaced with the value of the PRODUCT_ID field.

For a more detailed explanation of how APEX page URLs are constructed, please refer to the Tech talk sidebar on the next page.

The second column in the query is the label that will be used in the chart, and the third column is the value that will be used in the chart. You want to change both of these, along with the tables accessed in the query and the join conditions on those tables. Fortunately, you have all the required syntax in the SQL query that was used for the detail report.

21. If you saved the SQL query on the clipboard, select the text following the from keyword and paste it into the query text field in the wizard page. If you saved the query into a text document, cut and paste it from that document into the query text field.

22. Modify the SQL query text to match the text that follows, which is also available as the file Chapter_6_Chart_URL.txt. (You will have to change the page number to the page for your chart.) The text of the URL has been changed after the IR_CATEGORY field.

```
select 'f?p=&APP_ID.:10:'||:app_session||':::::IR_CATEGORY:'||CATEGORY||':' link,
  CATEGORY label,
  SUM("ORDER_ITEMS"."UNIT_PRICE" * "ORDER_ITEMS"."QUANTITY") value1
from "CATEGORIES" "CATEGORIES",
 "PRODUCTS" "PRODUCTS",
 "ORDER_ITEMS" "ORDER_ITEMS",
 "ORDERS" "ORDERS",
 "CUSTOMERS" "CUSTOMERS"
where   "CATEGORIES"."CATEGORY_ID"="PRODUCTS"."CATEGORY_ID"
and "PRODUCTS"."PRODUCT_ID"="ORDER_ITEMS"."PRODUCT_ID"
and "ORDER_ITEMS"."ORDER_ID"="ORDERS"."ORDER_ID"
and "ORDERS"."CUSTOMER_NAME_ID"="CUSTOMERS"."CUSTOMER_NAME_ID"
group by CATEGORY
```

Tech Talk – Understanding APEX URLs

The URL that is used to call a page in your APEX application looks a bit complex, but once you understand everything you can specify with it, you can begin to appreciate the power and flexibility encapsulated in this URL call.

The first part of the URL, as mentioned, is the URL for the Oracle database running APEX, followed by a directory named pls and any subdirectory indicated for the APEX services. For instance, the first part of the URL for the hosted APEX the examples in this book are using is:

```
Apex.oracle.com/pls/otn/
```

The parameters begin after this part of the URL with the characters f?p (which initially stood for a flow and a page), and then the equals sign (=). Following this, there are nine parameters, separated by colons (:):

- ❑ *Application* **identifier:** Is the number assigned to the application. As you did for the link in your chart, this value can be retrieved using the internal variable APP_ID*Page* identifier—which is the number of the page that is the target of the link*Session* identifier — which gives the called page access to session-based information, such as the user name.

- ❑ *Request* **identifier:** Can be used to pass the name of the button which caused the URL to be called. For the chart report, this parameter did not have a value.

- ❑ *Debug* **identifier:** Can only be YES or NO. Please refer to the documentation for more details about this parameter. This parameter can also be blank, which assumes the NO value.

- ❑ *ClearCache* **parameter:** Normally, APEX maintains information about the state of a page in a memory cache, which means that the page will have the same state and contents when you return to the page. With this parameter, you can clear those values for a page, or pages, or for the entire application. You can also use a special value for this parameter to clear cached items for an interactive report, which you will see in action later in this session.

- ❑ *itemNames* **and** *itemValues* **parameters pairs:** Specifies values for items in the target page. You can have more than one name-value pair, with the entries separated by commas.

- ❑ *PrinterFriendly* **parameter:** Can have a value of Yes to optimize the display of the page for printing, such as suppressing the display of tabs and navigation bars.

You basically have to make five changes:

a. Change the column name passed to the report from PRODUCT_ID to CATEGORY.

b. Change the second column from PRODUCT_ID label to CATEGORY label.

c. Change the third column from SUM(QUANTITY) value1 to:

```
SUM("ORDER_ITEMS"."UNIT_PRICE" * "ORDER_ITEMS"."QUANTITY") as
    "Total price"  value1,
```

which is a sum of the calculated value you brought over in the SQL from your report.

d. Change the syntax from `"BOOKSAMP"."ORDER_ITEMS"` to:

```
from "CATEGORIES" "CATEGORIES",
 "PRODUCTS" "PRODUCTS",
 "ORDER_ITEMS" "ORDER_ITEMS",
 "ORDERS" "ORDERS",
 "CUSTOMERS" "CUSTOMERS"
where    "CATEGORIES"."CATEGORY_ID"="PRODUCTS"."CATEGORY_ID"
and "PRODUCTS"."PRODUCT_ID"="ORDER_ITEMS"."PRODUCT_ID"
and "ORDER_ITEMS"."ORDER_ID"="ORDERS"."ORDER_ID"
and "ORDERS"."CUSTOMER_NAME_ID"="CUSTOMERS"."CUSTOMER_NAME_ID"
```

which you brought over from your report.

e. Change the final `order` by clause to the `group` by clause using `"CATEGORIES"."CATEGORY"`.

Don't worry about making a mistake in this SQL, at least not too much. By default, APEX will perform a query validation when you click Next, so any invalid SQL will be flagged. The complete text of the SQL script is included in the text file `Chapter_6_chart_URL.txt`, *although the page numbers (the* `Pn_` *at the beginning of bind variables) may be different, depending on whether you followed this book from the beginning or not.*

23. Click Next and then confirm that the chart is finished by clicking the Finish button.

If you are not that familiar with SQL, that last step may have been a bit difficult. But look at the bright side. SQL in a very powerful language, and you can use all of that power in specifying sophisticated queries as the basis for your charts and reports. And, as you will now see, you have built some pretty cool functionality into your chart.

How It Works

Now that your chart is properly associated with a detail report, you can see this magic at work.

1. Click on the Run Page icon to bring up the chart, which will look like Figure 6-13.

The chart took a moment to appear, with the dissolve effect that you specified, and the Flash runtime environment kept the user informed that the data was loading. The data looks like it is properly aggregated, with labels outside of each section of the pie and a legend to the left. Now you can see if the link works as planned.

2. Move the mouse over the section of the pie chart labeled `Computer`. You can see that a tip box appears with the value for the aggregation.

3. Click on the `Computer` segment to bring up the interactive report shown in Figure 6-14.

That worked nicely. You can see that the `Control Break` condition for `Category` appears as one of the conditions, along with the selection condition of `Category = 'Computer'` that was passed by the link.

4. Click the Back button to return you to the chart. Click on the `Audio` segment of the pie chart to bring up the report shown in Figure 6-15.

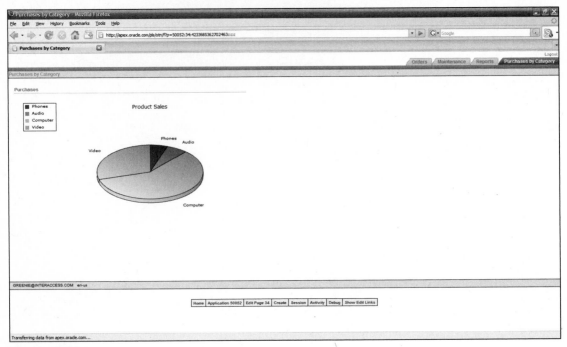

Figure 6-13

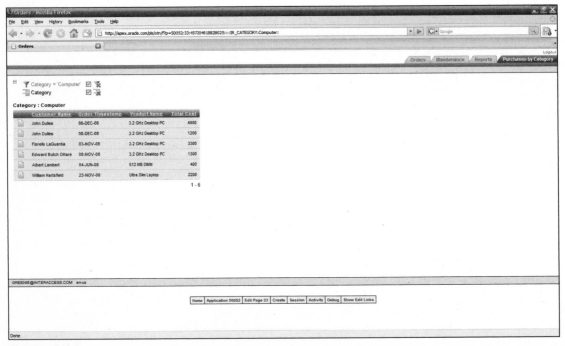

Figure 6-14

Figure 6-15

Once again, the interactive report with the correct selection conditions shows up. The selection for the Audio category is correctly checked, and the previous selection is not. This may seem a bit confusing to your users, but this behavior is one that can be easily modified by changing the way that the link to the interactive report is constructed.

5. Return to the chart page, and click on the Edit Page link to return to the development environment.

6. Bring up the attributes for the Flash Chart, and click on the Edit link for the Series Query.

As mentioned in the Tech Talk section previously, the syntax for the APEX URL can carry quite a few options, including the ClearCache option. By modifying that parameter in the link URL, you can call a fresh, new version of the interactive report each time.

7. Change the value of the link parameter just before the IR_CATEGORY item to RIR, which stands for Refresh Interactive Report. The new syntax for the link should look like this:

```
select 'f?p=&APP_ID.:10:'||:app_session||':::RIR:IR_CATEGORY:'||CATEGORY||':' link,
```

8. Click on Apply Changes and then the Run icon to bring up the chart.

9. Click on the Phones category in the pie chart to bring up the detailed report. Click on the Back pushbutton to return to the chart.

10. Click on the Audio category in the pie chart to bring up the detailed report again, which now looks like the report shown in Figure 6-16.

Figure 6-16

The report page called by the newly modified URL starts from scratch each time, which means the earlier filter condition is no longer part of the cache nor is it visible in the report.

You may have noticed that the number showing up on the report is not formatted like a currency value. You can correct this easily with another set of attributes.

1. Return to the development environment for your chart.

2. Click on the `Flash Chart` option in the attribute page and click on Display to isolate this section of the attributes.

3. At the bottom of this section, enter $ for the Prefix, select Yes for the `Show Group Separator` and 0 for `Decimal Places` and click Apply Changes.

To finish off this piece of your application, you will have to make a few more small changes to bring breadcrumbs into your chart for easier user navigation.

Try It Out   Perfecting Navigation

Remember that you did not add a breadcrumb for the report page, and that your defined the tab for these two pages with that report page. A little modification will complete your work on this section.

1. In the development environment, navigate to the interactive report page you created earlier in this chapter. Click on the plus icon (+) in the `Breadcrumbs` section in the `Shared Components` column on the right.

2. Leave the default choice for `Breadcrumb Entry`, and click Next.

You have to have a region of the page defined for breadcrumbs, but you will create this region as part of the Breadcrumb Entry Wizard.

3. The next page in the wizard asks for information about the breadcrumb region. You can accept all of the defaults and click Next.

4. Accept the defaults for the additional attributes on the next page, and click Next to bring up the page shown in complete form in Figure 6-17.

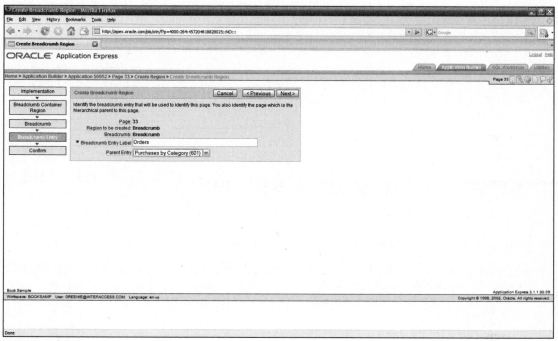

Figure 6-17

5. Set the `Breadcrumb Entry Label` to `Orders`, and select the breadcrumb for the chart page `Purchases by Category` as the parent entry. Click Next and then the Finish button to complete the creation of the new breadcrumb.

You have added a breadcrumb to navigate back to the Purchases chart. The only small additional change to make is to another shared component, the tab for both of your new pages.

6. Click on the Edit Page icon to return to the development environment.

7. In the `Tabs` section of the `Shared Components` column, click on the tab you created for these two pages.

When the attributes page comes up, you will see that the entry for the `Tab Page` is the report, while the chart is listed as a `Tab Also Current`. This listing means that a user clicking on the tab will bring up the report, rather than the chart, which is not the expected behavior.

   8. Swap the position of the two pages, making the chart the `Tab Page` for this tab, and change the page number in the Tab Also Current text box instead to the number of the report page.

   9. Click Apply Changes, return to the chart page, and run the application to see the new refinements at work. Click on the Purchases by Category tab, drill down to the report, and use the breadcrumb to return to the chart.

This small exercise has just scratched the surface of the sorts of things you can do by linking together pages to drill down for more detail. For instance, there is a ink column in the interactive report that, by default, brings up a single-row view of the row. You could just as easily change that link to go to another report for even more detail, with a breadcrumb trail to point the way home.

Drilling down for more detailed information is a way to get multiple pages to work together. You can implement the same type of cooperation between two different regions on a page, as you will see in the next section.

Interaction between Regions

The previous section illustrated how you can get two pages to work together to give users a more complete exploration of their data. In this section, you will see how you can implement a similar approach by using a select list to impose a filter condition on a Flash chart.

You are going to give your users another version of the chart you created in the previous section, which will show the breakdown of purchases, by category, for individual customers. The users will be able to select a customer from a dynamic selection list, so additional customers will instantly be available for this type of analysis.

Try It Out   Copying a Page

Since this chart will have a selection condition imposed on its data, you should start by copying your previous chart.

   1. Return to the development environment for your chart page.

   2. Click Copy to bring up the page shown in Figure 6-18. Accept the default choice of copying a page in the application, and click Next.

   3. On the next page, change the `New Page Name` to `Purchases by Customer` and select `Breadcrumb` from the selection list. Change the `Entry Name` for the breadcrumb to `Purchases by Customer`. You can use breadcrumbs as you did before, and click Next.

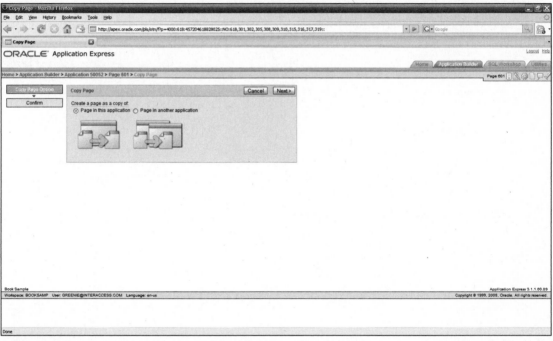

Figure 6-18

4. Leave the default names for the regions in the next page, and click Next.

5. This chart will be used to look at the data from a different viewpoint, so select the choice to use an existing tab set and create a new tab within the existing tab set. Click Next, and on the next two pages select the default tab set and give the new tab a label of Purchases by Customer. Click Next and then the Finish button to confirm the creation of the page.

You could run the page now to see what it looks like, but aside from a change in some of the text, your new page looks exactly like the last chart you created. But not for long.

Try It Out   **Adding a Region with a Select List**

As mentioned above, you want to add a select list to allow your users to select the customer whose orders they wish to view. You start this process by adding a new region to the page.

1. Click on the Edit Page link to return to the development page for your new chart.

2. Click on the plus sign (+) in the upper-right corner of the Regions section of the Page Rendering column on the left to bring up the page shown in Figure 6-19.

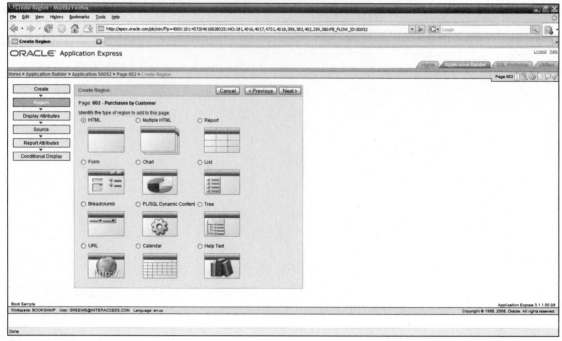

Figure 6-19

This page looks very similar to the page used by the Page Creation Wizard. You can have the same basic types of entities in a region as in a page.

3. Leave the default selection of HTML, and click Next.

Since this region will not be bound to any table in your database, you can use a standard HTML region to hold the select list.

4. Leave the default choice of HTML as the type of region container, and click Next.

The next page, shown in Figure 6-20, gives you a couple of important configuration options.

5. Enter `Customer` as the `Title` of the region, and enter 5 as the `Sequence` number.

You have probably noticed this sequence number in quite a few other configuration pages, and always left it as the default. Why the change now? As you might expect, the sequence number controls the order in which entities are displayed on a page. Normally, you built the page in sequential order, so the automatically generated sequences worked out fine. This time, though, you want the new region to appear above the existing chart region, which has a sequence number of 10. Any sequence number lower than 10 would accomplish this purpose, but the number 5 leaves room for changes down the road.

> *Take care to not use the same sequence number for components in the same functional area, as there is no guarantee as to the order in which these sequences will be executed.*

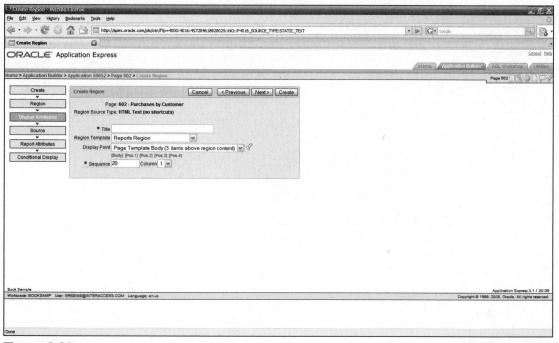

Figure 6-20

6. Click Create to add the region to the page, without going through the next two pages, which would have allowed you to add some HTML to the page and to limit its display based on a condition.

You can see the new region listed in the `Regions` section of the attribute page. You could look at your new region right now, but the region will only display in the region heading, so why not add the select list to the region so you can see it all.

7. Click on the plus sign in the `Items` section of the `Page Rendering` column to bring up the page shown in Figure 6-21.

8. Choose the `Select List` option, and click Next.

9. On the next page, choose the `Select List with Submit`.

Of all the choices for a type of select list, you should use this option. Normally, a page is submitted whenever you click on a pushbutton, but this option will save your user valuable keystrokes by automatically submitting the page when a value is selected. With this choice, the page will be submitted to the server whenever the user selects a new value, and the chart will change in response.

10. Click Next to bring up the page shown, in its completed form, in Figure 6-22.

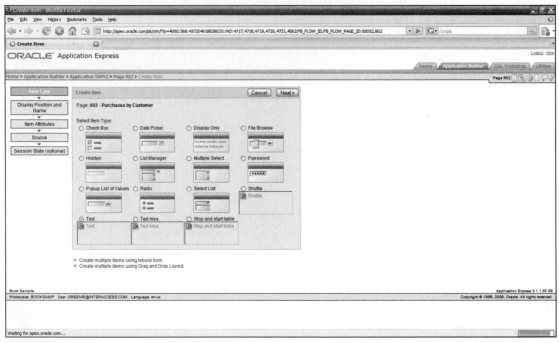

Figure 6-21

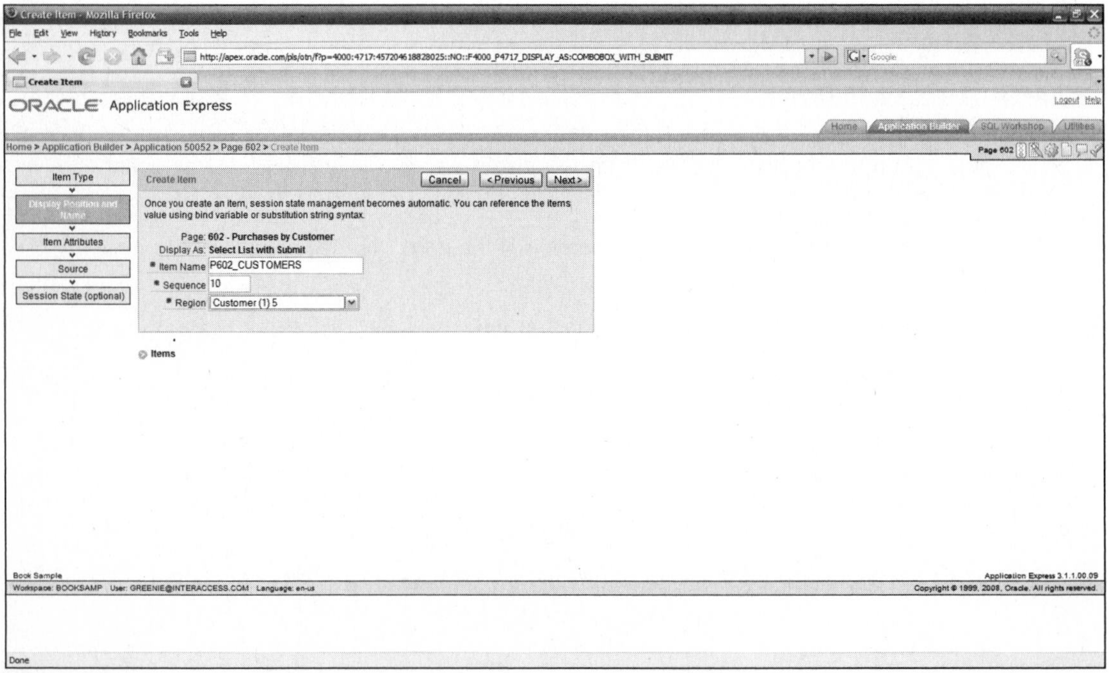

Figure 6-22

11. On this page, give the select list item a descriptive name, such as Pn_CUSTOMERS, and make sure to select the Customer region you just created as its region. Click Next.

The Pn_ naming convention is used through APEX for all default items, so you should use the same convention.

The next page should again look familiar. This page is used to define the values used in the selection list.

12. Click on the Create Dynamic List of Values link below the List of Values Query text box. Use the Dynamic LOV Wizard to select the default schema, the CUSTOMERS table, the CUSTOMER_NAME as the display column and the CUSTOMER_NAME_ID as the return value, and then click Next and the Finish button to add the newly created query to the Identify List of Values page. Make sure that the Display Null Option selection is set to Yes and click Next.

13. The next page allows you to change the characteristics of the item display. You can accept the defaults by clicking Next.

14. The final page in this wizard allows you to associate the item with a source or give it a default value. You will not need to do either one of these things, so you can just click Create Item to finish your work.

Now you are ready to try out your new page.

15. Click on the Run icon to run your newly created and modified page. The page will look like Figure 6-23.

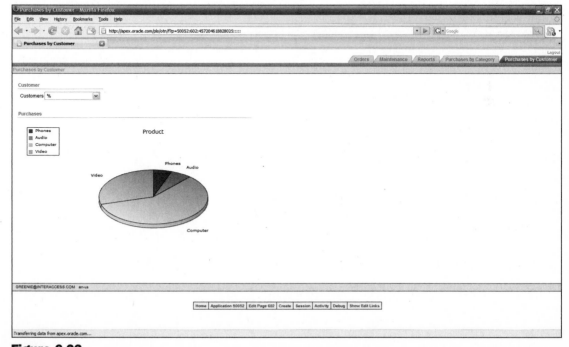

Figure 6-23

You can see the new region at the top of the page, with the select list you just created. The chart below still displays the aggregate values for all the orders, because you have not added a selection criterion for the chart. But while you are here, you might as well see your nice new select list in action.

16. Select any customer in the selection list.

Ooops. Uh, looks like an error. Thankfully, the error message, `Page nn provided no page to branch to`, points the way to the problem. Remember, when the user selects a value in this particular selection list, the selection list automatically submits the page. And whenever a page is submitted, APEX looks to the branching instructions to understand where to go next.

17. Return to the development environment by using the Back button and the `Edit Page` link.

Sure enough, there are no entries in the `Branches` section. You can fix this easily enough.

18. Click on the plus sign in the `Branches` section in the `Page Processing` center column to bring up the page shown in Figure 6-24. You can leave the defaults for a `Branch Point` to the default after all the processing is complete, since there will be no processing for this simple page, and the `Branch Type` of a branch to a page or a URL. Click Next.

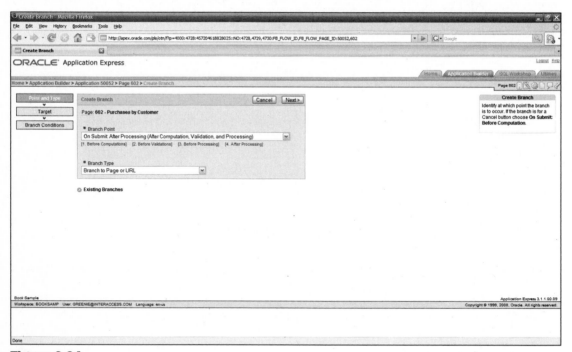

Figure 6-24

19. The next page prompts you for a target for the branch. Set the `Page` to the current page, and click Next.

20. On the next page, you have the option of adding a selection condition for the branch. You will want this branch to work in all situations, so you can simply click the Create Branch button.

Although you did not use any of the flexibility available in the final page of the Branch Definition Wizard, you have seen conditional branching, and the sequencing of those conditions, at work in pages that were already created for you automatically. You can go back and examine some of those branches to gain a more complete idea of what you can accomplish with branching logic.

These few steps should have fixed the problem you previously encountered.

21. Click on the Run icon, and then select a customer in the Customer selection list.

That's better. When you select a customer, the page does refresh. The only problem is that the page refreshes with the same chart that was shown before. The new region gives the user the ability to easily define a selection criterion. You can modify the chart to accept the value the user chooses in the next section.

Try It Out   Modifying the Chart

Changing the previously created chart to use the selected customer as a filter is a pretty easy task, now that you are familiar with how charts and reports are built from SQL statements.

1. Return to the development environment, and click on the `Flash chart` label to access the attributes of the chart.

2. Click on the Edit icon for the `Chart Series`.

Modify the existing `Series Query` to include the new line with the screen:

```
select 'f?p=&APP_ID.:10:'||:app_session||':::RIR:IR_CATEGORY:'||CATEGORY||':' link,
    CATEGORY label,
    SUM("ORDER_ITEMS"."UNIT_PRICE" * "ORDER_ITEMS"."QUANTITY") value1
from    "CATEGORIES" "CATEGORIES",
"PRODUCTS" "PRODUCTS",
"ORDER_ITEMS" "ORDER_ITEMS",
"ORDERS" "ORDERS",
"CUSTOMERS" "CUSTOMERS"
where   "CATEGORIES"."CATEGORY_ID"="PRODUCTS"."CATEGORY_ID"
and "PRODUCTS"."PRODUCT_ID"="ORDER_ITEMS"."PRODUCT_ID"
and "ORDER_ITEMS"."ORDER_ID"="ORDERS"."ORDER_ID"
and  "ORDERS"."CUSTOMER_NAME_ID"="CUSTOMERS"."CUSTOMER_NAME_ID"
and  "ORDERS"."CUSTOMER_NAME_ID" = :Pnn_CUSTOMERS
group by CATEGORY
```

The line you added to the existing WHERE clause acts as a filter to limit the data aggregated for the chart to the order information for the customer selected in the selection list above, using the bind variable indicator (:) to point to the value of the selection list item in the other region and replacing nn with the page number of the current page. The user makes a selection, the page is submitted with the customer selected, and the refreshed page is returned with a chart reflecting that user's orders.

At least that's the way it's supposed to work.

How It Works

After making that one small change to the code, the modified page is ready for a test run.

1. Click Apply Changes and then click the Run icon, and select `Albert Lambert` as the customer to bring up the page shown in Figure 6-25.

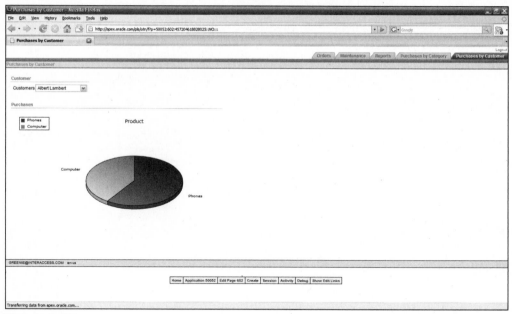

Figure 6-25

Something is definitely happening here, and you do know what it is. To make sure that the chart is working properly, try another customer name.

2.   Select `Edward Butch OHare` in the Customers selection list to produce the page shown in Figure 6-26.

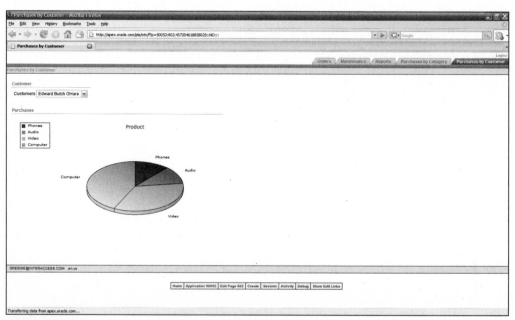

Figure 6-26

O.K. now — this is what you were looking for.

3. Select the wildcard (%) to indicate that no customer was chosen, to produce the page shown in Figure 6-27.

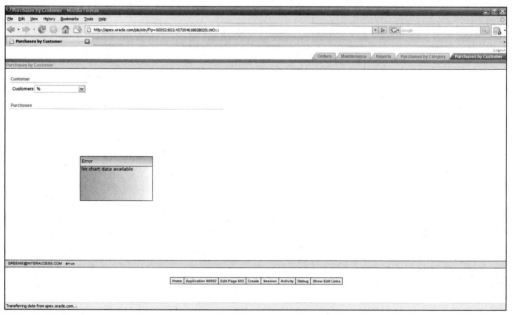

Figure 6-27

Even this result seems appropriate, you probably want to make the message produced when no customer is selected a little more descriptive.

4. Return to the development environment, and click on the `Flash` chart link.

5. Click on the Edit icon for the `Chart Series`.

6. Enter the following text in the `Series Query` in the text box for the `When No Data Found Message`:

    No orders found for this customer.

7. Click Apply Changes and then the Run icon.

The page should come up with the same selection in the Customers selection list from the previous run.

8. The % symbol in the Customers selection list produces the page shown in Figure 6-28.

Figure 6-28

This result reflects the new error message you created for the page. You have accomplished your goal of integrating a user selection with your Flash chart.

If you were to use this new chart in a production scenario, your work would not be done. This chart links to a detailed report, based on the category selected in the chart. You would at least have to add another filter that took into account the selected CUSTOMER_NAME_ID. More likely, you would make a copy of that interactive report and change the control break, to get the customer name to appear in the heading of the report, rather than on each line, as well as changing the breadcrumb. Remember, the breadcrumb defined for that particular detail report has a parent breadcrumb that links back to the chart for all orders, not the chart you just created.

These enhancements are pretty simple to make — you could no doubt do them yourself on your own. The completed sample application has that new report with those changes implemented, if you want to see them at work. For now, though, you have learned enough about coordinating between specific regions in a page. The next area to explore is another automatically generated type of page, the calendar.

Calendar Pages

The sample application you are creating has a time-based aspect to its data. It's certainly not unusual to have a date as a key element in one or more data tables.

When there is a date, there is frequently a user request to use this date in the presentation of data. APEX includes a calendar object, which is ideal for this type of display.

You have already learned most of what you will use in creating this page, including the creation of specific SQL statements to provide the required data to the page and creating links from the data displayed on the page.

Try It Out   Creating a Calendar

Your new calendar will be on its own page.

1. Return to the development environment, and click the Create button.

Clicking the Create button from an existing page gives you the choice of whether you want to create a new entity for the page, a shared component, or a new page.

2. Change the selection to New Page, and click Next.

3. Select the Calendar option, and click Next to bring up the page shown in Figure 6-29.

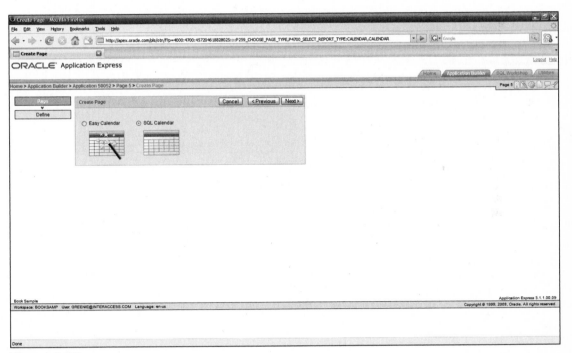

Figure 6-29

At this point in your career as an APEX developer, you probably don't need to use the Easy Calendar option. This option is a tiny bit easier than the SQL Calendar option, but the price you pay for avoiding a few mouse clicks is a decrease in the flexibility of the resulting calendar object. Even if you were unfamiliar with SQL before starting this book, with the help of the Query Builder you should be able to construct the statement for this calendar without much trouble.

4. Leave the SQL Calendar option selected, and click on Next.

5. On the `Page Attributes` page, enter `Orders by Date` for the `Page Name`, and `Orders` for the `Region Name`. You don't have to change the `Breadcrumb` selection, although you probably would include breadcrumbs for all your pages. Click Next.

6. Choose `Use an existing tab set and create a new tab` in the next page, and then accept the default tab set and give the new tab the label of `Orders Calendar`. Click Next.

7. On the next page, you can either enter the SQL directly or use the Query Builder to build a query with CUSTOMERS and ORDERS linked through the CUSTOMER_NAME_ID columns, and that contains the CUSTOMER_NAME, ORDER_ID, and ORDER_TIMESTAMP columns. When you finish entering the SQL or using the Query Builder, your SQL statement should look like this:

```
select  "CUSTOMERS"."CUSTOMER_NAME" as "CUSTOMER_NAME",
  "ORDERS"."ORDER_ID" as "ORDER_ID",
  "ORDERS"."ORDER_TIMESTAMP" as "ORDER_TIMESTAMP"
from      "ORDERS" "ORDERS",
  "CUSTOMERS" "CUSTOMERS"
where    "ORDERS"."CUSTOMER_NAME_ID"="CUSTOMERS"."CUSTOMER_NAME_ID"
```

8. Click Next to bring up the page shown in Figure 6-30.

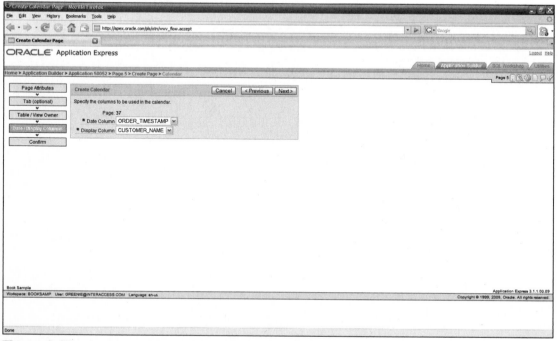

Figure 6-30

This page contains the two columns required for APEX to properly construct the calendar object: a column with a data value and a column to display for that date. If you use the select list for the Date Column, you can see that only selected date columns appear.

9. Accept the defaults, ORDER_TIMESTAMP for the Date Column and CUSTOMER_NAME for the Display Column, and click the Next button.

10. Click Finish to create the new calendar page, and then on the Run Page icon to see it in action, as shown in Figure 6-31.

You will probably want to go to the page for November, 2008, as shown in the Figure, which has quite a few entries.

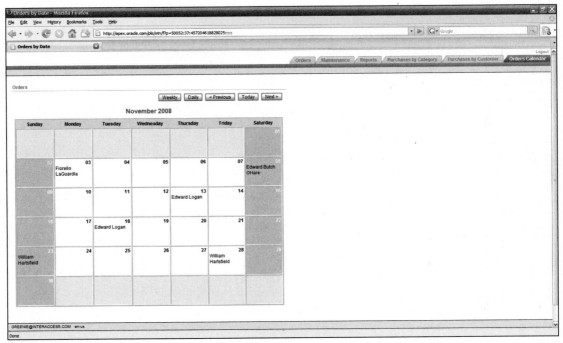

Figure 6-31

A single glance tells you that there is quite a bit of functionality in this automatically created object. The page has buttons to provide the options of seeing a monthly, weekly, or daily view, immediately going to today's date, and advancing through whichever calendar view you are currently using.

But you have grown greedy, gorging yourself on the capabilities of APEX. You want your calendar to do even more, such as providing a link from the calendar entry to the display of an order. And you can already probably imagine how simple expanding the calendar to include these features is going to be.

1. Return to the development environment by clicking on the Edit Page link, and select the Calendar link in the Regions section to bring up the page shown in Figure 6-32.

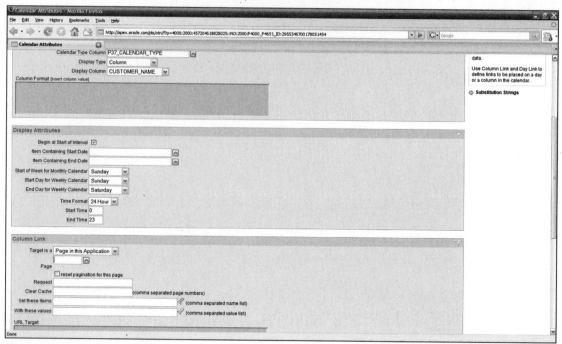

Figure 6-32

Figure 6-32 shows the attribute page for your calendar, scrolled down just a bit to show the most important parts. The Display Attributes area gives you control over how the calendar will be shown. Notice that you have the option of setting the default start and end dates for the display of the calendar, based on the value of items in the page. You could leverage these configuration options to shape the calendar to fit the more specific needs of your application, for example, the display of dates for the duration of a project. You also have the ability to change the overall format for the week and time displays.

The next section should look a bit familiar. You can define a column link for the entries within the calendar, just like you defined a link for other APEX entities.

> **2.** In the Column Link section, select the master-detail page you created for the ORDERS and ORDER_ITEMS tables earlier in this book.

You could, of course, create a report as the destination for your link, but for the accelerated purposes of this book, you might as well reuse a page you have already created. As in the previous link, you will want to pass the value of the ORDER_ID to the master-detail page, so that the destination page will display the correct information.

> **3.** Click on the flashlight icon to the right of the Set these items text field and use the lookup functionality in the resulting dialog box to link the #ORDER_ID# value (the right-hand column) in the calendar page to the corresponding item in the detail page, Pnn_ORDER_ID. Click Apply to add these entries to the Column Link section.

You have added the proper link to connect the calendar with the form for the order and its items. You didn't have to worry about clearing out the page cache, since the link will be passing a unique ORDER_ID value to the target page every time it is called.

Before leaving the attributes for the calendar, though, you might want to change the value that is displayed in the calendar. Right now, the only information showing for a particular date is the name of the customer. The entry might be a little more useful if it showed the customer's name along with the number of the order.

Fortunately, you can make this change without even having to touch the SQL statement underlying the calendar.

4. In the `Calendar Display` section, change the `Display Type` to `Custom`, which will enable the Column Format text box below.

5. Use the `Insert column value` link to the right of the `Column Format` label to add the columns for #CUSTOMER_NAME# and #ORDER_ID#, and then put a space, a dash, and a space between the two to end up with the following string:

```
#CUSTOMER_NAME#  -  #ORDER_ID#
```

If you are familiar with Oracle SQL, you might notice that you did concatenation of values without using the concatenation operator (||). The ## delimiters indicate that CUSTOMER_NAME and ORDER_ID are actually substitution strings, so APEX treats the result as a single string that does not require concatenation.

6. Click Apply Changes and then the Run icon to bring up the page shown in Figure 6-33.

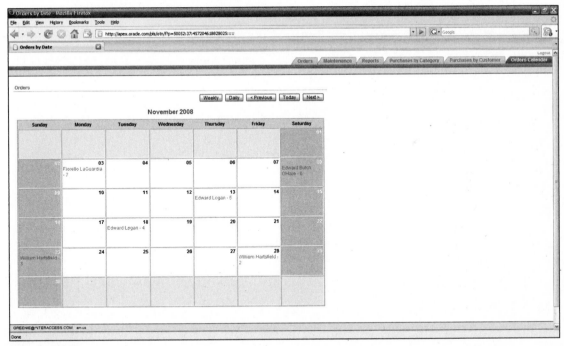

Figure 6-33

7. Click on one of the orders to properly bring up the master-detail form.

After those easy changes, your calendar object looks even better. As with the discussion of charts previously, there is a lot more you could do with calendars. For instance, your users may love this method of navigating around their orders, and they might want to use the calendar interface as their starting point for working with all orders. You could specify a link for the day (in the attributes under Day Link) that would call the same master-detail page with the selected date but no ORDER_ID, which would cause the page to appear in Create mode for orders.

You have accomplished a lot in terms of bringing together different pages to provide a richer user experience. But there is one more topic to cover, one that can really make your users happy — adding rich media to your applications.

Rich User Interfaces

In the past few years, users have come to expect rich media, such as images, as a standard part of their applications. These expectations had to be met with enhanced functionality in underlying databases as well as application development environments. With APEX, you can add graphical and multimedia user interface elements as easily as using more standard types of data.

Before you can use, in this case, images in your APEX application, you will have to modify a table in which to store them and then use an SQL script to load them.

Try It Out   Adding Columns to Support Images to a Table

Your first step is to go to the SQL Workshop and add some columns to your PRODUCTS table to store images of the products. You will have to add a column to hold the image, and also a few more columns to support the automatic functionality used with images in an APEX application.

1. Return to the development environment and go to the SQL Workshop by clicking on the appropriate tab.

2. Use the Object Browser to access your tables.

3. Select the PRODUCTS table in the left-hand panel. Click the Add Column button to add the first column.

The page shown in Figure 6-34 shows the completed page for the first column you will add, the column that will hold the actual image.

4. Give the new column the name of PRODUCT_IMAGE in the Add Column field, allow it to be NULL, and set the type to BLOB. Click Next and then confirm the addition by clicking the Finish button.

If you are unfamiliar with relational database terminology, you may not have encountered the term BLOB before. Technically, the word stands for Binary Large Object, and allows storage of large amounts of binary data, although the sound of the word implies a kind of, well, blobiness. The binary descriptor is an important part of the name. Normally, the data type for a column implies certain qualities for the data stored in that column, such as the requirement that a date value fit a certain format. A BLOB, though, allows the storage of any binary information, and many gigabytes of that information in an Oracle database. The Oracle database even allows BLOBs to take part in transactions. For the purposes of this section, your BLOB will hold an image of a product.

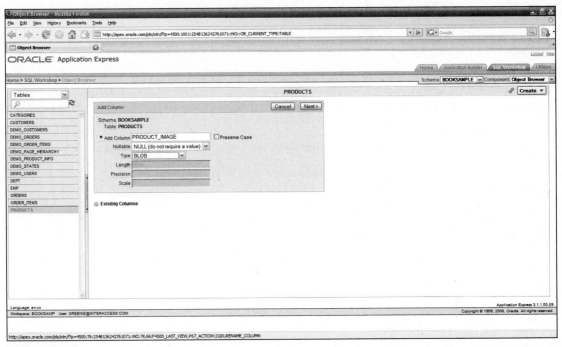

Figure 6-34

Why store BLOBs in the database? The best reason is that the BLOB then receives all the care and data protection of your other data, such as backups.

You will need to add three more columns to the PRODUCTS table to support the use of images.

5. Add the columns listed in Table 6-1 to the PRODUCTS table, following the same procedure used for the PRODUCT_IMAGE column.

Table 6-1

Column Name	NULL?	Data type
MIMETYPE	Yes	VARCHAR2, 255 characters
FILENAME	Yes	VARCHAR2, 255 characters
IMAGE_LAST_UPDATE	Yes	DATE

Why three more columns? As mentioned above, BLOBs fall outside the range of normal data, and, in a normal scenario, require specialized processing to handle their use. The APEX environment has eliminated the need to perform all that specialized processing with these three columns.

As you will see, the APEX implementation is really easy to use for users and developers alike.

Try It Out	Adding Image Capabilities to a Form

Now that you have prepared the PRODUCTS table to use BLOBs, you can use this new field in a form and a report.

Previously, you created a report and form combination for the users to interact with the PRODUCTS table. You modified the original form and report after you created the CATEGORIES lookup table. To include the new image capabilities, it will be just as easy to generate those two pages with a wizard, and then change the navigation list which referenced them.

1. Return to the Application Builder environment, select your application, and click Create Page.

2. Select the Form option, and click Next, and then select the Form on a Table with Report option, and click Next.

3. Accept the default schema, and click on Next. Select the PRODUCTS table as the base for the report and form, and click Next.

4. Set the Page Name for the Report Page to Products. You might also want to give the page a Page Number, which you will remember, since you will be adding this page to your navigation list shortly. Click Next.

5. Accept the default choice of no tabs, and click Next.

6. On the next page, deselect the MIMETYPE, FILENAME, and IMAGE_LAST_UPDATE columns. Your APEX application will use these columns while handling the images, but you should not display them in the report or form pages. Click Next.

7. Accept the default Edit Link Image, and click Next.

8. Give the Form Page a Page Name of Products. You might again want to give this form a recognizable Page Number. Click Next.

9. Accept the Primary Key, and click Next.

10. Change the primary key source to Existing sequence, and use the PRODUCTS_SEQ sequence you used in the earlier version of this page. Click Next.

11. As with the report, deselect the MIMETYPE, FILENAME, and IMAGE_LAST_UPDATE columns, and click Next.

12. Accept all the default buttons, and click Next, and then click the Finish button to complete the creation of the pages.

Using the wizard was once again fairly painless, and you will now begin to see how these new pages work.

How It Works

Time to see how these new pages are different.

1. Click on the Run Page icon to bring up the report page, as shown in Figure 6-35.

2. The report looks the same, except for the final column with the heading of Product Image.

3. Click on the Edit icon for the MP3 player to bring up the page shown in Figure 6-36.

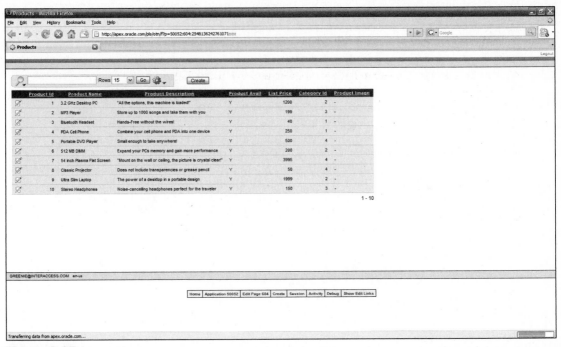

Figure 6-35

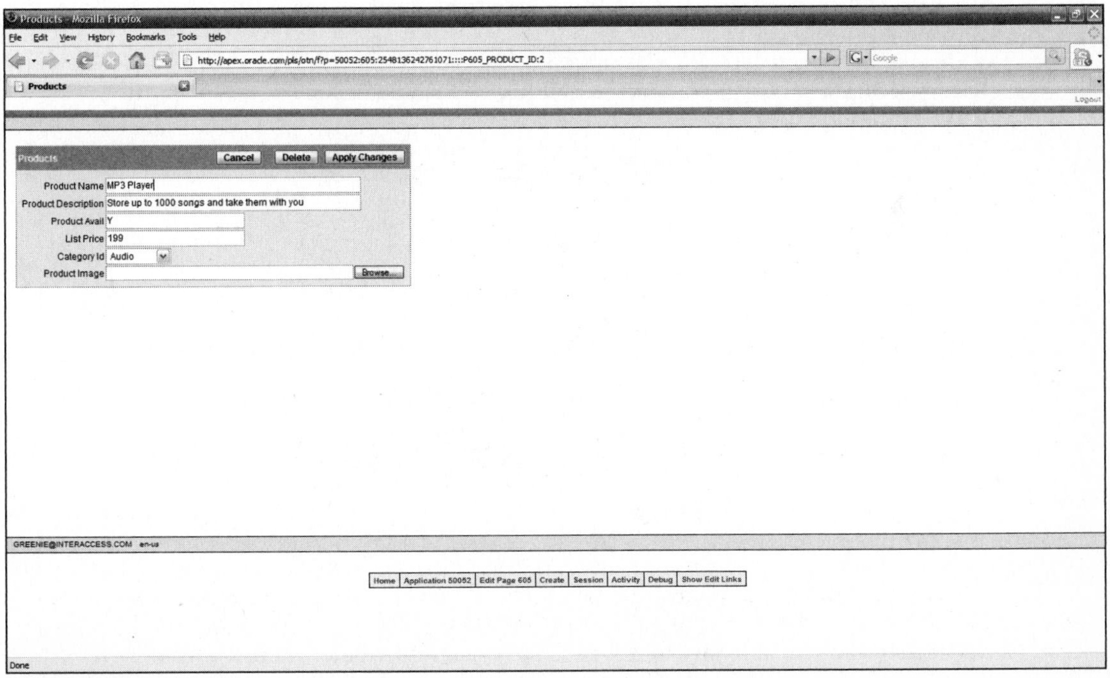

Figure 6-36

This page looks different from the original version of your generated form page for PRODUCTS. The first difference is the new Product Image field. You can see that this field has a Browse button next to the field, which you will see at work in a minute.

Tech Talk – The Power of Data Design

Do you notice another change? If you recall, your original form page for the PRODUCTS table was created before you added the lookup CATEGORIES table and the foreign key that connected it to the PRODUCTS table. That original form had a simple text field for the CATEGORY column. In this new version of the form, APEX has automatically included a selection list associated with a correct list of values. The APEX Page Wizard recognized the relationship and created the page accordingly. This little twist will hopefully drive home the message that APEX can really leverage a good data design, so you should spend some time thinking about your tables and their relationships before jumping into building an application.

The form and report pages are built to handle images, which you can check out next.

1. Click on Browse and navigate to the files for this book. Select the file named mp3_player.gif and click on Open, which will return you to the form.

2. Click on Apply Changes, which takes you back to the report.

When you come back to the report, you can see that the Product Image column now has a Download link. This link is shown when there are values for the four columns that handle the images.

3. Click on the Edit link for the MP3 player to return to the edit page. You can see the Download link on this page, too.

4. Click on the Download link, which will bring up the dialog box shown in Figure 6-37.

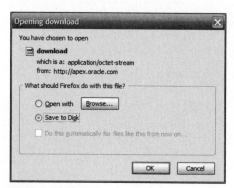

Figure 6-37

This result seems great, except for one little thing. The file name shown in the dialog box is simply download, without any identifying file type at the end. In order to get these pages using images in a completely robust way, you will have to return to the pages and modify them slightly.

Try It Out   Adding Image Display to a Report

The functionality in the form page allows your users to easily upload images to be stored in the
PRODUCTS table. Now that the images are stored, you would like to display them in the report, which
you can accomplish with one more simple modification.

1. Click Cancel in the dialog box for the download, return to the application development envi-
    ronment and click on the report page you recently created for the PRODUCTS table.

2. Select the Interactive Report region, and click on the Edit icon for the PRODUCT_IMAGE col-
    umn to bring up the page shown in Figure 6-38.

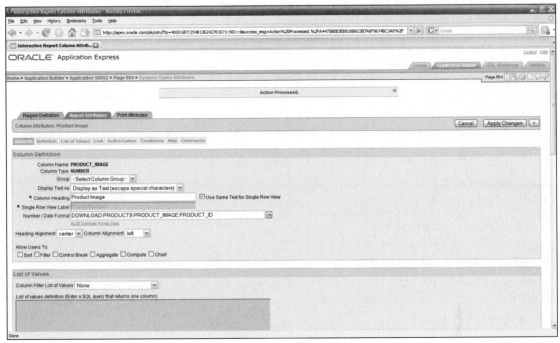

Figure 6-38

You should note two things in the Column Definition section of the page. The first is the
Number/Date Format, which seems to be a series of parameters, since they are separated by colons.
In fact, this format specification is a series of parameters, which will change as you change the BLOB
specification.

The second thing to note is a new link just below the Number/Date Format field, which has the label of
BLOB Download Format Mask.

3. Click on the BLOB Download Format Mask to bring up the page shown in Figure 6-39.

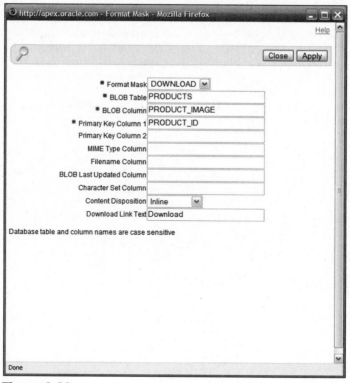

Figure 6-39

Although you have not seen this page before, you should not be too surprised by some of the fields in it. There are fields for the BLOB table and column, as well as the primary key column, which you already specified. There are three more fields to fill in.

4. Enter `MIMETYPE` for the `MIME Type` Column, `FILENAME` for the `Filename` Column, and `IMAGE_LAST_UPDATE` for the `BLOB Last Updated` Column.

Your APEX application will use these three columns to properly process the BLOB column.

5. Change the `Format Mask` at the top of the page to `IMAGE`, which will allow the display of the actual image, rather than a download link.

6. Click Apply to return to the main attribute page. You can see that the `Number/Date Format` has changed, and the first parameter is now `IMAGE`.

7. Click on Apply Changes to save your work.

You are ready to see if these modifications achieved the desired report. (I wouldn't mislead you!)

How It Works

Those last few changes were not that big a deal. If they give you the images on the page as you hope, it will all be well worth the time.

1. Click on the Run icon to bring up the new report, as shown in Figure 6-40.

Figure 6-40

Voila! The images are part of the report, just as you hoped.

You may not be completely satisfied with the appearance of the report, since the images themselves are fairly large, and cause the rows to be too high. You could reduce the size of the images but not with the default functionality built into a standard APEX page. You can use an APEX PL/SQL function designed to display images, and this function will allow you to specify any size you like for an image. For more information on this function and its use, please refer to the APEX documentation. The standard demo application for APEX also has an example of the use of this function in its report on products.

To round out the use of your new pages, you would want to go to the new form for PRODUCTS and change the BLOB Download Format Mask parameters for the form. Although you cannot display an image in a form, changing the BLOB parameters would cause the downloaded file to have the proper file name and be recognized by the appropriate reader. If you specified that the BLOB was inline for a form, the image would open up in a browser window, if the browser was able to handle the MIME type of the BLOB.

Try It Out	Cleaning up

If you want to use your newly created interface pages for PRODUCTS in your application, you will have to perform two cleanup functions to keep the navigation in your application correct and to clean up pages that are now no longer used.

1. Return to the application development environment, and click on the Shared Components icon.

2. Select the Lists link, and click on the list you created with links to the maintenance pages.

3. Click on the link for the list entry of Products, and change the target page to the report page you just completed.

4. Click Apply Changes to save the new target.

5. Select the master-detail page for the application, run the application, and test the new navigation from the list.

You would also have to adjust the tab settings for the new pages, adding them to the Maintenance tab.

This little demonstration highlights that using shared components, which can help enforce standardization, is even handier when you have to maintain some facet of your APEX application in the future.

Your last task is to delete the previous versions of the form and report used to maintain the PRODUCTS table, which you can do by selecting the page and clicking the Delete button. At this point in your APEX career, you probably don't need step-by-step directions to accomplish this.

Summary

This chapter has been like adding another story to a structure you are building or, even more relevantly, like growing older and wiser. You have learned how to create basic pages and work in the APEX development environment in the previous three chapters, but in this chapter you brought those parts together to make a larger, more valuable whole.

You have learned:

❑ How to link to a drill-down report from a chart

❑ How to allow a user to specify filters for a chart

❑ How to take advantage of rich data types, like images, in your Oracle database and APEX application

The next chapter will take you to another level of productivity, when you explore how to modify the appearance of an individual page or your entire application, while keeping all the valuable functionality you have already created in place.

Customizing User Interfaces

As an Application Builder, you should never overlook the key functionality required in your APEX applications. The first five chapters of this tutorial section have focused on including that functionality in the sample application.

But your users may not appreciate the elegance of your design and implementation. For them, beauty is page deep, and their expectations might require you to spend time sprucing up the appearance of your APEX components.

The APEX user interface enforces a standard look and feel, and you do have productive ways to modify the appearance of individual pages as well as your entire application, or even groups of applications. This chapter will cover the ways you can satisfy your users' look and feel desires without interfering with any of the capabilities you have already included in your application.

Page Layouts

In a browser, the atomic unit of display is a page. Pages are sent from the APEX server to your users' browser. Every APEX page has a page layout, which you can customize to change the appearance of the page.

Up until this point in the book, you have been accepting the default page layout for forms and standard reports. It's time to look at how you can change the layout of a page to give your users a more pleasing and logical interface.

Try It Out   **Drag- and-Drop Page Layouts**

The APEX development environment includes a simple drag-and-drop interface for item layouts.

1. Go to the main development page for your application, and double-click on the form you created for the CUSTOMERS table.

2. Run the page to refresh your memory of the appearance of the default page, as shown in Figure 7-1.

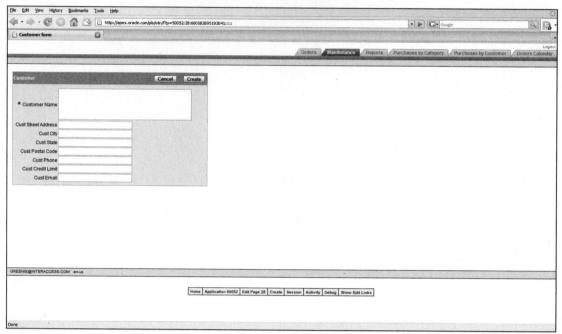

Figure 7-1

You can readily see that the layout of this page could be improved.

3. Return to the development environment by clicking on the `Edit Page` link.

In the `Items` section under the leftmost `Page Rendering` column, you will see three icons to the right of the `Customers` region. The first two allow you to move an item up or down in the item list, which will change the order of the items displayed on a page. The icon on the right looks kind of like a moving box, and this icon will lead you to the drag-and-drop interface.

4. Click on the rightmost icon to the right of the `Customers` region in the `Items` section to bring up the page shown in Figure 7-2.

The first thing you notice about this new page is that the fields are arranged in what looks like a table, with each field on its own line. This impression is accurate — APEX used HTML-based tables to determine the layout of a page. You will be adjusting some of the table-specific attributes of the fields on this page in this section.

5. Move the mouse over the item for the `CUST_STATE`. Hold the left mouse button down and drag the item up a row so that it is next to the `CUST_CITY` item.

6. Drag the `CUST_POSTAL_CODE` item up so that it is to the right of the `CUST_STATE` field. The layout page should now look like Figure 7-3. Click Next.

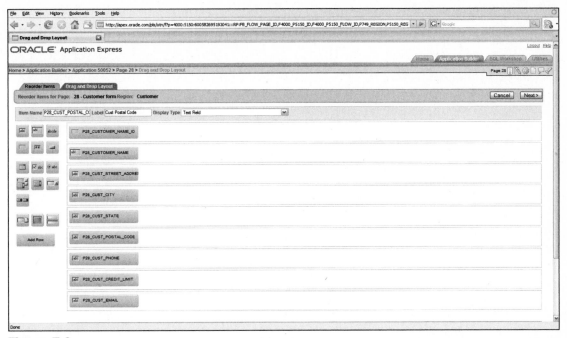

Figure 7-2

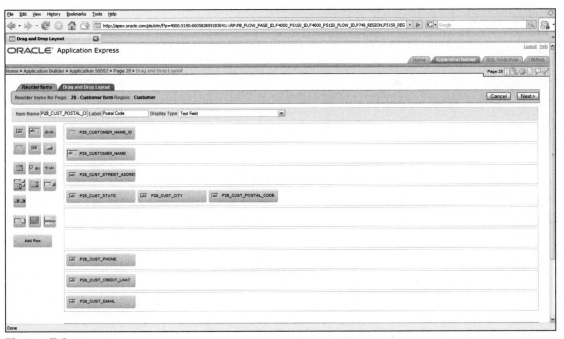

Figure 7-3

The layout looks better, but moving the columns left two rows blank. Don't worry, APEX is smart enough to know that those rows can be dropped in the creation of the page layout.

The next page displays the name of the items, the labels for the items, and the item type. For this particular table, all the column names are preceded by the prefix CUST_, which is probably not helpful for your users. You might as well use this page to reset these labels to something a little more user-friendly.

7. Change the labels for the items in the page to match the labels shown in Table 7-1.

Table 7-1

Column Name	Label
CUSTOMER_NAME	Customer
CUST_STREET_ADDRESS	Street Address
CUST_CITY	City
CUST_STATE	State
CUST_POSTAL_CODE	Postal Code
CUST_PHONE	Phone
CUST_CREDIT_LIMIT	Credit Limit
CUST_EMAIL	E-mail

8. Click Apply Changes and run the page, which should now look like Figure 7-4.

The new page layout is certainly an improvement, but you could do even better. For instance, the width of the entry fields for City, State, Postal Code, Credit Limit, Phone, and E-mail fields are way too wide, and the height of the entry field for Customer is too great. You can quickly change all of these factors in the column edit grid.

9. Return to the development environment, and click on the link to the Customers region in the Items section, which will bring up the page shown in Figure 7-5.

10. The grid view shown in this page gives you ready access to most of the important attributes of your columns. You can see that using the drag-and-drop page layout editor has changed the value of the New Line choice for the State and Postal Code fields.

11. Change the Width of the items for CUST_CITY, CUST_STATE, CUST_POSTAL_CODE, CUST_PHONE, CUST_CREDIT_LIMIT, and CUST_EMAIL items to 20. Click Apply Changes and then the Run icon to bring up the page shown in Figure 7-6.

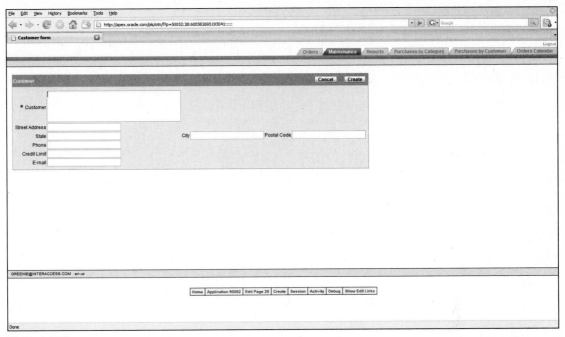

Figure 7-4

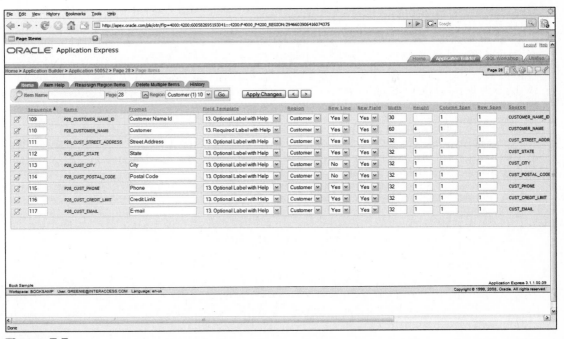

Figure 7-5

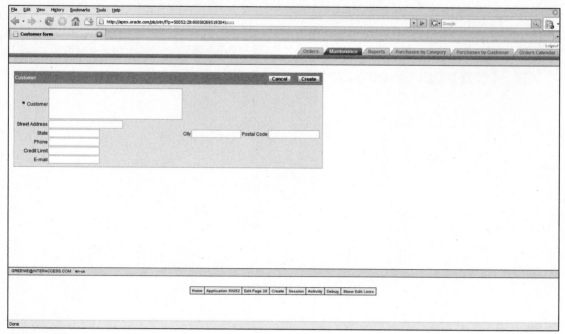

Figure 7-6

This page looks better, but the results may not be exactly what you expected. The field for the Name item is still too tall, which you can fix by changing the item type in a moment. The other disparity in the display comes with the placement of the label for the State item. You would like this label to begin just to the right of the City item — how come it is placed to the right of the end of the Name item?

The reason comes back to the use of HTML tables as the basis for page layouts. An HTML table has columns, which, by default, automatically adjust to the width of the widest field in the column. In the current layout, the greatest width is the width of the Name field, so the label for the State field begins in the next column.

You can easily fix this problem by adjusting the column span of the Name and Street Address items. By specifying that these items span more than one column, you will prevent their greater width from setting the width for the first column.

1. Return to the development environment and click on the CUSTOMER_NAME link in the Items section.

2. Change the Display As value to Text, and click Apply Changes.

3. Return to the page layout grid. Change the Col Span for the Name and Street Address items to 3.

Why 3? Why not 2? Be aware that the label for an item is in one column, with the field for that item in the next column. If you want the larger fields to span the width of two fields with their labels, the field column will have to span three columns.

4. Click Apply Changes and then the Run icon, which will show you the new version of the page in Figure 7-7.

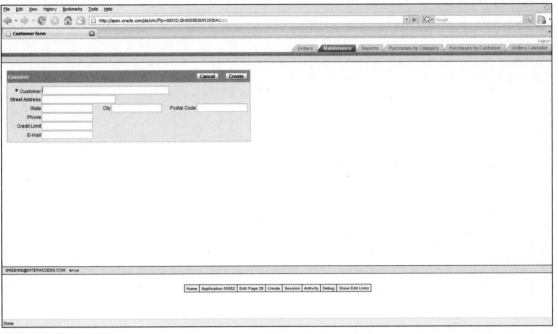

Figure 7-7

That's more like it. But before you take leave of this section on page layouts, you should return to the drag-and-drop page layout to understand another attribute you can use to adjust the appearance of your pages.

Try It Out   Adding a Text Area with Its Own layout

As a way to learn more about formatting pages, you will add a text area to your Customers page.

1.   Return to the development environment, and bring up the drag-and-drop editor for the page.

2.   Click on the Add Row icon in the left-hand panel, and drag it to a position underneath the CUST_EMAIL field. Release the mouse button to place the row.

3.   Grab the Text Area icon, in the middle of the top row of the left-hand panel, and drag it to the blank row you just added.

4.   Click in the Item Name field at the top of the layout area and extend the default name with the name of COMMENTS.

5.   Click on the select list for the Display Type, and change the item type to Textarea with Character Counter & Spellcheck.

This display type was selected to show you a bit more of the functionality built into APEX component types. You could have also made the text area an HTML Editor, which would give your users more formatting flexibility.

6. Click Next and then Apply Changes.

7. Once the changes are saved, click on the new text area item in the Items list. Set the Label to Comments. Change the Horizontal/Vertical Alignment option in the Label section to Above and the template to Optional Label with Help. While you are here, you can also make the area bigger by changing the Width to 70 and the Height to 5 in the Element section. Click Apply Changes.

8. Click on the Run icon to bring up the page shown in Figure 7-8.

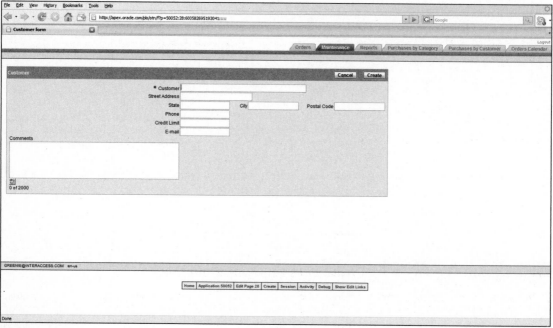

Figure 7-8

Whoa, that doesn't look so great. The new text area is nice, but all the rest of the labels and fields are suddenly pushed way over to the left. The new alignment makes sense when you think back to the way HTML tables work. When you put the label for the text area above the field, you caused both of these elements to be placed in the first column. This new arrangement caused that column to expand in width and pushed the second column over to the right.

What you really want is for these new elements to fall outside the scope of the HTML table. You can get to this layout with a few more tweaks in the drag-and-drop editor, while learning a little bit more about how to shape the overall APEX page layout.

1. Return to the development environment and bring up the drag-and-drop editor.

2. Move your mouse over the rightmost icon in the second-to-last row of the left-hand panel. You will see the icon represents `Stop` and `start table`.

As the title implies, this icon will stop the use of one HTML table and add another. By dragging one of these attributes before the text area and its label, you will effectively place each of them in their own table, which will allow their placement to be independent of the previous items.

3. Drag a `Stop` and `start table` item to a position before the COMMENTS item. You could give this item a name if you want to document it. Click Next and Apply Changes to return to the main development page and then click on the Run icon to bring up the page shown in Figure 7-9.

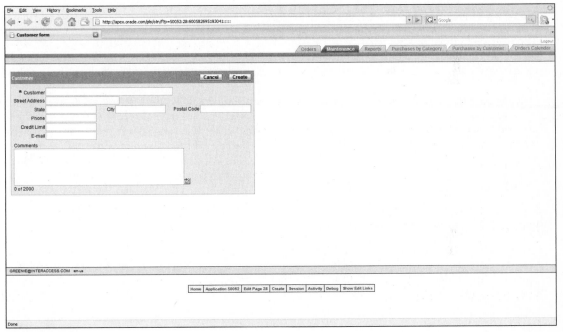

Figure 7-9

This final result is what you were looking for. The label for the text area is directly above the area, and both of these items are resting against the right side of the page.

If you are wondering about those field templates you just changed, you will only have to hold on a little while before it all becomes clear. You will learn the basics of using templates later in this chapter, but first you can explore a way of increasing your productivity by reducing the number of changes you have to make on individual pages.

> ### What about the Data?
>
> In this section, you created a new text area to accept comments on a customer. But, as it currently stands, that text area only exists on a page in your application. The item is not associated with a column in the database. If you were to bring up the attributes page for that text area and look in the Source section, you would see that the Source Type is Static Assignment. If you wanted to save this information in the database, you would first need to identify an existing column or create a new column to store the data. You would then change the Source Type to DB Column and identify the column in the Source value or expression field, as the APEX wizards did for other items that are bound to database columns. By setting this attribute, you are instructing APEX to retrieve values for the item from that database column and to save values entered in this item to that database column.

User Interface Defaults

The pages that the APEX wizards generate provide a fairly complete set of capabilities for interacting with your data. The wizards use information in the *data dictionary*, which holds information about the structures in the database, to create the appropriate field types and labels for the items in your pages.

But, as you already saw, sometimes the default assumptions made by the APEX wizards are not exactly what you want. In the last section, you changed the labels for all of the fields for the CUSTOMERS table — but you only changed them on one page. In other places where the data from that table is referenced, the automatic labels still exist, and you would have to find each of them and change them by hand.

In a real development process, though, you have the ability to change those defaults before ever generating a single page.

Try It Out   Changing User Interface Defaults

The APEX page that allows you to change default attributes for a data column can be accessed from several different places, including the Shared Components page and links from some attribute pages. Since the user defaults are connected with distinct columns, for the purposes of this section, you can get to them from the SQL Browser.

1. Go to the SQL Workshop and bring up the Object Browser to browse Tables.

2. Click on the PRODUCTS table and then on the UI defaults button to bring up the page shown in Figure 7-10.

The contents of the right panel now contain a partial list of the user interface defaults for the columns of the PRODUCTS table. You can see that these defaults include the standard label for the fields, the order in which the fields will appear in a report or form, and the type of display used for the field. You want to change some of the labels and the display type for one of the columns in the table.

3. Click Edit to bring up a report on some of the user interface defaults, and then click Grid Edit to bring up the page shown in Figure 7-11.

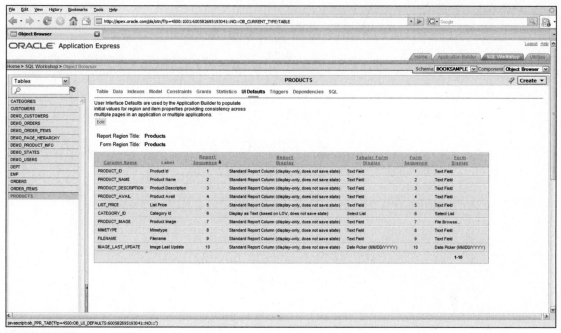

Figure 7-10

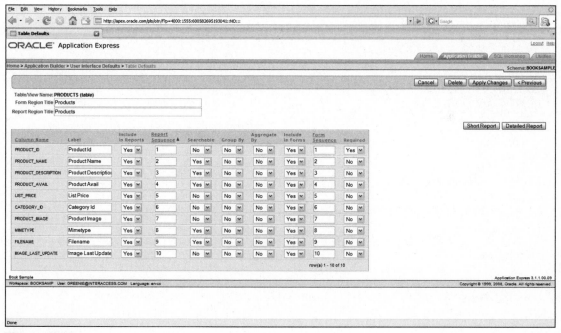

Figure 7-11

4. Change the `Labels` for `PRODUCT_ID` to `Product ID` and `CATEGORY_ID` to `Category`. Click Apply Changes to save the new labels.

You have changed the default labels for the ID fields, but it makes sense to change the display type used for the `PRODUCT_AVAIL` column, since this product will only have two possible values, an ideal candidate for a radiogroup.

1. Click Short Report, and then on the `PRODUCT_AVAIL` link to display the page shown in Figure 7-12.

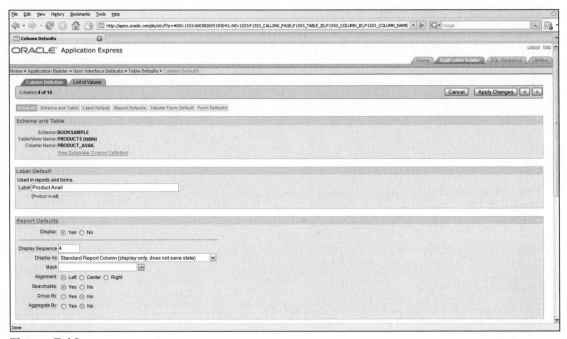

Figure 7-12

On this page, you have access to all of the user interface defaults.

2. Change the `Display As` entry for the `Tabular Form Default` to `Select List`, and the `Display As` for the `Form Defaults` to `Radiogroup`.

3. Change the `Label` to `Product Availability`.

Since you will be limiting value selection for these fields, you will also have to define a list of values for the column.

1. Click on the List of Values tab on the page. Select `Static` as the `List of Values Type` to change the display to look like Figure 7-13.

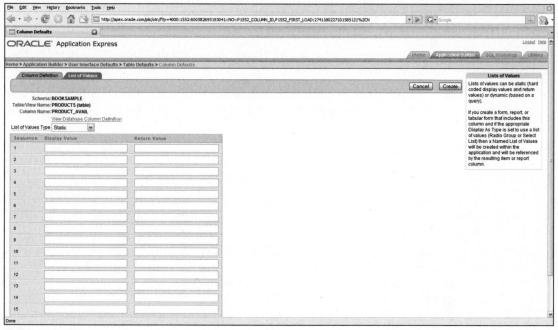

Figure 7-13

2. Enter Display Values of Yes and No and Return Values of Y and N, respectively. Click Create and then Apply Changes.

3. Click on the LIST_PRICE column. Change the Mask in the Report Defaults and Form Defaults section to represent currency. Click Apply Changes and return to the Application Builder main page.

Now that you have changed some of the user defaults, you can create some new pages to show the results of your work.

1. Select your application in the Application Builder home page, and then click Create Page.

2. Select Form for the page type, and click Next. Select Form on a Table with Report on the next page, and click Next.

3. On the next two pages, accept the default schema and select the PRODUCTS table, clicking Next on both pages.

4. Change the Report Page Name to Products, and click Next. Accept the default of no tabs on the next page by clicking Next. On the next page, deselect the MIMETYPE, FILENAME and IMAGE_LAST_UPDATE columns and click Next.

5. Accept the default Edit icon, and click Next.

6. On the first Form Page, set the Page Name to Products and click Next. Accept the primary key and click Next.

7. On the next page, select the Existing sequence choice and the PRODUCTS_SEQ as the source, and click Next.

8. Once again, deselect the MIMETYPE, FILENAME, and IMAGE_LAST_UPDATE columns, and click Next. Accept the defaults on the next page, and click Next, and then click Finish to complete the creation of the pages.

9. Click Run Page to run your most recent creation.

The report page should look like Figure 7-14, and the form should look like Figure 7-15.

The newly created pages serve as an illustration of how the user interface defaults work. You might want to use these new pages instead of the ones you created earlier, in which case you would simply have to edit the links in your navigation list.

Please, don't feel betrayed by this late discovery of a better way to do things. The purpose of this book, as stated from the very beginning, is to teach you how to use APEX to create applications. At this point in your explorations, you can understand and appreciate how user interface defaults work, whereas introducing them earlier might have complicated the learning process.

As noted previously, several times, APEX applications spring from the data that the applications access. User interface defaults are yet another example of this philosophy — time spent setting the proper defaults for your data before you create any pages is time very well spent.

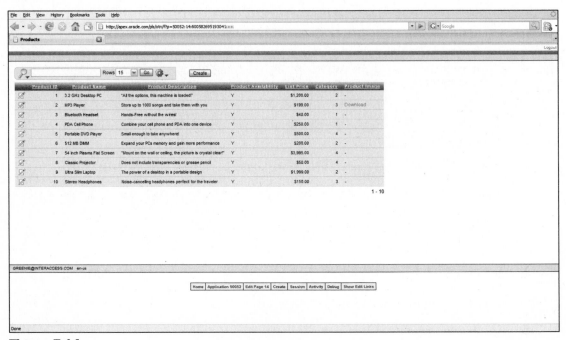

Figure 7-14

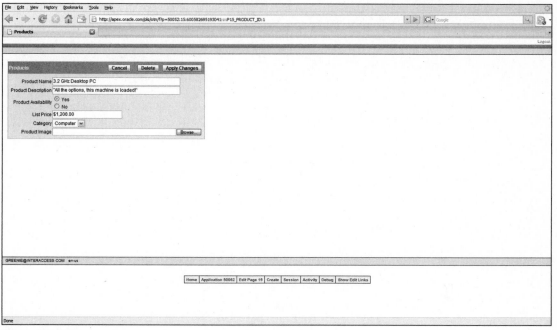

Figure 7-15

Tech talk – Comparing User Interfaces for a Column

Having a consistent user interface representation for a column is almost as important as having the best user interface for the column. You can compare the attributes of the user interface for all the occurrences of a column in all pages in an application with a built-in report. Go to the User Interface Defaults page from the Shared Components area. On the right, you will see a link for a comparison report, which will show you all the characteristics of every instance of a column in your application.

User interface defaults apply to all usage of particular pieces of data, across all applications. What if you wanted to add an element to all the pages in your application? APEX provides a special page that handles this task.

Try It Out   Using Page Zero

You may have noticed that the first page you create in an application will, by default, have a page number of 1. You may have also noticed that one of the options when you are creating a page is to create a Page 0. What is this mysterious Page Zero?

Rather than representing nothing, Page Zero is a place where you can add user interface components which will appear on all pages in the application. Although an application does not need to have a Page Zero, only one Page Zero can exist for an application.

The interface elements described on Page Zero could be specific regions or items with defined text, or they could be regions that use information local to the specific page. You will use this latter capability of Page Zero in this exercise, adding a region for page-level help, which will display the help defined for the page.

1. Return to the development environment for your application, and click Create Page.

2. Select the `Page Zero` option for the page type, and click Next. On the next page, click Finish to confirm your desire to create Page Zero, which will take you to the attributes page for Page Zero, as shown in Figure 7-16.

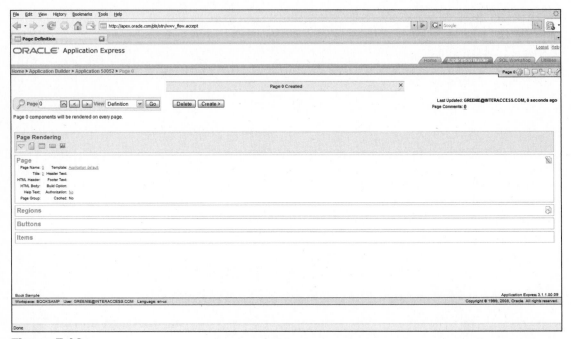

Figure 7-16

You can see that Page Zero has a much more limited set of attributes, since this page will never actually run. Even the attribute sections for Page Zero have fewer available configuration options, based on the special nature of Page Zero. For a simple demonstration of the type of thing you can accomplish with Page Zero, you will want to create a region to display help text on every page, rather than requiring your user to ask for it.

1. Click on the plus sign (+) in the upper-right corner of the `Regions` section.

2. Select the `Help Text` region type, and click Next.

3. Enter `Help for this page` as the `Title` of the region, and select `Before Footer` as the display point. Click Next to bring up the confirmation page, where you can click Create Region to finish your task.

With these small steps, you have added a region that will appear at the bottom of every page in your application with the help for the page. Before you can see how this region works, you will have to add some specific help text for some of your pages.

1. Return to the main application development page, and select the report for PRODUCTS that you just created. Click on the Help Text link in the Page section of the left-hand Page Rendering column to modify the help text for this page to something like This is a report on all products. Click Apply Changes.

2. Repeat the previous step for the form called by the PRODUCTS report, except make the help something like This form allows you to edit product information. Click Apply Changes.

3. Return to the main development page for the application, and select the PRODUCTS report. Click on the Run icon to bring up the page, which should look like Figure 7-17.

Figure 7-17

4. Click on the Edit icon to bring up the form for the individual product, which should look like Figure 7-18.

You can use Page Zero for many purposes, such as including corporate logos on every page in your application. You can also use another APEX feature to shape the way all pages of a certain type are shown in your application — the feature known as templates.

Figure 7-18

Templates

Every time you have created a page, a region, a report, or many other entities in APEX, you have accepted the default choice for a very powerful feature, the template. An APEX template is used to provide the look, feel and, in some cases, the functionality of a type of APEX entity.

Templates provide a framework for the target type of entity, a framework that is combined with the items and attributes specified for the entity to produce the result shown to the user. APEX comes with templates for:

❏ Pages

❏ Regions

❏ Reports

❏ Calendars

❏ Lists

❑ Popup List of Values

❑ Labels

❑ Buttons

❑ Breadcrumbs

Templates act as a kind of container for different types of objects. For instance, a page template can include HTML code for the header and footer of a page, as well as HTML that goes before and after any attribute-specified feature of the page. You could even include JavaScript routines in a page template to add functionality to your application pages.

Templates can take advantage of Cascading Style Sheets (CSS), which are used to define the look and feel of HTML pages. The complete understanding and modification of templates is a fairly complex topic, one that is beyond the limited scope of this book. But you can explore the way that templates affect pages, in particular, as well as see the way that templates work with other APEX attributes in the creation of those pages.

Try It Out   **Changing a Page Template**

The quickest way to see templates at work is to change different templates for a region and page and observe the effects.

How It Works

The master-detail page you created way back in Chapter 4 presents a good candidate to see how templates affect both regions and pages.

1. To see the full effect of a template change, edit the master-detail form for entering Order Items, which was named Order Items in the example. Click on the Maintenance Pages region, then the Delete and Delete Region buttons to remove the region.

2. Now run the master-detail form. If the page is in Create mode, without any order items showing, hit Cancel to return to the previous report and then select the first order to return to the page.

3. Click Show Edit Links in the page to make it easier to see the results of your template changes, if the links are not already showing.

4. Click on Edit Link for the upper region of the page next to the title in the upper-left corner of the page.

This region shows the fields for the ORDERS table. The region is defined as an HTML region with a Reports Region template, as shown in Figure 7-19.

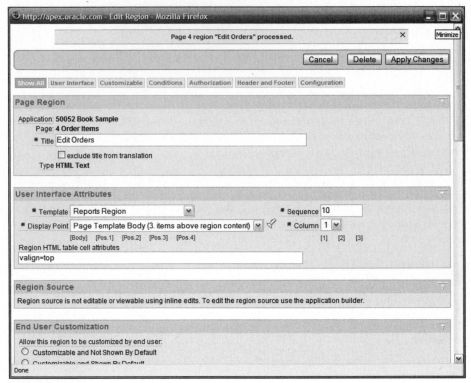

Figure 7-19

5. In the `User Interface Attributes` section of the attributes page, change the `Template` to `Reports Region 100% Width`. Click Apply Changes to save your new choice and leave the attributes page open.

6. Refresh the `Order Items` page to display the new version of the page, shown in Figure 7-20.

The change that occurred was not that dramatic, with the line under the heading of the page extending across the entire page, and the buttons moving, as a group, to the far right of the page. But you should realize that this template change only affected the user interface of this region, not any of the functionality.

Templates control the look and feel of a functionality container, be it a region, page or a button, without interfering with the functionality embedded in that container. Although templates only change the user interface to a container, that change can offer additional features, at least to the user.

7. Change the template for the HTML region to `Hide and Show Region`, and click Apply Changes. Refresh the `Order Items` page to show the new version of the page, as illustrated in Figure 7-21.

Figure 7-20

Figure 7-21

What happened to the body of the region? That body is not gone, it's just hiding, as the name of the template implies.

8. Click on the plus sign (+) to the right of the `Order Items` label, which will change the appearance of the page to that shown in Figure 7-22.

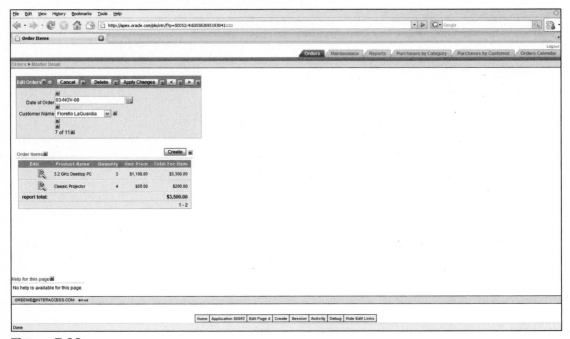

Figure 7-22

Although this region template may not be appropriate for all situations (it's not that appropriate for this one, for instance, where the user will always want to see the fields for the ORDERS table), using this template for the region is a more dramatic change.

9. Change the template back to the `Reports Region`, and click Apply Changes to return the region to its original state.

The actual code used to define templates is a combination of standard HTML and special tokens which are interpreted by the APEX runtime environment. An explanation of the complete syntax and use of templates is beyond the scope of this brief tutorial, but you can get some idea of how templates operate by changing a template for the page, and then looking at the template code that produces that change.

10. Return to the development environment for the page, and click on the `Application default` link for the `Template` entry in the `Page` section of the `Page Rendering` column.

The selection of `Use Application Level Default` indicates that the `Page Template` is following the standard selected for the entire application.

11. Change the `Page Template` to `One Level Tabs`, which is the application default, and click Apply Changes. Run the page to show that the appearance has not changed.

12. Return to the page attributes and change the template for the page to `Printer Friendly`. Save the changes and run the page, which will now look like the page in Figure 7-23.

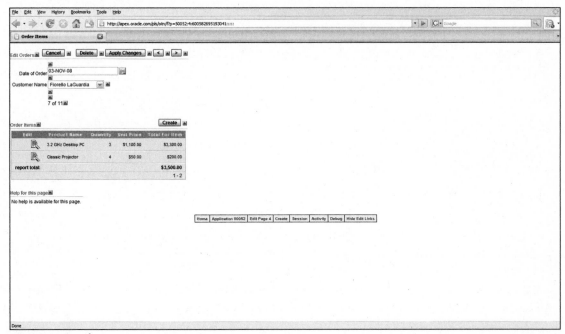

Figure 7-23

Although this new look for the page doesn't look as good in your browser, you can readily see that this appearance is more appropriate for a page destined for printing. There is no need for navigation tabs on a printed page, so the template simply gets rid of them.

Comparing the code for these two templates will give you a taste of how templates are assembled.

1. Return to the attributes for this page and change the template for the page back to the application default to return the page to its original state. Click Apply Changes to return to the main attributes page.

2. In the right-hand `Shared Components` column, you can see that the actual template used for the page is displayed, with a link. Click on the link to bring up the attributes of the template, and then on the Definition button to show the section in Figure 7-24.

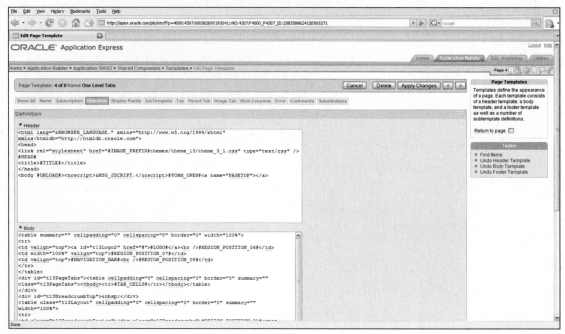

Figure 7-24

If you are familiar with HTML, you will probably understand a lot of what you can see in these fields. If you are not that familiar with HTML, don't fret — you are only going to look at a single piece of this code.

The HTML for the Header, Body, and Footer is combined with the HTML generated for your pages, based on the attributes you specified for the page, region, or other area. You can see where the bulk of the code for a page is placed by scrolling down the Body field until you see the #BOX_BODY# substitution string. APEX replaces this variable with all the code for the items on a page.

If you scroll back up to the top of the code, you can spot the #NAVIGATION_BAR# substitution string. This seems like a likely candidate to be missing in the Printer Friendly template.

> **3.** Click on the Templates breadcrumb to go to a listing of templates. Scroll down to the page template area of the listing and click on the Printer Friendly template.

You can see that the template code for the body of this template is quite a bit simpler, and that, sure enough, the #NAVIGATION_BAR# substitution string is missing.

This small examination should give you a taste of how templates can be used, as well as an inkling of the way template code works. Before leaving the area of templates, you can try making a change that will be reflected through the use of templates.

Try It Out   **Adding a Logo to Your Application**

Templates are used for customizing the look and feel of your application, while providing a consistency to the various components in the application. One of the most frequent customization requests is to add a logo to the application.

APEX provides you with a simple way to specify a logo for your application, and that specification is used in many different templates.

Before leaving the attribute page for the Printer Friendly template, notice the #LOGO# substitution string near the top of the Body code. This variable will be replaced with the logo you are about to specify.

1. Click on the Shared Components breadcrumb to return to the main page for shared components.

2. Click on the Definition link in the Application section of the page.

3. Click on the Logo button to present only that section on the page, as shown in Figure 7-25.

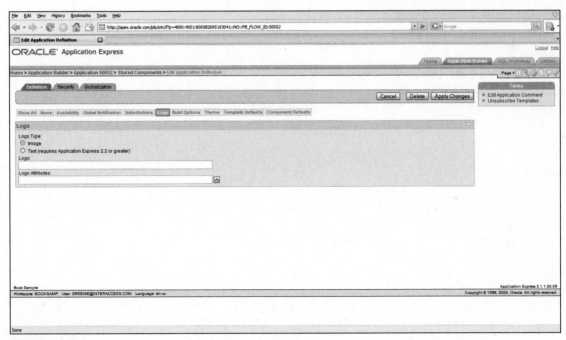

Figure 7-25

If you have a logo for your organization handy, you could enter the complete filename in the Logo field. For the purposes of this book, this example will use text for a logo.

1. Select the Text option for the Logo Type, and enter Learning APEX as the Logo.

2. Use the Logo Attributes select list popup to choose Blue Text as the type of logo. When the Logo Attributes are returned to the attributes page, you can recognize these attributes as standard HTML attributes.

3. Save the changes by clicking Apply Changes, and then run the application, which will bring up a page with your new logo, as shown in Figure 7-26.

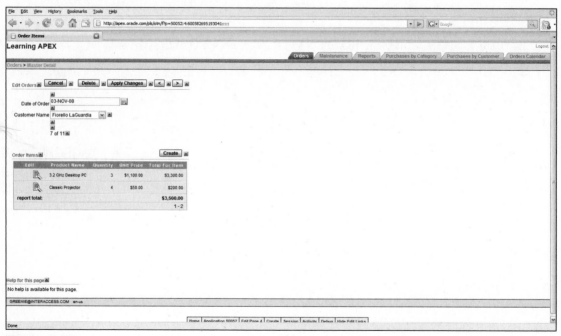

Figure 7-26

The logo substitution string is in most of the standard page templates, so adding a logo is somewhat similar to using Page Zero. However, since the logo is represented in a template as a variable, which could be placed anywhere in the code for a page, using templates gives you a lot more flexibility than the brute-force method of Page Zero.

Templates give you plenty of power to control the look and feel of your application, but templates are a shared component in an application. If you only want to change the template in one specific place, for example, a specialized report layout, then the best practice would be to copy an existing template that closely matches what you want and save it with a distinct name for use in that specialized situation. You very well may want to develop and use a look and feel for multiple applications across your organization. You can do this through themes, which are covered in the next section.

> **Tech Talk – Subscribing to Templates**
>
> What if you want to create a new template that is a lot like another template but that varies in some small ways? You could copy the template by clicking on the icon on the right of the template entry. When you copy the template, the resulting template has a link to its parent, which is referred to as *subscribing* to that parent, with the parent *publishing* to the child template.
>
> The template list page allows you to display only parent templates by clicking on the `Published` link, and only children templates by clicking on the `Subscription` link.
>
> Once this relationship is set up, you can refresh the child template from its attribute page. Refreshing a template means that the current version of the parent replaces the current version of the child completely, so any changes that you made to the child will then be lost.
>
> You can subscribe to any template in any theme for an application, and you will learn about themes in the last section of this chapter.

Themes

Throughout this chapter, you have learned about modifying the user interface of APEX pages, from an individual page layout to a template which can shape the appearance and functionality of a particular type of APEX entity. The highest level of APEX interface aggregation is the theme.

A theme consists of a collection of templates. Each theme generally has templates in all of the same nine categories listed for templates in the previous section.

A theme can have more than one option for a particular template type, with one template designated as the default for that type. Themes provide the "universe" of templates for an APEX application. The only template options available to an application are those that are part of the overall theme for the application. Through the use of multiple templates in a theme, developers can have flexibility in their design, while still remaining within organizational standards.

You can export a theme, which copies the theme contents to an SQL file. Other applications can import and install themes, which makes the theme available to the application. Once the theme is installed, you can switch themes for an application, during which you will be asked to map the currently used templates in the application to templates in the new theme.

Themes are used to provide a common look and feel across multiple applications. Themes are frequently used to provide a "corporate standard" look and feel to all the applications for an organization. If you customize the templates to create your own corporate theme this collection of templates can be published as a custom theme and available across your workspace. Since themes can be exported to SQL files, you can even share themes and their templates across multiple workspaces.

Since the theme associated with an application can change large portions of the layout of all the pages in an application, you should spend some time planning how to use themes to get the maximum benefit from their flexibility.

Summary

In this chapter, you learned about many different ways of affecting the way that your pages present information to the user.

❑   Page layouts, which are specific to an individual page

❑   User interface defaults, which provide a default value whenever a field for a particular column is used in a form or a report

❑   Page Zero, which gives you the ability to include interface components or code on every page in an application

❑   Templates, which provide enormous flexibility to format all the pages of a certain type in an application

❑   Themes, a collection of templates, which can be used to provide an overall look and feel for all your applications

All of these options work together to give you a great deal of flexibility in the user interface used by your APEX applications. In the next chapter, you will explore one last area of additional functional flexibility through the use of PL/SQL procedural code.

PL/SQL

In the previous chapters, you have learned a lot about the powerful default functionality provided by the APEX environment and how to shape that functionality through the use of parameter-driven configuration. You haven't really written any code to implement any of this functionality.

But you are not limited to the capabilities designed into the APEX world. You can add your own specific functionality through the use of code using the PL/SQL language. In this chapter, you will write some PL/SQL code to provide a more subtle validation scheme for the ORDER_TIMESTAMP field, automatically calculate totals for each order, and check to see if a customer's current order would exceed their credit limit.

This chapter will provide you with a few examples of using PL/SQL to extend your application with specific logic. The use of PL/SQL is a vast topic, with many books available describing its use, including *Professional Oracle Programming*, Rick Greenwald, 2005, from WROX, for an introduction to the language, or the definitive series of books by Steven Feuerstein published by O'Reilly and Associates. This chapter will provide you with some experience using the language and, more importantly, a framework for understanding how PL/SQL can be used to extend your applications.

PL/SQL

PL/SQL is the language used to add logic to an Oracle database. The name of the language stems from its status as a way to add procedural logic to extend standard SQL statements.

The syntax for PL/SQL should not be that strange to anyone who has used either another database-resident procedural language, such as TransactSQL, or another standard programming language. PL/SQL includes the ability to define variables, implement repeated logic (loops) and switch between different options (IF-THEN-ELSE).

As you will learn in the second and third examples in this chapter, PL/SQL also includes very tight integration with the SQL statements used to access and manipulate data. This close connection has several implications. The first implication is that you will find it easy to combine the power of SQL with the logic of PL/SQL, since the language was designed from the ground up to fulfill this purpose. Another implication is that PL/SQL runs in the Oracle database server, which makes it ideal for using logic tightly connected with data efficiently. The final implication is that all PL/SQL routines are triggered by data operations.

You have already been using PL/SQL extensively, although you may not be aware of it. Everything that APEX provides you — from the pages your application provides to users to the data interaction that underlies their operation — is provided by PL/SQL code generated by the APEX server in your target Oracle database. When you define components within APEX, the characteristics of these components are stored as metadata in tables in your Oracle database, with all the processing being performed by PL/SQL programs operating based on this metadata and the operations performed by the end users.

Setting a Variable Default

The first place to use PL/SQL within your application is to set a default value for a new column in the database. You will have to use procedural logic to set this default, since the value of the default changes, depending on the value of fields in the page.

Way back in Chapter 4, you added a default value for the ORDER_TIMESTAMP column. In this section, you will add a new field to the ORDERS table to hold the promised ship date and then create logic to calculate what this ship date should be.

Try It Out   **Adding a New Column**

Your first task will be to add a new column to the ORDERS table to hold the ship date.

1.   Return to the development environment, and click on the SQL Workshop tab. Bring up the Object Browser by using the cascading menus to browse existing tables.

2.   Click on the ORDERS table to bring up the description of the table.

3.   Click on the Add Column button to begin the creation of a new column for the table with the page shown in Figure 8-1.

4.   Enter ORDER_SHIP_DATE in the Add Column field, make the Type a date, and click Next.

5.   On the next page, click Finish to create the column.

Now that you have a new column in the table, you will have to add an item to the page to display the value.

1.   Click on the Application Builder page, go to the application you are building, and select the master-detail page for the ORDERS and ORDER_ITEMS tables.

2.   In the Items section of the Page Rendering column on the left, click on the plus icon (+) to bring up the page shown in Figure 8-2.

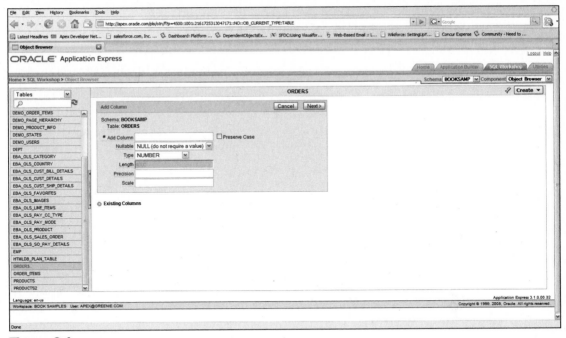

Figure 8-1

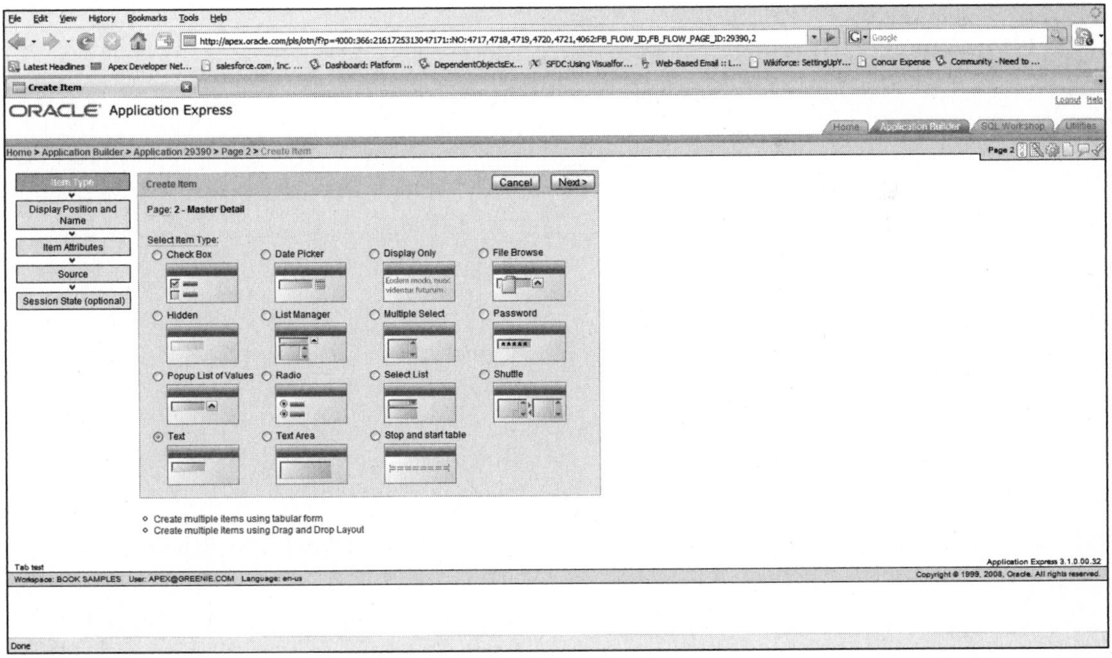

Figure 8-2

3. Select the `Display Only` default item type, and click Next.

Since this column value will be calculated later, you will only want to display the value.

But, you say, what if someone wants to set the value of the ship date to something other than the default? Not to worry — you will learn how to allow users with the right security level to do just that in the next chapter.

4. Accept the default for the `Display Only Type` on the next page, and click on `Next` to bring up the page shown in Figure 8-3.

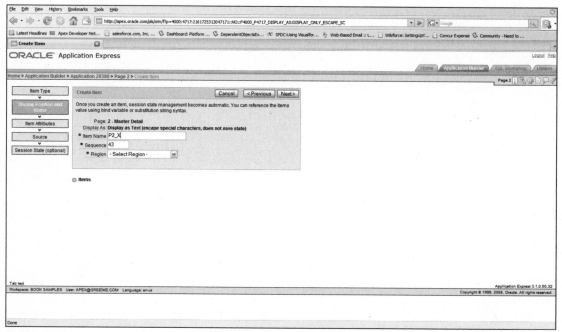

Figure 8-3

5. On this page, enter an Item Name, such as `Pn_ORDER_SHIP_DATE` for the Item Name, select `Edit Orders` as the Region, and click on `Next`.

6. Accept all the default values on the next page and click Next.

7. Connect this item with the column you just created by changing `Item Source` to `Database Column`, and make sure that the `Database Column Name` is the column you just created. When you are done, click on `Create Item` to finish your work and return to the main development area for this page.

When you get back to the page, take a closer look at the `Items` section shown in Figure 8-4.

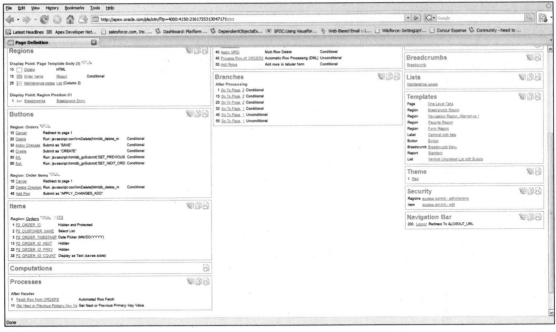

Figure 8-4

You can see that the new item is, by default, placed at the end of the items, by virtue of its sequence number. You will actually want this item to be displayed just below the ORDER_TIMESTAMP item, so you will have to modify this sequence number.

You could also use the drag-and-drop editor, which you saw in the last chapter, to accomplish the same goal.

As you can see in Figure 8-4, this item is followed by some hidden items, and you want your new item to come before them. Note the sequence number of the CUSTOMER_NAME item, which should be 3, and the first hidden field, which should be 13.

8. Click on the Pn_ORDER_SHIP_DATE item to edit its attributes.

9. Change the Sequence number to one more than the number for the CUSTOMER_NAME field.

10. Click Apply Changes to save your work.

Before moving on to the computation, you should take a quick look at the new appearance of your page.

How It Works

Time to run your newly modified page.

11. Click on the Run icon to bring up the new page, ready to create a new order, as shown in Figure 8-5.

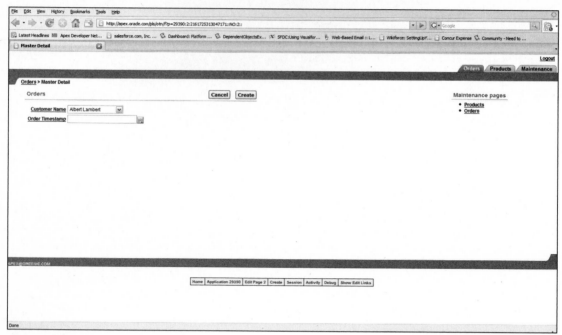

Figure 8-5

You can see there is no input field for the new; instead, the item will display as text, once it has a value. Your next step is to write the PL/SQL computation to create that value.

Try It Out   Computations with PL/SQL Code

You have already added some processing to this particular page when you added a validation for the ORDER_TIMESTAMP item earlier in this book. In this section, you will create a computation that will determine the ship date for an order three days after the order is taken, based on the value of the ORDER_TIMESTAMP item.

But not all three day periods are the same. Your shipping department doesn't want to have to work on weekends, but if an order was taken on Wednesday or Thursday, the order would be scheduled for shipment on the weekend. Further, as it takes three days to prepare the order, it is important to adjust the shipping date for those orders taken on Friday or Saturday as well.

You can change the routine to support the concept of weekends, but you will have to go from having a simple PL/SQL expression (e.g., ORDER_TIMESTAMP + 2) to actually writing a small bit of code to allow the routine to discover the day of the week and make allowances for Saturday and Sunday.

Problem Statement and Solution Design

Before jumping into our computational code, you should carefully define the problem you are trying to address. In the business scenario this computation is designed to address, you want to set the ship date to a day that is three business days after the date of the order.

In order to determine this ship date, you will have to go through three steps:

1. Determining the day of the week for the current date

2. Using IF-THEN-ELSE logic to determine how many days should be added to the order date

3. Returning the proper value, based on the previous logic and the order date

You will also need to define some variables to hold values used in the intermediate calculations. The next few sections will cover the code you will use to implement the solution. Once you understand all the PL/SQL code required, the final section will walk you through using the code for your computation.

But what about holidays? You could add in this functionality by performing a database query against a table of holiday dates to see if a holiday fell on one of the business days, but that logic is outside the scope of this exercise.

Defining Variables

PL/SQL code calls for defining any variables and constants your code will use at the beginning of the code block.

For this PL/SQL code, you will need two variables: a number that will hold the number of days after the order date that the order will be shipped and a string variable that will hold the current day of the week, which is used as a starting point for your logic.

The following code defines these two variables and sets up a space to hold the code block:

```
declare
  DAYS_FORWARD NUMBER;
  DAY_OF_WEEK VARCHAR2(3);
begin
end;
```

The code begins with the keyword declare, indicating the start of your variable declarations. The DAYS_FORWARD variable is defined as a number, while DAY_OF_WEEK is a variable length character field, which will hold the three-letter abbreviation for the week day.

You could have assigned a default value to either of these variables by including the keyword DEFAULT, followed by the desired value. The DAYS_FORWARD variable could have had a default value of 3, but this particular implementation will assign that default as part of the logical testing.

Once all the variables have been defined, you add keywords to indicate the beginning (begin) and end of the code block.

Notice that all PL/SQL statements are terminated with semicolons (;). With this structure in place, you can move on to your first logical task.

Determining the Day of the Week

You already used a PL/SQL function in your validation. SYSDATE is a PL/SQL function that returns the current system date. Another PL/SQL function will come in handy in determining the actual day of the week for the current date.

The following code includes that function as the first line of your PL/SQL code block:

```
declare
  DAYS_FORWARD NUMBER;
  DAY_OF_WEEK VARCHAR2(10);
begin
  DAY_OF_WEEK := to_char(to_date(:P4_ORDER_TIMESTAMP), 'DY');
end;
```

The to_char() function is used to convert nonstring values, such as numbers and dates, into character strings. The Oracle database checks if the variable passed to the function is a date value, and the second parameter, 'DY', instructs the function to return the first three letters for the day of the week, such as SUN, MON, or TUE.

If the value is not a date, the PL/SQL code will return an error when run.

The to_date() function is used to convert the value of the P4_ORDER_TIMESTAMP field to a date. Remember, that a field is simply a text string in an HTML page, and your PL/SQL procedure requires a date for the conversion to work properly.

Notice that the operator used to assign the value to the DAY_OF_WEEK is an equals sign preceded by a colon. In PL/SQL, the equals sign alone is used as a comparison operator to determine if the values on either side of the operator are the same. To assign a value, you have to use the := operator.

IF Constructs

Your code is ready to take on its first logical task, setting the number of days that will be added to the order date to determine the ship date.

To accomplish this task, you will use a logical structure that should be familiar to you if you have ever done any programming, the IF construct. The following code incorporates this construct to perform the logical test which will be used to properly prepare the DAYS_FORWARD variable for its final use in the computation.

```
declare
  DAYS_FORWARD NUMBER;
  DAY_OF_WEEK VARCHAR2(10);
begin
  DAY_OF_WEEK := to_char(to_date(:P4_ORDER_TIMESTAMP), 'DY');
  if (DAY_OF_WEEK ='WED' OR DAY_OF_WEEK = 'THU' OR DAY_OF_WEEK = 'FRI')
    then
```

```
       DAYS_FORWARD := 5;
   elsif (DAY_OF_WEEK ='SAT')
     then
        DAYS_FORWARD := 4;
   else
        DAYS_FORWARD := 3;
  end if;
end;
```

The IF construct starts with the keyword if and ends with the keywords end if. In this particular example, you can see that there are two logical comparisons, followed by a default action, indicated by the else keyword.

This code is illustrative of a nested if statement. A particular value is tested with the first condition to see if the value is 'WED', 'THU', or 'FRI'. Notice that the keyword OR is used to allow for any of these values for the DAY_OF_WEEK variable, and that these three alternate conditions are surrounded by parentheses to indicate that the combined tests will return a single logical condition. If this condition is met, the action that follows the then keyword is taken, and the code skips the remaining steps.

If the value does not meet the first condition, the second condition is begun with the keyword elseif. Once again, if the value meets this condition, the action following the then keyword is taken, and the code skips the remainder of the steps.

The else keyword is used to establish a default action — all values that do not meet the first two tests are subjected to the actions in this section, which are to set the DAYS_FORWARD variable to 3.

All the keywords used in this code are required and yes, you have to spell them correctly. After the current day has been used to assign the appropriate value for the DAYS_FORWARD variable, your value is ready to be returned so that we can populate the shipping date.

Computation

The final piece of PL/SQL, which actually performs the assignment of the computed value, has been added after the if construct in the following code:

```
declare
  DAYS_FORWARD NUMBER;
  DAY_OF_WEEK VARCHAR2(10);
begin
  DAY_OF_WEEK := to_char(to_date(:P4_ORDER_TIMESTAMP), 'DY');
  if (DAY_OF_WEEK ='WED' OR DAY_OF_WEEK = 'THU' OR DAY_OF_WEEK = 'FRI')
    then
      DAYS_FORWARD := 5;
    elsif (DAY_OF_WEEK ='SAT')
      then
        DAYS_FORWARD := 4;
    else
        DAYS_FORWARD := 3;
  end if;
  return (to_date(:P4_ORDER_TIMESTAMP)+ DAYS_FORWARD);
end;
```

This line of code is pretty straightforward. You need to use the to_date() function on the Pn_ORDER_TIMESTAMP to convert the HTML text into a date. PL/SQL will perform a date addition of the timestamp with the number of days specified in the numeric PL/SQL variable DAYS_FORWARD. Since this is a computation, your APEX program knows that the result of the code should be the return of a value. The return statement does just that.

Your code is finished, and you are now ready to add it to your application.

Entering the Validation Code

The PL/SQL code you have just learned can now be used in a computation within APEX.

1. Return to the development environment for the page. Click on the plus sign (+) icon in the Computations section of the Page Processes middle column.

2. Select the Item on This Page choice, and click Next to bring up the page shown in its completed state in Figure 8-6.

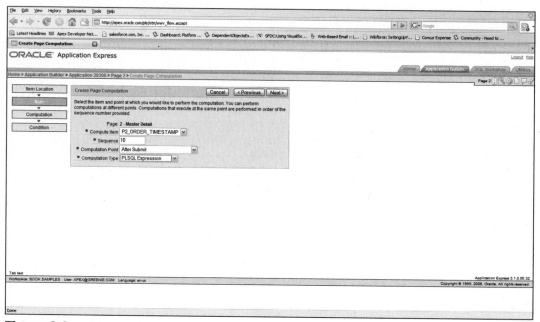

Figure 8-6

3. Select the item you just added to the page, and change the Computation type to PL/SQL Function Body. Click Next.

4. Enter the code described above into the Computation text area.

    If you would like to simply cut and paste, the code is included in a file named Chapter_8_Computation.txt.

5. Click Next, which will not only take you to the next page but also validate the code in the Computation text area as valid PL/SQL code.

For this particular computation, you will not want to add any type of condition, since you will always want to set the ship date three business days after the order date.

In the next chapter, when you allow a certain class of user to enter a ship date other than the default, you will come back and add conditions to this computation.

6. Click on Create to add the computation to the page.

How It Works

You know that the PL/SQL code you entered was at least valid, or else you could not have saved the computation. But being valid and working properly are two separate things. Time to check out the operation of your computation.

1. Click on the Run icon to bring up your page, which should come up in entry mode.

If you are not in entry mode, click Cancel to return to the report, and then click Create.

2. Select an order date on a day of the week that should exercise the logic of the computation. Click Create to create the order and return to the Orders report.

3. Click the Edit icon for the newly created order to return to the page and see the calculated ship date, as shown in Figure 8-7.

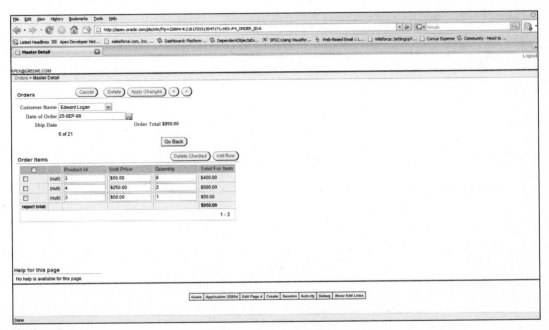

Figure 8-7

You can test the logic of your computation more if you like, just to make sure — a good practice when developing your own code.

Tech Talk – More Flexibility

Wait, you say, three-day delivery? That seems a bit long to wait in this day and age. You could easily add a radio group for the user to select the type of delivery requested and use the value of that group to add a little more logic to your computation. Along these same lines, you could have another table with holidays listed and run an SQL query using the BETWEEN operator to see if any of those holidays would impact overall delivery times.

There is, of course, one thing missing here. The orders that were already in the database do not have a ship date. You could run an SQL script to calculate dates for each existing order. In the next section, you will learn how to use PL/SQL code in a database trigger and then run a script to update existing orders.

Server-Side PL/SQL

As mentioned at the beginning of this chapter and throughout this book, PL/SQL is the procedural language used in the Oracle database, and the applications you create with APEX are materialized with PL/SQL code. This code can be thought of as application-side code, in that the code responds to application side interactions.

However, you can also use PL/SQL code to implement *triggers*, which respond to database activities. A trigger is fired when the data is inserted, updated, or deleted from the database, and triggers fire either before or after these events.

> *The Oracle database also supports* INSTEAD OF *triggers, which, as their name implies, are used instead of database actions. This type of trigger is used less commonly than* INSERT, UPDATE, *and* DELETE *triggers, and are beyond the scope of this book.*

If you are a developer, you are probably already familiar with the distinction between application code and server code, but the distinction between PL/SQL in APEX and in the database is a little less clear. For instance, application code typically runs on a client machine, while PL/SQL application code used by APEX still runs in the Oracle database. And PL/SQL code that runs as part of an APEX application has a slightly different syntax than PL/SQL database triggers, as you will soon see.

But there are still times when it makes more sense to use database triggers than PL/SQL APEX triggers.

Problem Statement and Solution Location

You have already added totals for each order in your interactive report, but those totals only exist within the report. There might be times when your overall systems environment would want to have access to that information, which would require you to store the total as part of the ORDERS table.

Conceptually, you can understand the problem fairly simply. If a new ORDER_ITEMS row is inserted into the database, you would want to add the amount of that order item to the total field on its parent ORDERS record. Similarly, a delete action would require you to reduce the total field by the amount of the order item, and an update would require you to adjust the value of the total by the difference between the old value and the new value.

This straightforward scheme becomes a little more complicated when it confronts the flexible user interface of your APEX application. When you create a process in your APEX application, you can specify the conditions that would cause it to be fired. The conditions are based on the object which made the request to the server. The object is identified by the type of request received by the server, which is included in the request. Request names are typically the name of the action performed by a user interface, usually the click of a button.

You could handle these logical options with checks in the code, but it would be simpler to just associate the totaling action with database actions. You can create a trigger that will fire whenever a row is inserted, updated, or deleted, and that trigger could simply recalculate the total for the order after each of these database interactions. In addition, database triggers fire whenever anyone accesses data in the table, through an APEX application or any other tool or utility or other applications, such as native .NET or Visual Studio applications. For these reasons, implementing this logic as database triggers is a cleaner and less complex way to achieve your goal.

Try It Out   Adding a New Column to Hold the Total

Your first step in the solution is to create a new column to hold the new information. Since you already added a new column to the ORDERS table in the previous section, this operation should be familiar to you now.

1. Return to the development environment, and go to the SQL Workshop. Use the Object Browser to browse tables and select the ORDERS table.

2. Click on Add Column to begin the process.

3. Give the column the name of ORDER_TOTAL with a precision of 9 and a scale of 2. Click Next.

4. Click Finish to add the column to the table.

As in the previous section, you will want to add an item to the master-detail page to hold the new column's values.

1. Click on the Application Builder page, select your application and the master-detail page.

As in the previous section, you will want to place this item just after the ORDER_SHIP_DATE item. Before you start to define the new item, note the Sequence number for that item so that you can add it yourself as part of the definition process.

2. Click on the plus sign (+) icon in the Items section and then the Display Only option icon, which will move you to the next page.

3. Accept the default for Display Only Type, and click Next.

4. Give the item the name of Pn_ORDER_TOTAL, change the Sequence number to one that will place the item into the proper position, and select the Edit Orders region. Click Next when you have completed these entries.

5. Accept the defaults on the next page, and click Next.

6. As with the previous example, this item will take as its source a Database Column. Select that option, and accept ORDER_TOTAL into the Database Column. When you are finished, click Create Item to add the item to your page.

At this point, adding an item to your page should be familiar. You can run the page to take a quick look at the new page layout, but there is no need to show it here in the book. You probably want to get to the new part here, creating a database trigger.

You would probably also want to modify the Format Mask of the new item, which is in the Source section of the item definition, to display the total as currency.

Try It Out   **Creating a Database Trigger**

Now that you have a column to hold the total for the orders and an item to show it on your page, you want to create a trigger on the ORDER_ITEMS table to calculate the total for all order items for an order whenever a row in the ORDER_ITEMS table receives a new value. As with your previous PL/SQL code, it makes sense to follow the same process here, first ensuring that you have a complete understanding of the problem, and then implementing the code in smaller portions.

Solution Design

The problem you are trying to solve is fairly basic — you want to include a total for all of the order items in the ORDERS table. If you know SQL, you probably already understand the type of SQL statement you will use to accomplish this.

But there is still a dimension of the problem that needs consideration: when you want this type of totaling to take place, which in turn affects how you want the operation to take place.

You could perform different calculations based on the type of database action. For an insert, you would add the new value to the existing total. For a deletion, you would subtract the deleted value from the existing total. And for an update, you would compare the old and new values and adjust the total accordingly. In a database with a lot of activity, or one where orders have a lot of items, you might want to go through the "effort" of creating these three separate logical paths.

But in this demonstration application, you can take more of a brute-force approach. You can simply recalculate the ORDER_TOTAL each time there is a change in the ORDER_ITEMS table. This type of solution will allow you to use a simple SQL statement and focus on understanding how to implement triggers.

If you are thinking that this will only work for new changes to the ORDER_ITEMS table, you are perfectly correct. Before the end of this section, you will use the same SQL statement you use in the trigger to bring all existing orders up-to-date.

The SQL Statement

If you are familiar with SQL, you already know that the language was designed to access and modify sets of data, exactly the task that is before you. If you are not familiar with SQL, you will be happy to see that the statement to implement the totaling action is very simple, as shown here:

```
update ORDERS set ORDER_TOTAL =
   (select sum(UNIT_PRICE * QUANTITY) from ORDER_ITEMS
      where ORDER_ITEMS.ORDER_ID = ORDERS.ORDER_ID);
```

The SQL begins with the update keyword, indicating that you will want to update columns in the ORDERS table. The next portion indicates that the statement will set the value of the ORDER_TOTAL column. You use another SQL statement to calculate the value you want to use for the ORDER_TOTAL column, with the statement enclosed within parentheses. This type of statement is referred to as a *sub-select* as you are selecting a collection of records and in this case summing them.

Surround this SQL statement with begin and end, and you have all the code you will need to write your trigger, as shown here:

```
begin
   update ORDERS set ORDER_TOTAL =
      (select sum(UNIT_PRICE * QUANTITY) from ORDER_ITEMS
         where ORDER_ITEMS.ORDER_ID = ORDERS.ORDER_ID);
end;
```

It's trigger time.

Try It Out   **Creating a Database Trigger**

A trigger is another type of database object, so you will use SQL Workshop for the task.

1. Go to the SQL Workshop section of the APEX development environment, and use the Object Browser menus to select the Create option for a trigger.

2. Select the ORDER_ITEMS table in the Table Name selection list, and click Next, which will bring up the page, shown in its completed state in Figure 8-8.

3. Give your new trigger a descriptive name, like CALC_ORDER_TOTALS, and set the Firing Point to AFTER. You can leave the Options as the default of insert, update, and delete.

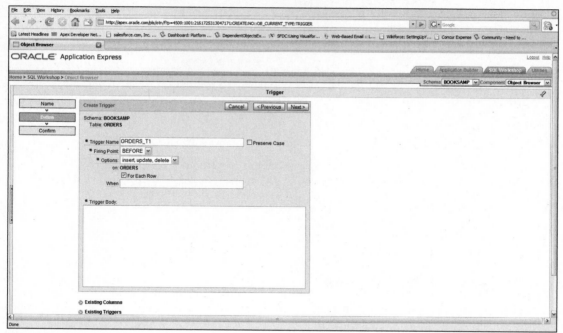

Figure 8-8

These two options describe the key timing elements of your trigger. As mentioned previously, you can specify a trigger to execute for inserts, updates, or deletes, and you can take the action before or after any of these options. You will only want to calculate the total for an order once the action on the ORDER_ITEMS table has been completed, since there is no need to perform this operation if the attempted action on the ORDER_ITEMS table does not complete.

4.   Uncheck the For Each Row checkbox.

This small action is very, very important. If you forget to perform this step, you will get an error at runtime about a mutating trigger, explained in the sidebar.

Mutating Triggers

If you properly unchecked the For Each Row checkbox, you will not have to worry about mutating trigger errors. But what causes a mutating trigger error anyway?

Your Oracle database is very concerned with the integrity of your data. One of the protections it offers is assurance that any row you are about to change with PL/SQL code has not been changed since your PL/SQL transaction began. If Oracle detects that a change has occurred, the PL/SQL operation will be terminated, and a runtime error returned. This change is called a mutation, hence the mutating trigger error.

This error could (and can) occur if you leave the For Each Row checkbox checked. The trigger changes the parent ORDERS record with the first ORDER_ITEMS row, and then goes to change it again with the next record. Ooops — mutation.

When you uncheck that box, the trigger is only fired once per transaction, so the trigger only updates the ORDERS row once.

5. Add the code from the previous section to the Trigger Body text area. This code has been included in a file named Chapter_8_Order_Total.txt, if you would like to simply cut and paste it. Click Next.

6. Click Finish to complete your work, which will return you to the page shown in Figure 8-9.

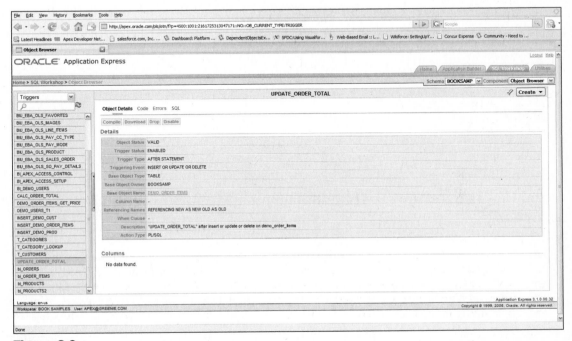

Figure 8-9

This page summarizes the trigger you just created. You will see some lines that are familiar and some that you didn't really enter. For instance, the TRIGGER STATUS is set to ENABLED. All triggers can be enabled or disabled. SQL Workshop makes the assumption that you are defining a trigger because you want to use it. In a moment, you will see the actual SQL code that was generated, which will include a separate SQL statement to enable the trigger. You can also see the Disable button at the top of this page, which you can use to turn off this trigger.

You can also see a field labeled Referencing Names, with a value displayed of REFERENCING NEW AS NEW OLD AS OLD. This particular attribute of the trigger is not relevant to you in this case, but will be when you make some calculations based on the old and new values for columns in an update statement.

To see the actual work that SQL Workshop did for you, click on the SQL link at the top of the page to bring up the page shown in Figure 8-10.

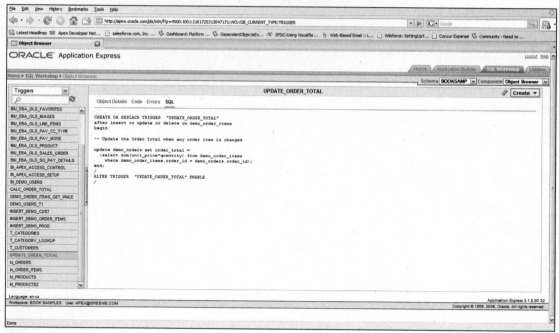

Figure 8-10

The code you entered makes up the bulk of the code in the trigger, but there are a couple of additional lines that were created by SQL Workshop. The first line assigns the name to your trigger, with the specification that the trigger should be created if the name does not exist, or the existing trigger should be replaced with this new code. You don't have to worry about replacing an existing trigger by mistake, though, as the Trigger Creation Wizard will stop you if you specify a trigger name that already exists.

And if you want to edit an existing trigger, you can select the Code button on the trigger page and then the Edit button on that subsequent page.

The final line of code in your trigger creation statement enables the trigger.

If you did not enter a valid trigger code for your trigger, the Trigger Creation Wizard will still allow you to finish the creation of the trigger and save it. To check for errors, you would have to select the Compile button at the top of the trigger page, which will compile the trigger and list any errors after selecting the Errors link at the top of the trigger listing. In addition, SQL Workshop would put a red bar at the beginning of the name of the trigger in the left-hand panel list.

But you should not have any errors in this trigger, so it's time to see it in action.

How It Works

You have your database trigger in place, and the field to hold the value calculated by the trigger. You can run the application and add a new order line or two to see the effect of the new trigger.

1. Go to the application and select the master-detail page for ORDERS and ORDER_ITEMS. Start the application by clicking Run.

2. If the page does not display an existing order, return to the report page for ORDERS by clicking Cancel, and then select an order to return to the master-detail page in Edit mode.

3. Add a new Order Item record by clicking Create, adding a row, and clicking Apply Changes. You should see the value of the Order Total field now display the calculated total value of all the order items for that order, as shown in Figure 8-11.

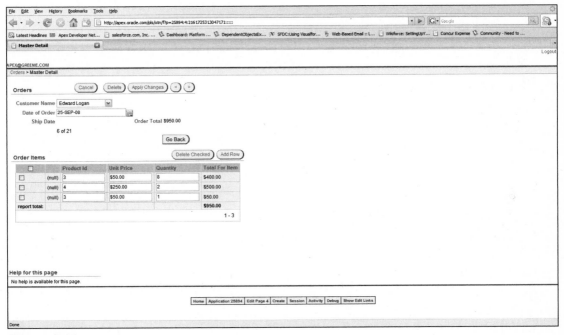

Figure 8-11

Because the trigger works by calculating the total for an order each time a row associated with that order changes, the Order Total field acquires the right value whenever any order item rows for that order are added, deleted, or changed. But you will probably not want to visit and change order items for every order record in order to calculate the ORDER_TOTAL column. You can run an SQL statement to initialize the totals for every order, the same SQL statement used in your trigger.

Try It Out   **Initializing Totals**

You have written all the triggers you will need to implement order totals, but one problem remains. What about the data already resident in the ORDER_ITEMS table?

You will only have to perform this initialization action once, and you can do it through the power of SQL.

1. Return to the development environment and go to the SQL Workshop.

2. Click on the SQL Commands icon to bring up the page shown in Figure 8-12.

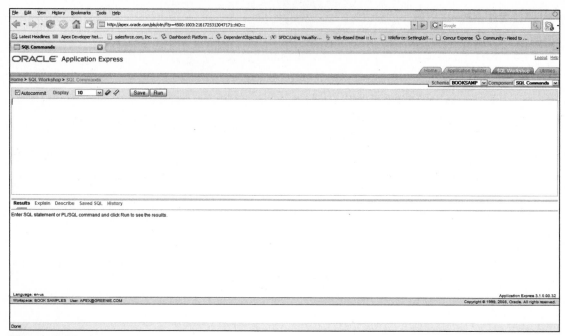

Figure 8-12

This page has two main areas, with the upper area acting as a scratch pad where you can enter SQL statements and then run or save them, and the lower section returning the results of the statement run, along with some associated information about the run.

Enter the following SQL statement in the upper panel, and click Run.

```
update ORDERS set ORDER_TOTAL =
  (select sum(UNIT_PRICE * QUANTITY) from ORDER_ITEMS
   where ORDER_ITEMS.ORDER_ID = ORDERS.ORDER_ID);
```

In the lower panel, you will see the result of the run, indicating the number of records in your ORDERS table that have been updated, and the time it took to execute the statement. The remainder of the links in the lower window are:

❏ Explain: Displays the actual steps used by the Oracle database to execute the statement. Those of you who are familiar with SQL will recognize this information as the *explain plan* for the statement.

❏ Describe: Allows you to get information about the contents and type of any SQL object, such as the columns within a table.

❏ Saved SQL: Lists all the SQL statements you have saved with the pushbutton in the upper panel, and

❏ History: Lists all the SQL statements which have been run from SQL Workshop. Each statement is a link which will place that SQL into the upper panel. This feature is a useful way to rerun any statement created by SQL Workshop, either in this page or by a wizard.

How It Works

Before leaving this section of the chapter, you should go back and check to make sure all the order totals have been properly set.

1. Return to the Application Builder, select the initial report page for orders, which should be page 1, and click on the Run icon.

2. Select the Edit icon for an order, which should bring up the page shown in Figure 8-13.

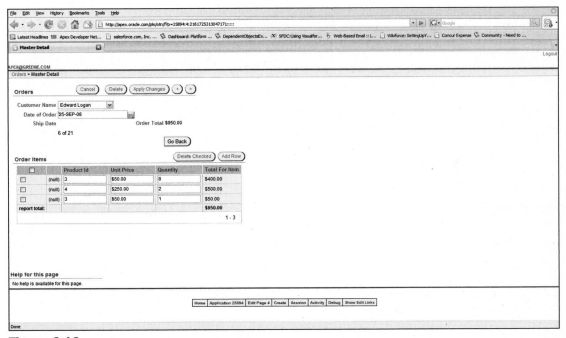

Figure 8-13

There you have it, all your orders have their totals properly set. You could add the new value to the report if you wanted, but you can do this at your leisure. The final section of this chapter will walk you through the creation of one more trigger, which combines SQL and logic.

Checking against Credit Limit

The observant among you may have taken notice of a field on the CUSTOMERS table called CREDIT_LIMIT. The imaginative among you may have theorized that this value was intended to place an upper cap on the amount of an order for the given customer — and you would be right.

Your final PL/SQL challenge will be to create another validation, which will check to see whether a change to an ORDER_ITEMS row would cause the order to be over the credit limit, and to return an error in the event that it does.

Problem Definition and Solution Design

The problem you wish to address is easily stated — you don't want to let a customer submit an order where the total of the extended prices of each order item line exceed the customer's credit limit.

Since you want to prevent this event from occurring, it makes sense to use a validation to implement this logic. The validation will have to collect some information from related tables, such as the credit limit from the CUSTOMERS table and the current ORDER_TOTAL from the ORDERS table.

Once you have these values, you will have to figure out how much the current extended price adds to the overall total for the order. For a new order item, you can simply add the new extended price to the existing order total. For an updated order item, you will have to calculate the difference between the old extended price and the new extended price and apply that to the current order total. You will not have to run the validation for a row deletion, since there is no way that this action could cause the overall order total to increase.

Defining Variables

You will start your PL/SQL code by declaring the variables you will need in the validation. The code to accomplish this follows. As with the earlier example, you can always just cut and paste the code from the text file named Chapter_8_Credit_Check.txt.

```
declare
    l_customer_id number;
    l_order_total number;
    l_credit_limit number;
    l_new_order_total number;
begin
end;
```

The first two variables will hold information you will be retrieving from the ORDERS table. Since you will need these values later in the validation, you will have to store them somewhere. The next variable, l_credit_limit, will hold the credit limit retrieved from the CUSTOMERS row for this order.

The next variable will hold the new value of the order total, which will include the increase brought about by the current action.

The next two variables hold the original value of the extended price for the order item and the new value of the same calculation. You will need both of these to properly process updated order items. The l_order_item_dif will hold the result of this calculation.

With these variables defined, you can move to the first logical step in your validation.

Retrieving Values with SQL

The current APEX page you are modifying has a row that either came from or will eventually find its way into the ORDER_ITEMS table, but you will need information from related rows in some other tables to properly validate this information.

> ### Tech Talk – Why SQL Here?
>
> Some of these values, such as ORDER_TOTAL, are also available in fields on other pages in the application. You could use those fields instead of some of the SQL retrievals detailed in this section, as long as no one else was accessing the same data. For instance, the order total for an order could have been increased since you retrieved that row into a page in your application. The foolproof way to avoid exceeding the credit limit is to go to the source, the database table.

You will execute two SQL statements to retrieve the values you will need in this validation. The code for these statements has been added to the previous code in the following listing:

```
declare
    l_customer_id number;
    l_order_total number;
    l_credit_limit number;
    l_new_order_total number;
begin
    select order_total, customer_name_id into l_order_total, l_customer_id
        from orders where orders.order_id = :Pn_ORDER_ID;
    select cust_credit_limit into l_credit_limit from customers where
        customer_name_id = l_customer_id;
end;
```

The first of these statements retrieves the current total for the current order, as well as the CUSTOMER_NAME_ID, which you will need in the next SQL statement. The second statement uses this value to retrieve the credit limit for the customer purchasing this order.

These SQL statements use the INTO clause to place the retrieved values in the variables you defined previously. The SQL used to access Oracle data requires this clause between the list of columns and the tables in the statement.

In this code listing, as well as the remaining listings, the n in Pn represents your current page.

Calculating the Current Extended Price

For this next step, you can simply access the values in the current page. Since these values are coming from outside the PL/SQL environment, you will have to precede the field names with the bind variable indication (:).

The code for this calculation is added into the previous code in the following listing:

```
declare
    l_customer_id number;
```

```
       l_order_total number;
       l_credit_limit number;
       l_new_order_total number;
   begin
   select order_total, customer_name_id into l_order_total, l_customer_id
       from orders where orders.order_id = :Pn_ORDER_ID;
   select cust_credit_limit into l_credit_limit from customers where
       customer_name_id = l_customer_id;
   l_new_order_total := (:Pn_QUANTITY * :Pn_UNIT_PRICE) + l_order_total;
   end;
```

Checking the Result and Returning an Error

You now have everything you need to start the real work of determining whether the changes to the current row will cause the order total to exceed the credit limit for the customer.

This code is pretty straightforward. You check to see if the new order total is greater than the credit limit. If the new total has exceeded the credit limit, the code returns an error message indicating the amount by which the credit limit has been exceeded.

When you actually add this code to your page as a validation, one of the choices you will have is to define a PL/SQL procedure that returns an error message. With this specification, your APEX page understands that if the procedure returns a value, that value is an error message, which means that the validation failed and the row should not be processed. If the procedure returns a null value, the row passed the validation and the processing should proceed.

You implement this final step with the return value, which is executed if the new order total exceeds the credit limit. If this condition is not met, the procedure returns NULL.

The code to accomplish this is highlighted in the next code listing.

```
   declare
       l_customer_id number;
       l_order_total number;
       l_credit_limit number;
       l_new_order_total number;
   begin
   select order_total, customer_name_id into l_order_total, l_customer_id
       from orders where orders.order_id = :Pn_ORDER_ID;
   select cust_credit_limit into l_credit_limit from customers where
       customer_name_id = l_customer_id;
   l_new_order_total := (:Pn_QUANTITY * :Pn_UNIT_PRICE) + l_order_total;
   if l_new_order_total > l_credit_limit
       then
         return 'Credit limit exceeded by ' || to_char(l_new_order_total -
            l_credit_limit);
       else
         return null;
       end if;
   end;
```

Try It Out   Adding a Credit Check Validation

You now understand all the code you will use to implement the credit check as a validation. You can use the same validation method you used in Chapter 5 to add this new validation.

1.   Return to the development environment for the order item form page, which is called from the master-detail page.

2.   Click on the plus sign (+) in the Validations section of the Page Processing column of the page.

3.   Change the type of validation on the next page to Page level validation, and click Next.

4.   Select PL/SQL as the validation method, and click Next.

5.   On the next page, expand the example code for the PL/SQL Function Returning Error Text Example at the bottom of the page to show the code as in Figure 8-14.

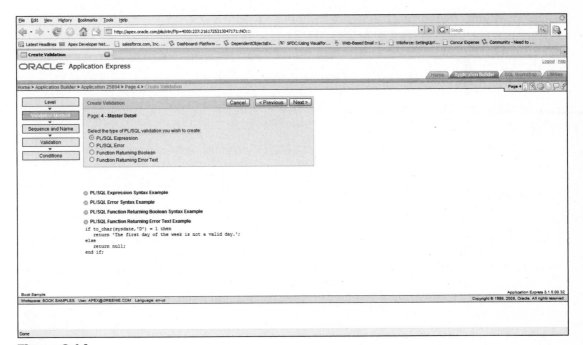

Figure 8-14

You can see an IF statement in this example with the same form as the IF statement at the end of the previous code example.

6.   Select Function Returning Error Text, and click Next.

7.   Accept the default, Sequence, and give the validation the name of CREDIT_LIMIT_CHECK. Leave the default Error Display Location, although be aware that with a page-level validation like this one, the error will only show at the top of the page. Click Next.

8. Enter the code for the validation, either directly or by cutting and pasting from the `Chapter_8_Credit_Check.txt` file. Remember to change the 3 references to `Pn` to replace the n with the page number of the current page. Click Next.

9. On the final page in this wizard, select a `Condition Type` of `Request != Expression 1`, and then enter `DELETE` in the `Expression 1` text area, as shown in its completed form in Figure 8-15.

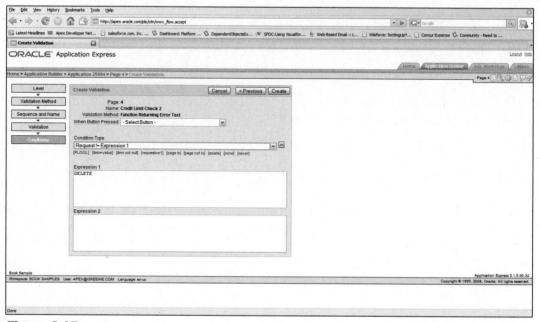

Figure 8-15

On this page, you have the option of specifying when a validation is run in terms of an individual button push, or when a validation is run in terms of one or more requests sent. If you drop down the selection list from the `When Button Pushed` field, you will see a list of requests, in capital letters, and their associated buttons. Since you want to run this validation for all requests (all buttons pushed) except the `DELETE` request, you will use the `Condition Type` instead. You could use the same approach to designate multiple `REQUESTs` in a condition.

10. Click Finish to create the validation.

Your most complex validation, up to this point, is complete. Time to see how well it works.

How It Works

If the validation code is right, it should prevent the user from creating or modifying an order that would result in the order total exceeding the credit limit for the customer.

1. Click on the Run icon to run the page.

2. Return to the report page by clicking Cancel.

3. Select an order to edit. When the edit page comes up, note the Order Total for the order.

4.   Click the Create button to add another order item.

5.   Add an order item where the extended price of the item would bring the order total over the credit limit of $1000 for the customer.

Remember, you set the credit limit to $1,000 for all customers when you loaded the customer data way back in Chapter 3.

6.   Click Create and return, to cause an error, as shown in Figure 8-16.

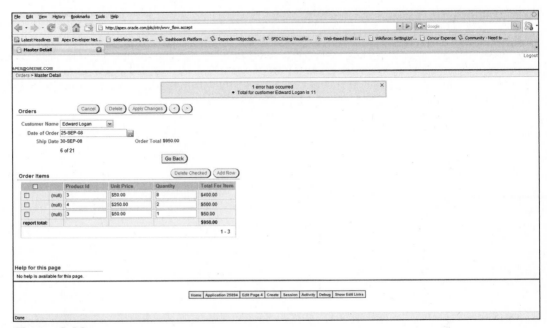

Figure 8-16

There you have it -- at least for an INSERT, your validation check worked perfectly.

1.   Click Cancel to return to the master-detail page. Select an existing order item to edit.

2.   Change the quantity for the order item to cause the order total to exceed the credit limit for the customer. Click Apply Changes, which should hopefully bring up the same error as you saw in Figure 8-16.

Since the validation check will work for either new order items or modifications of existing order items, you have to check both use cases to ensure that your enhancement is correct. In fact, you should also delete an order item (from your test data, of course) to ensure that the validation also worked properly for both activities: avoiding its use in this scenario and checking to make sure that the validation code did not fail in this scenario.

With this last validation, you put together a logical test that used several features of PL/SQL and APEX to achieve success.

Summary

In this chapter, you skimmed the surface of the deep and rich world of functionality you can implement with PL/SQL. The examples you used in this chapter provided the following functionality to your application:

❑   Added a calculation to determine the default shipping date for an order

❑   Added a trigger to your database to aggregate the extended price of each order item into an order total field

❑   Checked each time a user added or changed an order item row to ensure that they did not exceed their credit limit

Of course, there is much, much more you can do with PL/SQL, but you should always try to accomplish your goals without having to use code. The APEX environment was created to provide a lot of functionality, and that functionality is implemented very efficiently within the APEX framework. But having the ability to extend the built-in logic of your APEX application is an invaluable tool.

In the final chapter of this tutorial section, you will learn how to use the built-in security scheme to limit access appropriately for your APEX application.

Security

Up until now, your application has essentially been a single-user application. Although your APEX application has been created with the ability to support many users (and the underlying Oracle database can support hundreds of users simultaneously), you have not taken advantage of this capability.

In this last chapter of the tutorial section of this book, you will explore how to define users and security for your application. As with other chapters, the knowledge you will gain in this brief introduction will give you the ability to start to design and implement robust security features in your own applications.

Security Basics

Before you can start to implement security for your APEX application, you will have to understand some of the basics about how APEX implements security.

Authentication

Authentication is the process of establishing the identity of a user. You no doubt deal with authentication processes every day, from logging in to your network to using personalized web sites.

Typically, authentication is implemented by using a unique combination of a user name and a password. APEX applications use this type of approach. The exact method used for establishing and referencing the identities of users is implemented through an authorization scheme.

Authentication Schemes

All APEX applications use an authentication scheme. An *authentication scheme* describes the method APEX will use for authenticating the user name and password. An application can have more than one authentication scheme defined, although only one scheme can be used at any time.

APEX includes a number of preconfigured authentication scheme options:

❏ **Open Door Credentials:** Allow anyone to access the application. The application still uses a login page to capture a user name, but no password is required. This scheme is particularly useful when you are developing an application and want to test your access without using real user accounts.

❏ **Application Express Account Credentials:** You create and manage users for the APEX environment. This scheme gives you complete control over users and authentication but remains independent of any other authorization authorities that already exist in your environment.

❏ **Database Account Credentials:** Uses existing Oracle user accounts for authorization. Since APEX is built on an Oracle database, many users already have Oracle user accounts established that they wish to reuse.

❏ **LDAP Credentials:** Use an LDAP server to authenticate users.

There are several other preconfigured authentication schemes that allow you to integrate other Oracle technologies as part of your overall authentication process. In addition, you can define your own custom authentication scheme, using PL/SQL logic to return a Boolean value (TRUE or FALSE), which will control access to applications and application components.

APEX provides its own authentication, which is the topic of the rest of this chapter. However, you can use APEX with external authentication methods. Please refer to the APEX forum at the Oracle Technology Network (OTN) for more information on working with these methods.

Finally, you can choose to have no authentication for your application, making it a public application.

How It Works

The application you have created includes a set of authorization schemes implemented by default, including the APEX Account Credentials, which is the current method for your application and which you will use throughout this chapter.

You can take a quick look at the available authentication schemes in your application.

1. Click on the Application Builder tab of your development environment and then click on Shared Components.

2. In the Security section of the page, click on Authentication Schemes to bring up the page shown in Figure 9-1.

You can see that there are three schemes for this application: an APEX account credentials authentication scheme, which is currently in use, a scheme called DATABASE ACCOUNT which uses the preconfigured scheme of the same type, and a DATABASE scheme, which captures the user name from the Data Access Descriptor (DAD) for the target Oracle database.

For the purposes of this chapter and its exercises, you will continue to use the APEX authorization scheme. Your next step in exploring authentication is to create some users who will have different levels of access to your application.

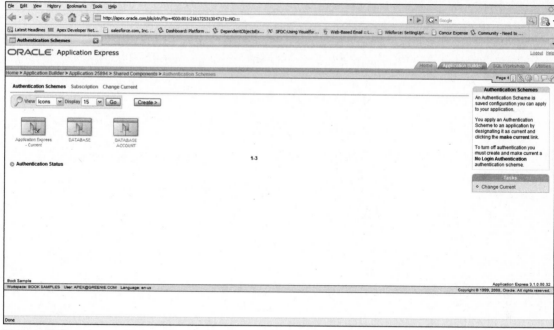

Figure 9-1

Tech Talk – Security Is Always There

If you have authentication enabled, your APEX application must know the identity of a user before that user can access any components in an application. If the user identity is not known (available in the session state), APEX will use the login page to prompt for user name and password when someone tries to access a page. You have witnessed this phenomenon at work when you have come back to run a page in your application after being gone for a while. When you go to run the page, you have to first log in before going to the selected page.

Creating Users

When you are using an APEX account credentials authentication scheme, you can define users within the APEX environment. For the exercises in this chapter, designed to demonstrate some common security practices, you will have to define four users: an administrator; a manager; a sales rep, who works for the manager; and a standard user.

Try It Out   Creating Users

Defining users is done through an administrative utility in the APEX development environment.

1. Click on the Utilities tab in the application development environment.

2. In the Tasks list on the right-hand side of the page, click on the `Administration` link, which will bring up the page shown in Figure 9-2.

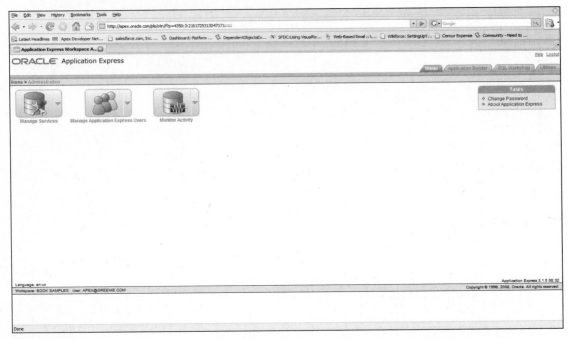

Figure 9-2

3. Click on the arrow on the right of the Manage Application Express Users icon to show two choices: Users or User Groups.

As you can probably tell by the name, User Groups allows you to combine multiple users into a single entity for easier management of security for large numbers of users. You will not need to use groups for the purposes of this book.

4. Select the Users and Manage Existing Users menu choices to bring up the page shown in Figure 9-3.

Ah, what a cute little icon! Each of those little weebles represents a user. Right now, all you can see is your user, which is colored red. The colors indicate levels of privilege for the APEX development environment, as you will see in the next page.

> In a smaller environment, you will probably be both the workspace administrator and a developer.
> When a single workspace is used for multiple application projects, there will more likely be some people
> who are developers within that workspace but without workspace administrator privileges.

5. Click on the Create button to bring up the page shown in Figure 9-4, completed for the first user.

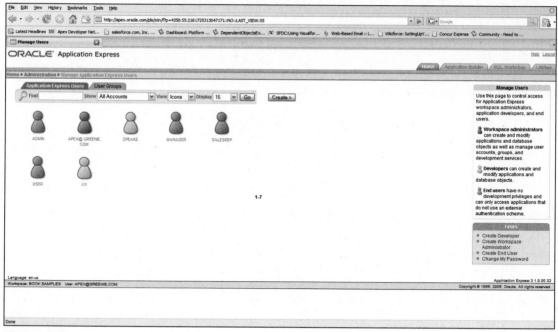

Figure 9-3

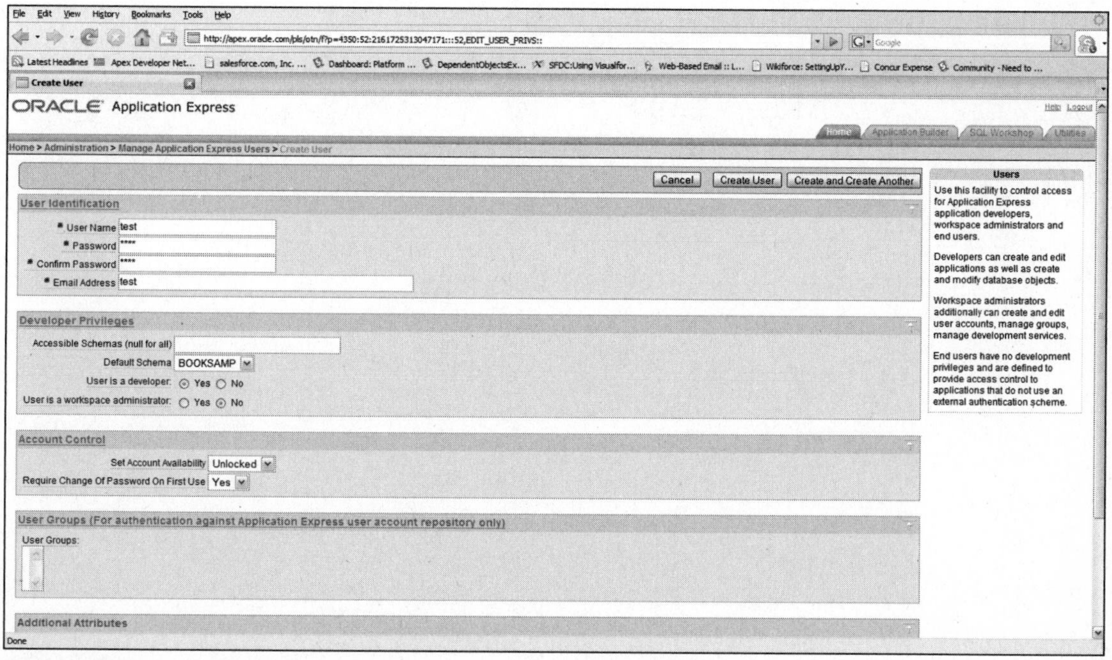

Figure 9-4

On this page, you add key information about the APEX user you are defining.

6. Enter ADMIN for the user name and an easy to remember password of at least six characters. Enter an email address, which does not have to be unique for each user.

7. Select No for the User is a developer, and leave the No selection for User is a workspace administrator.

Keep in mind the security privileges you are defining with these two choices are privileges that relate to the APEX development environment. You don't want any of these users to be able to access this development environment, let alone administer APEX workspaces, so it is important to make the appropriate selection.

In this area, you also specify that an account is currently locked and not accessible, and whether you want APEX to require users to enter a new password the first time they log in to the account. You can leave the default for the new password or set it to No for less confusion.

This requirement is only enforced if the user is trying to enter the application through the login choice available from the apex.oracle.com site. If the user is logging directly into the application, as you will in the next section, APEX does not prompt for a new password.

8. Once you have entered this information, click Create and Create Another to begin the process again.

9. Create three more users, with user names of MANAGER, SALESREP, and USER. For the last user, click Create User to return to the Manage Application Express Users page, which should now look like Figure 9-5.

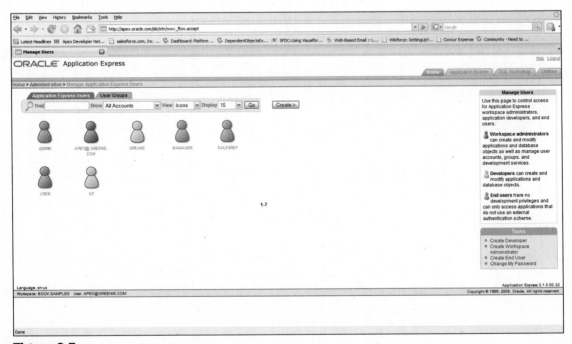

Figure 9-5

You have all the users you will need to start exploring how to use security with your application.

How It Works

There may have been a security thought tickling through your head even before this chapter. You have been running this application from the development environment, and you do not want to allow your users into this environment. How do your users get to the application directly?

Your users call up the APEX application you have been developing with the following URL:

```
http://apex.oracle.com/pls/otn/f?p=application_number
```

In other words, if the application number for your application were 29390, the URL would be:

```
http://apex.oracle.com/pls/otn/f?p=29390
```

1. Logout from the APEX development environment by clicking on the Logout link in the upper right corner. Enter the URL for your application into the navigation toolbar and press Enter to be presented with the login page for the application, as shown in Figure 9-6.

Figure 9-6

2. Enter one of the user names you just created, but with an invalid password.

3. When this entry is denied, enter the correct password to bring up the application, as shown in Figure 9-7.

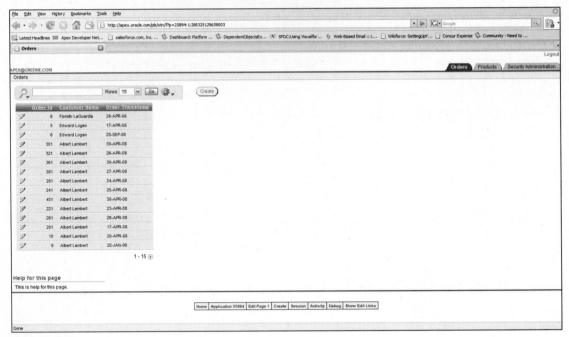

Figure 9-7

You will notice one big difference between the page shown in Figure 9-7 and the one you have been using all along — there are no links at the bottom of the page to go directly to the development environment, which is as it should be. This is called the Developer's Toolbar and is only displayed when you run an application from the Application Builder. Since your end users access the application directly and will not be able to log in to the Application Builder, they will never see this toolbar at the bottom of the page.

You could try out the rest of the user names and passwords if you want, but the result, for now, will be the same. All you have done so far is define users and how they are identified with the authentication process. Things get much more interesting when you use these user identities to restrain access to the application with authorization.

Limiting Access

Defining users is the necessary precursor for providing differential access to your application. Now that you have different users for your application, you can use this information to limit access to the application or its components.

Authorization

Authorization defines what type of access a particular user or user group will have to various application components. Most components, from the application itself to shared components, to individual items and buttons, allow you to define which users are authorized to use that component.

Authorizations are implemented by means of authorization schemes. As with authentication, the authorization scheme is used to associate users with a particular type of authorization.

Oracle APEX gives you an easy way to define and implement authorization schemes through the use of Access Control Lists, or ACLs. Although ACLs are not the only way to limit access to components, most applications can put this capability to good use.

ACLs

APEX comes with three built-in authorization schemes: view, edit, and administrator. The schemes are a hierarchy, from view to administrator. This hierarchy means that users in the edit ACL automatically have all access privileges of the view ACL, and administrator users have all the privileges of both the view and edit ACLs.

You implement Access Control Lists by creating an ACL page, which lets you specify users for different ACLs as well as how to implement the authorizations defined with the ACLs.

Try It Out   Defining Access Control

The ability to define access control for your application has been hiding in plain sight. The process revolves around the definition of an ACL page for your application.

1. Return to the development environment by logging out of the application and logging back in to the developer account with your developer name, and click on Application Builder. Select your application and click Create page.

2. On the next page, click on the Access Control icon to begin the creation of a page to control your ACLs.

3. Give the page a number, or accept the default number for the page, and click Next.

4. Choose to use an existing tab set and add a new tab called ACL. Click Next and then Finish to complete the creation of the new page.

This initial setup task was simple — now to see the details.

How It Works

The real meat of using Access Control Lists is revealed when you run the access control page you just created.

1. Click on the Run icon to bring up the Access Control page you just created, as shown in Figure 9-8.

There are two main sections to this page. The top of the page allows you to define the way that the ACLs will be used for this application. The first option simply ignores any ACL-based restrictions on any application component. The next level tightens security a bit by only allowing users defined as one of the ACLs to have access to the application, although any user defined in any list will have full access to all functionality.

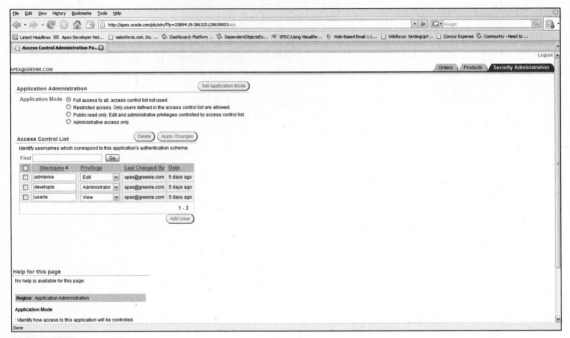

Figure 9-8

The third option enforces the restrictions described by the ACLs. By default, there are three ACL privileges: Administrator, Edit, and View. As mentioned earlier, these levels are a hierarchy, with each higher level having all the privileges of the underlying levels. This third option implements the access privileges defined for components in your application, a process you will go through shortly.

The final option limits access to the entire application to those users defined as Administrators, effectively locking down the application to all but the most privileged users.

Tech Talk – More Levels?

If you have designed robust security schemes before, you may be a bit nonplussed by this default functionality. After all, three different levels of security are not that much.

Keep in mind that these are the default levels, those that are provided for you automatically. These levels are implemented as authorization schemes. You can add more authorization schemes manually through the appropriate link in the `Shared Components` page. However, your new schemes will not automatically show up in the user definitions at the bottom of the page, due to the fact that the list of values is using a static list. Of course, you can simply add your authorization schemes to that static list to make them available in the user definition process.

The lower part of the page allows you to associate users with the three different ACLs, which you will do in the next section.

Try It Out   Defining Users

In order to see authorization schemes in action, you will have to associate the users you just defined with a particular scheme, which you can do in the `Access Control List` region of the ACL page.

This page should look familiar, familiar enough that you automatically understand how to add users, delete users, and apply changes with the appropriate pushbuttons and check boxes.

In the `Access Control List` region, you will add a user name for each of the users you created in the first part of this chapter.

1. Create an `ADMIN` user with the `Administrator` privilege.

2. Create the `MANAGER` and `SALESREP` users with the `Edit` privilege.

3. Create the `USER` with the `View` privilege.

4. Add your user name and give yourself `Administrator` privilege.

5. Click Apply Changes to associate the users with the ACLs. You may want to also define your development user as an `Administrator`, although you can get access to any page from the development environment by turning authorizations on and off.

You have laid the groundwork for using ACLs to shape the way users interact with your application.

Try It Out   Limiting Access to a Tab

Defining users and associating them with ACLs complete the framework for assigning access privileges in your application. But for these ACLs to have any effect, you will have to add the authorization schemes to components in your application.

Your first task will be to limit the use of the Administration tab to those users in the Administrator ACL.

1. Return to the development environment. Go to the `Shared Components` page and select `Tabs`.

2. Click on the Maintenance tab, and then on the Edit icon. Click the Authorization button to limit the display to the section displayed in Figure 9-9, shown with the select list visible.

You can see there are seven choices available to you — to allow or deny access to users on any of the ACLs, or to deny access to anyone not included on one of the ACLs, who would only be Public Users. For this tab, you will want to suppress the display of the tab to everyone who is not an administrator.

3. Select `access control - administrator` for this tab, and click Apply Changes.

Simple enough. Now take a look at how you new access restriction works.

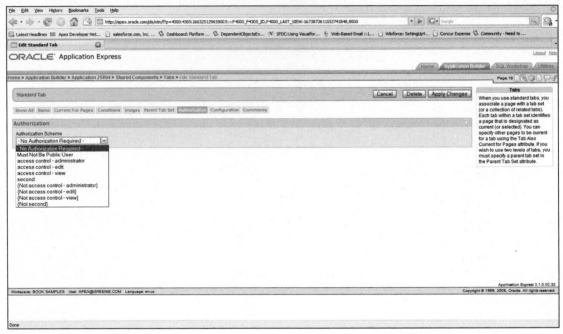

Figure 9-9

How It Works

Time to see ACLs in action for the first time.

1. Return to the application development area, select your application, select the first page in the application, and click the Run icon to bring up your first page, which looks like Figure 9-10.

A bit disappointing — the `Maintenance` tab is still visible. But wait, you forgot to log in as a user whose ACL membership would not allow him or her to see the tab.

2. Click Logout, and then login with the `USER` user name and password.

Ooops, still no joy. Why is the tab still visible? For a simple reason; remember, you have not turned on the ACL enforcement yet.

3. Click on the ACL tab, and change the application mode to `Public read only`. Click Set Application Mode to bring up the page shown in Figure 9-11.

There, that's more like it. You can log out and log back in as `ADMIN` to see that the ACLs are working properly to allow this user to see the ACL page. Nice. But, if you recall, you used the same list from the `Maintenance` page in one of your other pages. You will have to suppress the display of that with the same authorization scheme.

Figure 9-10

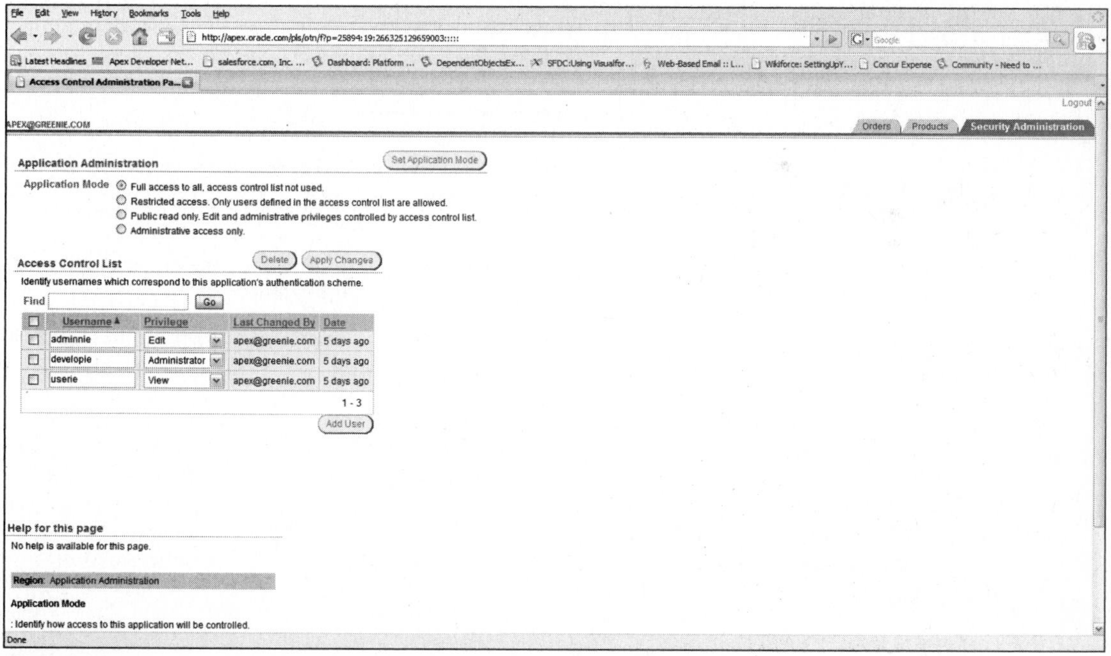

Figure 9-11

| Try It Out | **Limiting Access to a Region** |

When you created the shared component list with a list of all the maintenance pages, you also displayed that list in a region on the master-detail order entry page. You can follow the same procedure to hide that region.

1. Return to the development environment, and go to the master-detail page. In Chapter 7, you removed the `Maintenance` region from the page. Add it back onto this page; click the plus sign in the `Regions` area, indicating that the new region is a list region; give the region the Title of `Maintenance` and assign it to Region Position 03; and select the `Maintenance` list and click Create List Region.

2. Click on the `Maintenance` region and then the Authorization button, which will bring up a section that looks just like the one you saw for the tab.

3. Change the authorization scheme to `access control – administrator`, and click Apply Changes.

How It Works

Time to see if this second access limitation works like the first.

1. Log out from the application and log back in as any of the other user names. Go to the Orders tab and select an order to edit. The master-detail page will not display the list of links, as expected.

Using ACLs to simply hide pages and regions is a bit of a brute-force approach. You can use ACLs to shape the type of functionality available to different users by controlling access to the components that deliver that functionality.

| Try It Out | **Limiting Access to Functionality** |

For this application, you would like to prevent users in the View ACL from being able to add new orders or edit existing orders. Since both of these actions are triggered by specific components in the application, you can limit functionality by limiting access to those components.

The components in question are the Create button on the `Orders` report page, which allows users to create a new order, and the first column in the same report, which lets users edit existing records.

1. Return to the development environment and go to the `Orders` report, which should be Page 1.

2. Click on the Create button in the page, go to the `Authorization` section of the attributes page, and select `access control – edit`.

Selecting this option will give both `Edit` and `Administrator` ACL members access to this button, while preventing users defined on the View list from seeing the button.

3. Click Apply Changes to return to the main attributes for the page.

4. Click on the `Interactive Report` link in the `Regions` section.

5. Scroll down to the `Link Column` section, and choose access `control - edit` for the Authorization Scheme for the column.

6. Click Apply Changes to set the ACL limits in place.

How It Works

Time to check your work again.

1. Click on the Run icon for the page.

If you were last running the application as ADMIN, MANAGER, or SALESREP, you should not notice anything different about the appearance of the page.

2. Click Logout, and log back into the application as USER. The first page you see should look like Figure 9-12.

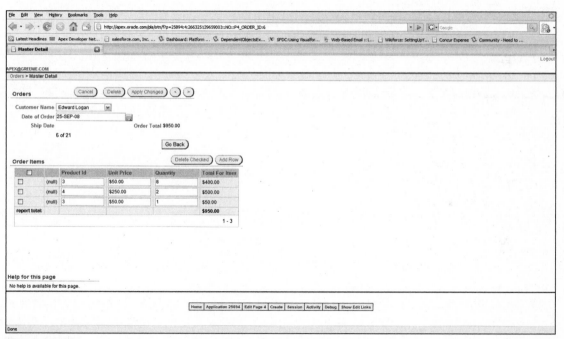

Figure 9-12

Voilà! Both the Create button and `Edit` link are gone, just as you wanted.

Try It Out   Limit Access to the ACL Tab

As you are starting to see, the use of authorization schemes and ACLs can have a powerful effect on your application — so powerful that you would very likely want to prevent all but the most privileged from making changes to ACL membership or the way that ACLs are used in the application. In other words, you want to prevent pretty much everyone from accessing the ACL tab and page.

In this particular application scenario, you have defined the Administrator privilege as one that allows its members to administer the content of the application, such as the products available for use in orders. But you certainly would not want to give all of these people the ability to turn ACLs off for the application or to change the membership in the ACLs themselves.

You can stop all users from accessing this tab, and its associated page, by making its display conditional.

1. Return to the development environment, go to the `Shared Components` area, and click on the `Tabs` link.

2. Select the ACL tab, and then click on the Edit icon for the tab. Click the Conditions button to bring up the section shown in Figure 9-13.

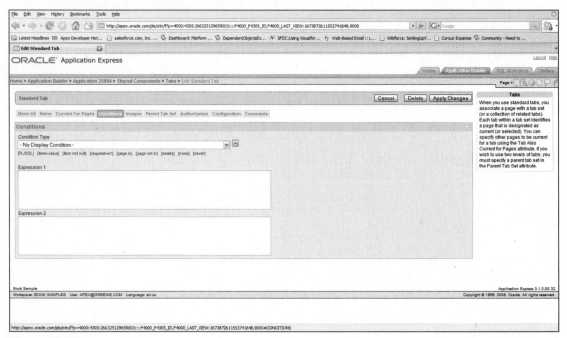

Figure 9-13

3. Click on the Condition Type selection list.

This list gives you a lot of choices, with the ability to create conditions based on SQL statements, PL/SQL, the name of the request submitted for the page, the values of two expressions in this section, and the type of client browser, to name just some of the options. For this particular task, though, you want to pick the most restrictive condition.

4. Select the second-to-last choice, Never.

Sounds pretty dire, and well it should. With this condition, no one will ever see this tab.

5. Click Apply Changes to save the new condition.

This exercise has not only given you a way to prevent users from getting to the ACL page, but also introduced you to the idea of conditional display, an idea that will be expanded upon in the final section of this chapter.

How It Works

You have shut the door on the ACL tab to all users. But for something this important, you might want to make sure that the door is really shut.

1. Run the application. You will not see the ACL tab. You can log out and back in as each of the users you defined to demonstrate that no one will be able to see the tab.

2. Return to the development environment. Select the ACL page, and click on the Run icon to bring up the ACL page.

By specifying that the ACL tab is never available, you have, in effect, blocked the only road to the ACL page. However, you can still run the page, if you can get there from the development environment.

This particular way of limiting access may not be appropriate for your application, but by using these attributes, you have gotten familiar with both another option for limiting access and the way that the development and deploy environments differ for APEX applications.

As you have seen in this section, ACLs bring a lot of flexibility to the table. You certainly would like to consider them in terms of broadly allowing or limiting access to application components. But there may be times when you want to use an even finer level of access control, and the final section of this chapter will show you how to accomplish this goal.

Shaping Access

In the previous section, you used a rather blunt approach to limiting access to entire components of your application. But you can set conditional display specifications on most portions of a page and region, down to the level of individual items or columns.

To allow you to discover the type of flexible access control you can implement with APEX, this section will walk you through changing the display of the Orders portion of the master-detail form to allow managers capabilities beyond those of mere sales reps. As you recall, you added a PL/SQL procedure in the previous chapter to automatically set the ship date on an order to three business days past the order date.

This consistent approach will guarantee a certain level of customer satisfaction, but there may be times when you want to allow more rapid shipping. However, you have to limit the people who would be allowed to change the ship date for an order. You can't let a sales rep change a ship date, since most sales reps want to do all they can to make their customers happiest, up to and including immediate shipment. You would also not want to allow the ADMIN user to change the ship date, since these users may not understand the business reasons why you would, or would not, want to stretch the rules for a particular customer.

The proper way in this scenario is to allow the MANAGER to change the ship date. The way you can implement this functionality is use another conditional display, one that will limit the field to read only access.

Try It Out   Limiting Access to Items

One of the principals behind the design of APEX is to offer up frequently needed functionality to developers in an easy, declarative form. The requirement of allowing some fields to be editable in some circumstances and not others is a prime example of this quest.

In this particular situation, you can use this configuration option to get the results that you want.

1. Return to the development environment and select the master-detail page to edit.

2. Click on the item for Pn_ORDER_SHIP_DATE and then on the Read Only button to isolate the section shown in Figure 9-14 in its completed state.

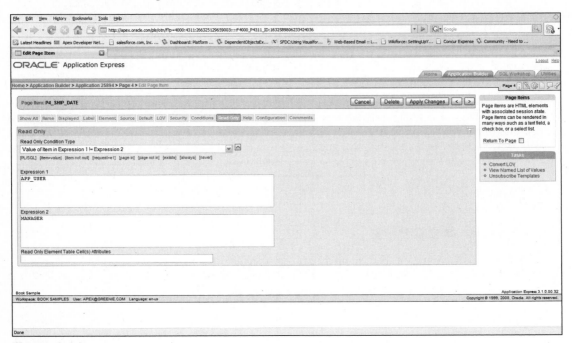

Figure 9-14

This page looks familiar, which is a tribute to both the consistency of the APEX development environment and your growing familiarity with it.

3. Select the Read Only Condition Type to be
    Value of Item in Expression 1 != Expression 2, and then
    enter APP_USER in Expression 1 and MANAGER in Expression 2.

This little change will deliver exactly the functionality you want. APP_USER is a session variable which contains, curiously enough, the user name of the current application user. If that user is anything but MANAGER, you do not want to allow access to the SHIP_DATE field.

This new arrangement is well and good, but you will have to go back and change the display type of the SHIP_DATE item to be appropriate for use by the MANAGER user.

4. Click the Name button to bring up the attributes section that contains the display type for the item. Change the Display As entry from Display Only to Date Picker (DD-MON-YYYY).

5. Click Apply Changes.

Since only the MANAGER user will be able to insert or edit a value into this field, you might as well give him or her the use of a handy date picker.

Before your application can properly run, you have to make one more change. Remember, the computation you created automatically derives the SHIP_DATE each time the record is saved. This operation makes sense as long as the user is not a manager. So you would want to add a condition to the computation that prevented it from operating if the user was the MANAGER.

But even if the user is the MANAGER, you would still want to give him or her the opportunity to let the application enter the default SHIP_DATE for them. You can adjust the operation of the computation with a simple compound condition.

6. Select the computation for the Pn_ORDER_TIMESTAMP item.

7. Click the Conditions button to bring up the section shown in Figure 9-15 in its completed form.

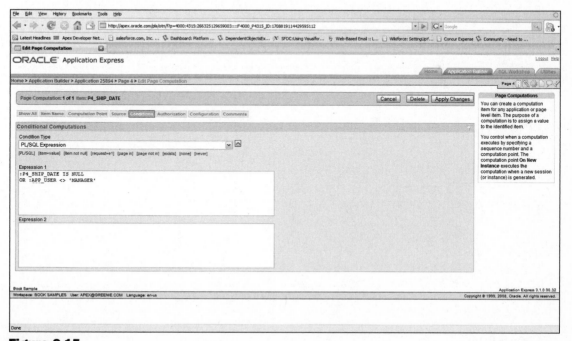

Figure 9-15

8. Select PL/SQL Expression for the Condition Type, and enter the following code for Expression 1:

```
:APP_USER <> 'MANAGER' OR :Pn_ORDER_SHIP_DATE IS NULL
```

replacing the n with the number of your master-detail page, and remembering to preface the field name with a colon (:) to identify it as a bind variable. With this code, you allow the computation whenever the user is anyone other than the MANAGER user, or when that user has not entered a value into the Pn_ORDER_SHIP_DATE field.

9. Click Apply Changes to save your work.

You've completed all the changes you will need to make to implement the functionality you want.

How It Works

For the last time in this chapter, it's time to see your work in action.

1. Click on the Run icon to bring up the master-detail page.

2. Log out of the application, and log in as MANAGER.

3. Click on one of the orders in the report to bring up the page shown in Figure 9-16.

You can see that the Ship Date field is a data picker.

4. Enter a date into the Ship Date field, and save the record.

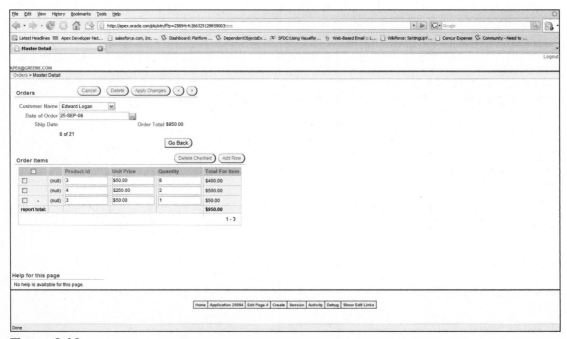

Figure 9-16

Notice that the date you entered remains as the value, as it should.

5.   Log out of the application, and log back in as the ADMIN user.

6.   Click on the Edit icon for any of the orders to bring up the page shown in Figure 9-17.

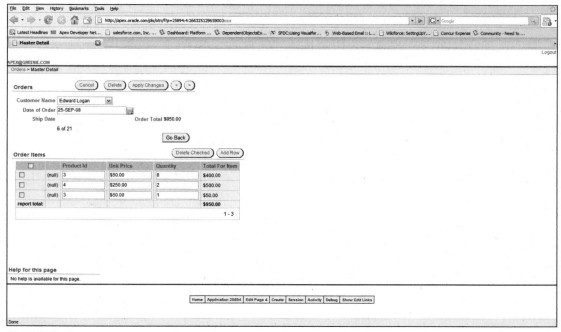

Figure 9-17

There you have it — the same page, but with the Ship Date field now shown as a display only field. The use of conditions on the field and the computation have delivered just what you want, all with a few simple entries.

Tech Talk – User Groups to the Rescue

Although you may like the functionality you have just implemented, in the real world you would have more than one person who would have the ability to edit ship dates. You could accomplish the same goal by having the condition based on a user group, rather than a user, and simply add all appropriate users to that group.

For a production scenario, you would probably want to add in some validation that would apply to the date entered by the manager, ensuring that the date chosen did not fall on a weekend or holiday.

In addition, you would probably want to add some read-only conditions to prevent the order date, or, for that matter, the order item information, if the SHIP_DATE had already passed. With the knowledge you have of the APEX environment, you should be able to implement these restrictions easily on your own, should you desire.

Summary

This chapter adds the final piece to your initial exploration of APEX development. You have learned how to use the built-in security features of the environment to shape the way that different users access data and application components.

In this chapter you:

❑   Defined additional users.

❑   Added these users to an authentication scheme.

❑   Created an ACL page and authorization schemes.

❑   Added users to the authentication schemes and used them to limit access.

❑   Used the conditions for different APEX components to put your new security to work.

You should step back and realize that the authentication and authorization capabilities of your application are built into the APEX environment. Although you had to create users and assign access control for different components, this process merely instituted specific limitations — you did not have to build or add the security framework.

This chapter concludes your quick tutorial on creating applications with APEX. In the rest of this book, you will learn more about managing APEX applications, using packaged APEX applications, and look at the possibility of migrating existing applications to the world of APEX.

Part III

Deploying the Application

Deployment and Administration

Throughout the previous eight chapters, you crafted a fairly nice application. For production purposes, that application probably needs some more refinement to meet the specific goals of your environment, but you have created enough value to think about giving the application to your users.

This chapter will cover that deployment process, as well as provide an overview of some of the administration options for your APEX environment.

Locking Down Your Application

Once you have finished your development efforts, or when you reach a temporary pause in your development efforts, you probably want to have some kind of lockdown of your application. In fact, you very well may want to limit some types of access to your application even during the development process.

Try It Out   Locking Down Your Application

Oracle APEX provides the capability to limit access through a configuration parameter for the application.

   1.   Go to the main development page for your application, and click on Shared Components.

   2.   Click on the `Definition` link under Application and then on the Availability button to isolate the section shown in Figure 10-1.

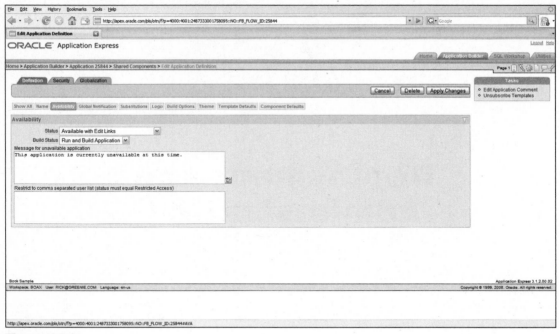

Figure 10-1

You can see that you have been working all this time with a particular availability setting of Available with Edit Links. This setting is the most generous, which is what you wanted when you were first learning about the environment. With this setting, you can access the edit menu links at the bottom of the page when you are logged into the development environment in the same browser session.

There are six other availability options:

❏ **Available:** The application is available without any specific restrictions to all, but without any access to the edit links at the bottom of the page for any users.

❏ **Available to Developers only:** Access is limited to those users defined as developers.

❏ **Restricted Access:** Access is limited to developers named in the comma-separated `Restrict To` list, the lower text area in this section.

❏ **Unavailable:** The application is not available to anyone, including developers. With this option selected, anyone attempting to access the application receives a simple text message in their browser informing them that the application is not available. This message is less than optimally useful, so the next two messages give you the ability to replace it with something else.

❏ **Unavailable (Status Shown with PL/SQL):** The application is still unavailable, but you can use PL/SQL to specify the message returned to anyone trying to access the application.

❏ **Unavailable (Redirect to URL):** Once again, the application is still unavailable for all, but anyone trying to access the application is directed to a URL, which could display a more informative message.

How It Works

In order to understand how these options work, you can quickly try them out.

1. Change the Status to Unavailable, and click Apply Changes. Click on the Run icon to bring up a page that looks like Figure 10-2.

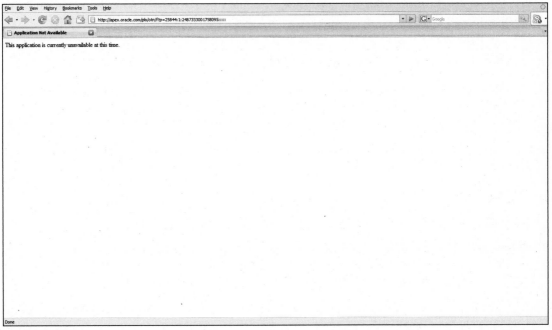

Figure 10-2

There — told you it wasn't very informative. You can see that unavailable means unavailable — no one can get to the application, even a workspace administrator like you.

2. Use the Back button in your browser to return to the Application Definition page, and set the Status to Available to Developers Only.

Build Status

Later in this chapter, you will learn how to deploy an APEX application to another environment. One of the most frequent reasons for this movement is to take an application from a development environment to a testing, training, and/or production environment.

The Build Status option gives you the ability to deploy a version of the application that does not allow users, regardless of privilege or status, to make any modifications to the application. Currently, this option is set to Run and Build Application, but the alternative is to only allow running the application. The Run Application Only option will prevent all access to the development environment for the deployed application, typically what you want in a production environment.

Version Tracking

In this overall discussion of application availability options, you may be thinking beyond the mere movement of your application from one environment to another. After you move an application, you will usually want to start on the next version of the application or continue work to enhance the current version. As soon as you have more than one version of your application, you will need to track different versions of your application as you move through one or more development cycles.

As you will learn later in this chapter, you can export your entire application into scripts, which can be used to recreate the application, either at another site or to recover your current application. If you want to save your development work at a point in time, you can simply export the application and save those files.

You can also use this method with most standard version control systems to compare different versions of your application by comparing the export scripts.

Structure of the APEX Environment

The next main topic to cover is to learn how to deploy your completed application. You are already familiar with the various components of an APEX application, but to fully understand deployment options, you should fully understand the structure of the APEX environment.

As you already know, APEX applications run on an Oracle database. In fact, the APEX environment can be understood as a hierarchy of environments, as shown in Figure 10-3.

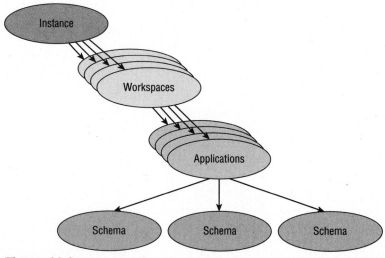

Figure 10-3

At the top level is the Oracle database *instance*. An Oracle instance is the entire world, the runtime environment of the Oracle database. When a user connects to any application in any workspace, or data in any schema, they are connecting to the Oracle instance. The Oracle instance contains the common systems, such as SQL parsers, the PL/SQL runtime environment, the overall security system and the network software which handles client connections.

Within the Oracle instance are individual APEX *workspaces*. An APEX workspace is like a virtual private database, fencing off all the information within the workspace from unauthorized access. A workspace can contain one or more applications, as well as shared objects that are used by one or more applications within the workspace. APEX users are also defined within a workspace, as you did in Chapter 9 on security.

An APEX application is implemented as a collection of PL/SQL procedures that hold and manipulate the metadata that defines the application

An APEX workspace can access one or more schemas. When you log into an Oracle database, you go to a specific schema. The objects in a schema are commonly available across the schema. Although you could access data objects in different schemas, you would have to qualify the names of the objects, a practice not normally done in the APEX environment. An Oracle schema is the functional equivalent of an Access database.

With a clear understanding of these different Oracle environments, you can understand the different deployment options for your APEX applications.

Deployment

Up to this point, most readers will have been running their application in a hosted APEX environment. This environment is fine for the development of your applications, with the significant caveat that Oracle Corporation does not provide any guarantees for the stability of that environment or its data.

> *Hey, It's free, right?*

Once you complete the initial development of your application, you will probably have to make a decision about where the production application will run. You will have to decide what deployment option you will use for the production application and then take the appropriate actions for that deployment.

The deployment process for APEX workspaces, applications, and components is a two-step process. You first export the desired entities to a script file, and you then import that script file and run it to create the entities in the new environment.

Deployment Options

You have a number of different options for deploying your APEX application:

❑ **No Deployment:** This deployment option is the choice of no choice. You could run your APEX application in the same environment that you used to develop the application. You could lock down the application and simply distribute the URL to access the application. This option has the virtue of being extremely easy — you don't do anything. But development environments are often more limited than production environments, in many ways, with less data, fewer users and less server horsepower to run your applications and store your data. And, of course, any changes you make to the application in this environment can be immediately visible to users, which is frequently not the most desirable approach. If you have been using Oracle's free hosted APEX environment, then this is provided for development purposes only and running production applications in this environment is strictly prohibited.

❏ **Deploy Only Your Application:** As your application is made from a collection of PL/SQL procedures and the parameters that guide them, you could choose to deploy only an application. Exporting an application, as you will later in this section, will also include any shared components that are used in the application. You would move the application to another Oracle instance. That instance would have to have all the data structures that your application is using, as well as any users whom you have specifically referenced in your code. This deployment option is one of the most popular options for users who have a production Oracle database before they start using APEX. Typically, these organizations will prepare a development environment that is a mirror of a portion of their production environment, although with less data.

> ### Tech Talk — Describing Your Data Requirements
>
> What if you are not sure whether the target Oracle database contains all the data structures you will need, or even which data objects are used by a particular application? You have a couple of tools you can use to help you figure out if the target will be a warm and welcoming environment for your APEX application. You can use the application report, described later in this chapter, to get a list of the data objects accessed by this application. You can also use SQL Developer, described in Chapter 12, to compare the schemas of your development environment and your target production environment.

❏ **Deploy an Entire Workspace:** You can also move an entire APEX workspace to a different environment. This action will *not* move any of the applications or shared components, only the user definitions and the workspace definition. Exporting and importing an APEX workspace into another Oracle instance allows you to import application components, such as individual pages, rather than importing complete applications. It is advisable to import your workspace into your testing, training and/or production environments only once. Deploying a workspace, like deploying an application, does not move any data or data structures.

❏ **Deploy Your Application and Data Structures:** This deployment option will require two steps, moving your application and then moving the data structures from your development environment. This option is the most popular option for new APEX developers, since they are frequently creating both new applications and new data structures. The example you created in this book would probably be best suited for this option. Keep in mind that you will load the data into a particular schema, and data object names only have to be unique within a schema, not an entire database.

❏ **Deploy Your Application, Data Structures, and Data:** There may be scenarios that would call for you to move your application, data structures, and data. You may be deploying an application that has been used for a while in the development environment, and you don't want to lose the data entered, or you may want to install seed data in the new environment.

❑ **Move the Entire Database:** Of course, exporting the entire Oracle database will move everything contained in it — workspaces, schemas, and all the data structures and data within those schemas. This type of move is sometimes used for migrating to a more powerful server. When importing the complete database the APEX engine must be configured by correctly defining the Webserver access as defined in the installation guide.

❑ **Deploy Individual Components:** The APEX environment includes the ability to select individual components of an application, from pages to logos to templates. Although this chapter will not be covering this type of selective export, this option may be the most appropriate if your development plan calls for enhancements to be limited to the addition of components rather than the enhancement of existing components.

Some of the deployment options listed above involve the export and import of different application and data components. For instance, you may export an application, some data structures, and some data. Each of these exports will result in separate scripts.

Oracle APEX has a way of combining scripts together, linking the script for an application with scripts for installing supporting objects. These combined scripts are called a *package*, and you will create a simple package as you deploy your application in the next section.

Typically, you will deploy an entire application to a production Oracle database, and the next section will walk you through that process for the application you have just created.

Try It Out	**Deploying Your Application**

As mentioned above, the process of deployment involves two basic steps: exporting components from the APEX development environment to a script file, and then importing and installing that application in a different environment.

This exercise will make use of a different APEX environment to receive the application. You may only have a single workspace in the hosted APEX environment you have been using for the development of your application, so you may not have another environment ready to receive your application. In this case you will only be able to follow the example in the following text.

If you have been using a hosted APEX account, as suggested, you could set up a local environment using the version of Oracle 11*g* included on the DVD for this book. The following example will use this scenario. Performing this task will not only allow you to practice the following deployment example but also give you your very own APEX installation, completely under your control.

Defining Your Package

Your first step is to decide what components are going to be in the package you create. For this application, you will want to export your application, the data structures used by the application, and the workspace users you have created.

You will have to create two export scripts to handle the data structures and workspace users and then combine these scripts into the package you will create when you export your application.

Creating Supporting Object Scripts

Your first step is to create the scripts that will contain the supporting objects for your application, your database schema, and workspace users.

The script that will be used to create your database structures is referred to as DDL, or Data Definition Language, a form of standard SQL.

1. Enter the APEX development environment, and click on the Utilities tab.

2. Click on the Generate DDL icon and then on the Create Script button in the next page.

3. Accept the default schema, and click Next to bring up the page shown in Figure 10-4.

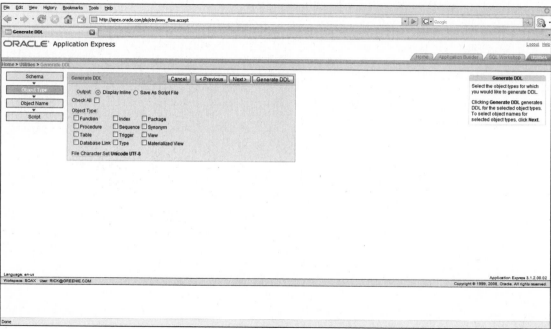

Figure 10-4

This page allows you to specify what types of objects you want to include in the generated DDL script. You will definitely want to include tables, indexes, sequences, and triggers.

1. Select Table, Index, Sequence, and Trigger, and click Next.

You could click on Generate DDL at this point, which would have the effect of including all objects of the type selected in the generated file. On the next page, you have the option of selecting any of the individual data objects for inclusion in the script file. Since you have only been working on your one application, and all the objects in the schema relate to that application, you will want to select all the objects.

2. Click Check All, and leave the Output selection set to Display Inline. Click Generate DDL to create the DDL file in the next page.

If you have worked with SQL in the past, the DDL file on the next page should look familiar. If you are not familiar with SQL, the DDL file will give you some idea of how this type of SQL works.

It is helpful, for the purposes of this book, for you to see the script file generated by this utility. However, what you really want to do is save this script in a file, an option available to you on the previous page.

1. Click the Back button of your browser, and change the Output option to Save As Script File. Click Generate DDL.

2. Give the script a Script Name and Description, and click Create Script. This action will save the script in the script repository in your development environment, as shown in Figure 10-5.

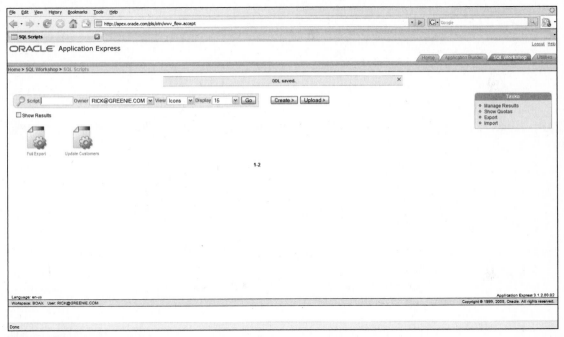

Figure 10-5

In order to create an installation script for this DDL, which you will include as a supporting object in your application package, you will need to have the script available as a file.

1. Click on the script you just created to bring up the edit window for the script. Click on the Download button to save the script as a file.

2. When prompted for a save location, you will probably want to create a directory for this script, as well as the other scripts you will use in your package, to make it easier to access them.

3. Save the script as a file and click Save.

Your next step is to create a script file to hold the application users you want to export.

1. Click on the Application Builder tab and then on your application.

2. Click on the Export icon at the top of the page and then on the Export choice again to bring up the page shown in Figure 10-6.

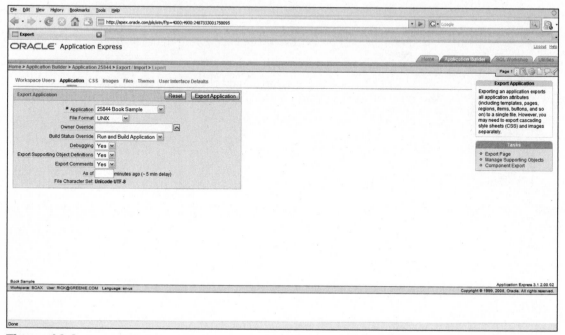

Figure 10-6

This page gives you the option to export your application or other types of components. You will return to this page shortly to export the application, along with its supporting objects, but first you have to create an export script for your workspace users.

1. Click on the Workspace Users choice at the top of the page and then on Export Workspace Users.

This time, you are prompted to save the export file immediately.

2. Save the file in the same directory as you saved the previous script.

3. Click on the application breadcrumb to return to the main page for the application.

One more script and you will be ready to go.

1. Go to the Shared Components page, and click on the Export Application Components task in the box in the upper left of the page.

2. On the next page, select the Application Attributes tab.

3. Click on the Logo choice, and then click the Add to Export button.

4. Click Next, accept the defaults, and then click Export Components.

5. Once again, you will be prompted for a file name for the export. Give the script file a name you can remember for a few minutes, and save it.

You are ready to add these supporting object scripts to your package definition.

Adding Supporting Objects to a Package

As explained previously, a package combines the export script for your application with additional scripts to install supporting objects.

1. Select your application and click on the Supporting Objects icon to bring up the page shown in Figure 10-7

Figure 10-7

As you can see from this page, you have a load of flexibility in creating a package. The topmost section provides a summary of the contents and operation of the package. The main work of the package is prescribed in the three sections on the left below the summary.

You will be creating a simple package, one that includes the DDL and workspace user export scripts. The choices under the Installation topic allow you to do many additional operations, from checking the target environment to see if certain objects exist, if the installation user has certain privileges, how much space should be available in the target Oracle instance, and whether the user will have to show proof of a license. If any of these prerequisites is not met, the installation of the application will fail.

You can add validations, similar to the validations you created in your application, to insure that certain logical conditions are met. You can also use a package to upgrade an existing version of your application, as well as including scripts to uninstall the application.

The Messages section on the right allows you to define custom messages to display to the user at different stages of the installation.

All this flexibility, and more, is beyond the immediate scope of this book. You will be using the Installation scripts choice to add the two scripts you created in the previous section.

2. Click on the Installation scripts link, and then on the Create button.

3. On the next page, click on the Create from File icon.

4. Give the script a name, such as DDL. You can accept the standard sequence, which will control the order in which the supporting objects are installed. Click Next.

5. On the next page, use the Browser button to select the DDL script you created. Click Create Script to add the script to the Installation Scripts window, as shown in Figure 10-8.

6. Click on the Create and Create from File choices again. Give the next script, which will be the workspace users script you created, an appropriate name, and click Next.

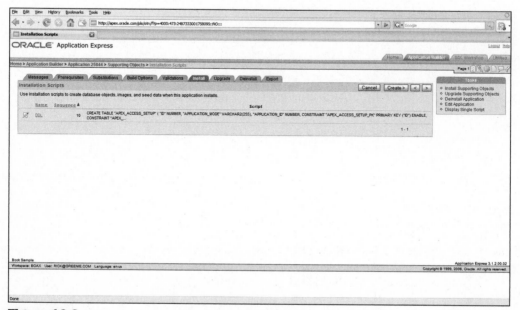

Figure 10-8

7. Select the export file you created for workspace users, and click Create Script.

8. Follow the same process for the script with your application logo.

You have now included these installation scripts as part of the installation process. Your final step in the export process is to create the installation package.

Creating an Installation Package

Adding the supporting object scripts is all you have to do to prepare this simple package. You are ready to create the master installation script.

1. Click on the Supporting Objects breadcrumb to return to the main page for this area.

2. Click on the Export Application task in the right-hand task box to bring up the page shown previously in Figure 10-6.

The page contains the basic choices for the export of an application. Notice that the application itself is displayed in the Application list of values. This option means that you can define a set of supporting objects that could support the deployment of more than one application from the same workspace.

You can also set the Build Status on this page, which was discussed in the first part of this chapter, and enable or disable debugging in the target environment.

3. Make sure that the File Format is properly selected. Set Debugging to No and Export Supporting Object Definitions to Yes.

   Notice that you can specify the application export will use the state of the application from an earlier time — this feature is available as part of Oracle's flashback capabilities, and it can be extremely useful in certain scenarios.

4. Click Export Application. Save the file in an appropriately named script in the same directory as your other scripts. Make sure that the script has the .sql identifier.

There — your application is ready for the next steps of importing and installation, which you will perform to see how this deployment process works.

How It Works

To see the results of your export work, you can install the package in a new environment.

   If you have been using the hosted version of APEX, this might be a good time to install a version of Oracle 11g , available for download at http://otn.oracle.com/apex. *Once you install the Oracle database, you will have to upgrade your APEX version, available from the same base URL, and download the latest version. (This book used version 3.1.2.) If you follow the instructions in the Installation Guide, you should end up with a complete version of APEX with which to perform these exercises.*

This example will install the application and supporting objects from the hosted environment to a local version of APEX running on Oracle 11*g*. This scenario assumes that none of the database objects or workspace users exist in the new environment, that APEX has been upgraded to the correct version, and that an APEX Workspace has been configured.

1. Log into your new APEX environment, and click on the Application Builder icon. The URL to access a default installation APEX on a local version of Oracle 11*g* is `http://localhost:8080/apex/f?p=4550:1`. The localhost specifies a local installation of Oracle. If you are accessing a version of Oracle on your network, replace that string with the network location. The default port for the internal Oracle listener is 8080.

2. Click the Import button to bring up the page shown in Figure 10-9.

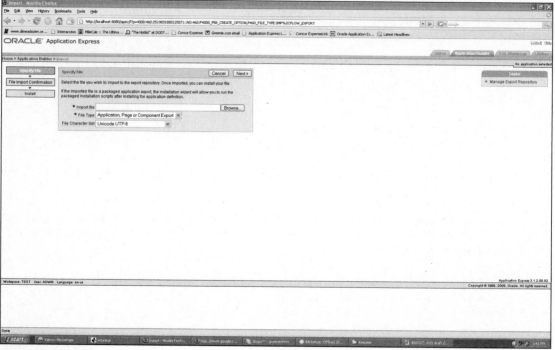

Figure 10-9

3. Use the Browse button to find the export file you just created and click Next.

The result of this action is to bring the import file into the Export Repository, where scripts are stored in your APEX environment. The script is now in your environment, but you will still have to run the script to install the application and its supporting files, which you can do directly from this page.

4. Once the file is completely imported, you will get a page that lets you know the import has been successful. Click Next to start the installation process on the page shown in Figure 10-10.

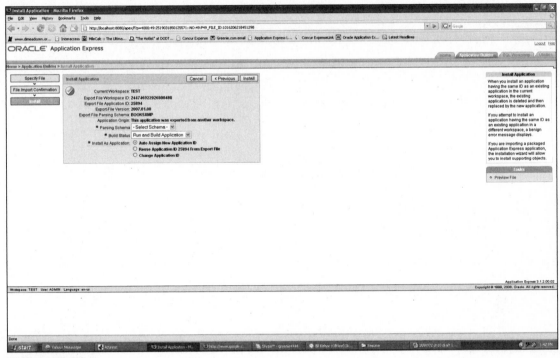

Figure 10-10

This page gives you an overview of the application you will be installing. You can select a schema to parse, or run, the script, which should be the schema for your workspace. You can also specify that the application should be loaded with the capability of both running and building the application, or just the ability to run the application, as discussed previously. Finally, you can automatically assign an Application ID to the new application, or you could choose to use the exiting Application ID or assign a different ID. As mentioned earlier, the Application ID has to be unique within an Oracle instance. You could leave the existing ID for the application, which might be a good idea for relating the application with other copies on other instances.

1. For this example, select a schema for parsing and leave the default choice of Auto Assign New Application ID. Click Install.

2. Once the installation of the application is completed, the page shown in Figure 10-11 will appear, which is the start of the process of installing the supporting objects for the application.

3. Note the new Application Number for the imported application. Accept the default choices, and click Next.

4. The next page will prompt you to confirm your choice of installing supporting objects, which you want to do to create the tables and the workspace users. Click Install to start the installation process. Once the process completes, you will see that some errors are reported. Click Install Summary to get to the results page, shown in Figure 10-12.

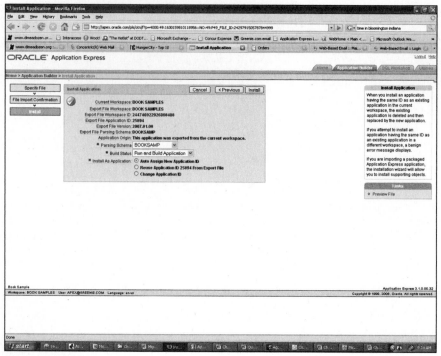

Figure 10-11

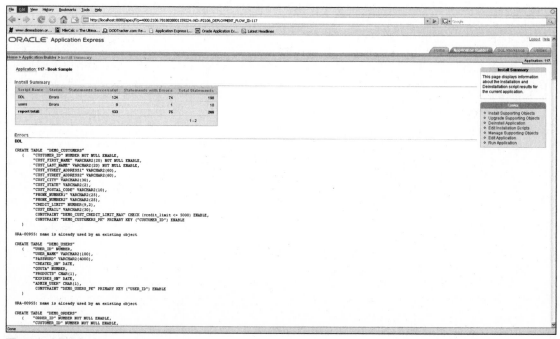

Figure 10-12

You can see that there were some errors for the import process, but all the errors are simply attempts by the supporting objects' scripts to duplicate existing indexes, which is not a problem for your run-time environment, or duplicate tables that were installed with this version of the Oracle database. If you were to export your source application again, for example after making some enhancements to your original application, then you should choose not to install the supporting objects, as the database objects already exist. When you are engaged in full-scale development, you may want to also incorporate update scripts and additional logic so that the installation process knows when to update the database objects rather than insert them.

5. Go back to the Application Builder, and click on the new application. Select a page or two, and run them to see the application in full bloom in your new environment.

The new application has all the functionality of the source application, but without any of the data. Normally, this type of migration would be supplemented with some installation scripts to load data for most of the tables that were the objects of lookup relationships, such as Products. You could have used SQL Developer, which will be covered in Chapter 12, to export the data files and add the scripts that resulted from that export as supporting objects, just as you did for the users and DDL in the current exercise.

Moving an APEX application to a new environment is really quite easy, making any of your deployment options simple to implement.

Tech Talk — Other Options

The process you used to import an application was nice and clean, first loading the script into the Export Repository and then executing the script. Be aware, though, that the script that you imported and ran was just an SQL script. The installation process also knew to run the supporting object scripts after installing the application. You could have accomplished the same task by using any SQL interface to your Oracle environment, including SQL Developer (which you will learn about in Chapter 12) to run the export scripts for the application and supporting object.

Administration

You have developed an application and deployed that application to a production instance. Before leaving the APEX environment, you will want to prepare yourself for the longer term by understanding some of the basic administrative tools available to you.

Administrator Levels

The administrative tools in APEX are only available to those who have the proper access rights, but there are different levels of administrator rights. You already saw one of these levels when you defined users in the last chapter. As you defined a user, you were asked if the user was to be a workspace administrator.

A *workspace administrator* can monitor and manage a specific workspace. When you signed up for a hosted APEX account, your user was automatically granted administration rights for your workspace. The subsequent sections of this chapter will examine the privileges given to workspace administrators, including the right to grant other users administrative rights to the workspace.

A higher level of administration rights gives a user APEX Administrator privileges. An APEX Admin can control privileges for the entire APEX installation, which cuts across all workspaces in that installation. These rights include:

❑ The ability to set login controls for all workspaces in the installation as a default.

❑ The ability to add specific tasks to the task lists that appear in the APEX development environment.

❑ The ability to add themes to public repository, making them available to all workspaces on the instance. Once a theme has been added to the public repository, individual users will not have to subscribe to the themes to use them.

❑ The ability to manage SQL Workshop attributes, such as preventing the editing of PL/SQL units for the entire installation. (A workspace administrator can implement the same limitation for a workspace.)

❑ The ability to establish policies for security, including the characteristics of user passwords and how they change, and limiting access to specified IP addresses.

❑ Create login and system messages. System messages are shown on the home pages for the workspace, Application Builder, SQL Workshop, and Utilities tabs.

❑ View and map schemas to workspaces.

❑ Only an APEX Admin can export workspaces, one of the strategies for deployment described above. This moves users and user groups as well as information about the workspace. You still have to export and move the applications and data.

APEX Admin rights can be turned off for all users, which will mean that no one will have access to these privileges. These high-level rights can be turned back on, but only through SQL*Plus, the standard interactive access tool for the Oracle database, and some API calls, as described in the documentation.

Since many readers will be using a hosted workspace, they will not be able to see the effects of being an APEX administrator, so the remainder of this chapter will focus on administration of an individual APEX workspace. For more information about the capabilities available to an APEX Admin, please refer to the Oracle Application Express User Guide.

Workspace Administration

A workspace administrator can manage their own workspace. As a workspace administrator, you have already used some of the standard privileges when you were creating users in Chapter 9. There are several other tools and capabilities frequently used by workspace administrators.

Application Builder Defaults

As the name implies, Application Builder Defaults are default choices that are applied for the entire workspace and all developers working within that space. You can set the few Application Builder

Defaults through clicking on the task with the same name on the main Application Builder page, which will bring up the page shown in Figure 10-13.

You can set the default tab setting, authentication and theme for all applications created within this workspace. Although a default is only a suggestion for usage, making your most frequently used option the default can save developers some time and improve consistency in the creation of multiple applications.

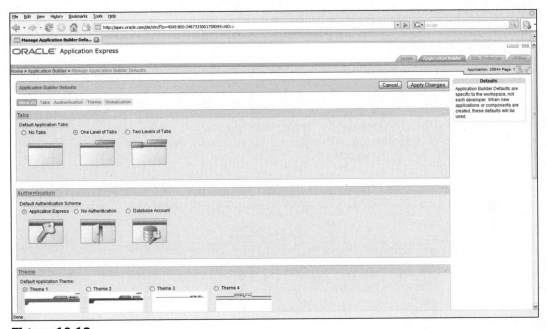

Figure 10-13

Application Models

The level of detail for defaults offered in the Application Builder Defaults section may seem like weak tea — they will save you a few keystrokes, but you would like to have a more robust set of defaults for creating applications.

You may have noticed, way back when you created your first application, that you had the choice of using an *application model* for your application. An application model is a predefined framework used to create your basic application.

Application models can include a number of standard pages, although the details of those pages may need to be modified to customize the application as part of the development process. Application models can be very useful to not only improve developer productivity but also establish application standards for your organization.

To understand the use of application models, you can create one on your own.

1. Return to the main Application Builder page.

2. Click the Create button to begin the creation of your application model.

3. On the next page, leave the default selection of Create Application, and click Next.

4. The next page prompts you for a name and schema for your application, and gives you the option of creating the application from scratch or from an application model. Since you are creating your first application model now, there would not be any available models for you to use, so leave the default choice of From scratch, give the application a Name, and click on Next.

The next page looks familiar — you can add pages to your application. You used this page way back when you created your first application, adding a page or two to your application.

5. For the purpose of this exercise, add a few pages to the application. As you add multiple pages, you will be given the option to make the subsequent pages subordinate to existing pages.

6. Click on the Next button and select your level of tabs. Click on the Next button.

7. On this page, you are prompted as to whether you would want to copy shared components from another application. If you click on the Yes choice, the page will change to give you the options shown in Figure 10-14.

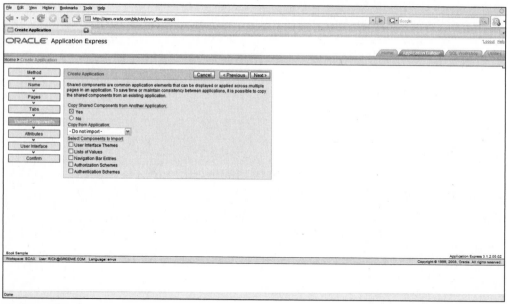

Figure 10-14

The detailed choices give you options as to which shared components you will want to import. You can easily imagine how you might want to include shared components in an application model.

1. For the purposes of this exercise, select your previous application and include the User Interface Themes and Lists of Values to import, and click Next.

2. The next page allows you to import a theme for the application. Leave the default and click Next.

3. The next page prompts you for an authentication scheme and some other defaults. These choices make more sense now than they did back when you created your first application. Choose a Date Format default, and click Next.

On the final page, you can see the standard summary information you have come to expect. But at the bottom of the page, you can see a check box that allows you to save this application as a design model.

4. Check the Save this definition check box, and click Create.

5. Return to the main Application Builder page. Click the Create button, select Create Application, and then enter a name for the application and select the Based on existing application design model choice. Click Next to see the use of the application model.

With the experience you gained in the previous chapters, you could probably come up with an application model that would act as a standard for other applications you plan to develop. Creating an application model is as easy as the initial definition of an application, and pays off in increased developer productivity.

Reports

In the earlier section of this chapter of deployment options, a mention was made of a report you could get on the overall data usage of an application. APEX gives you a fairly broad set of reports that give you visibility into the overall shape of your applications.

There are two main entry points to landing pads for a variety of different reports. On the main page for the APEX environment, the task area on the right has a link to Monitor activity under the heading of Administration. On the main development page for an application, you can click on Application Reports in the same task box.

The reports available for an application are shown in Figure 10-15.

Figure 10-15

There are three main areas of reporting listed here:

❑ **Page Views and Page View Analysis:** Gives you historical data on how many times each of the pages in the application have been viewed. You have a variety of ways to slice and dice this information, which can be used to understand usage patterns in your application, and potentially modify the application to better serve user needs.

❑ **Application Changes:** You can track the changes made to the application in a number of ways. This type of report is useful to both understand what a team of developers has been doing as well as tracking how your application is changing over time.

❑ **Environment:** Gives you an overview of environment usage by user agent, browser, operating system and clicks within the environment that led the user to an external site.

This page also includes the ability to monitor active sessions (e.g., end users) that are using this application, information which can be used to understand individual usage patterns at a detailed level

The reports available for the entire workspace are shown in Figure 10-16.

Figure 10-16

You have access to the same Page View and Application Changes reports here, but these reports are for all applications in the workspace. You also have a more granular level of analytic reports for Page Views, as well as the ability to monitor the login attempts by users to check on potential hacking attempts.

Finally, you can check out statistics on your overall user community, including the user agents, browser and operating systems that have been used to access applications in the workspace. One notable report in this section gives information on the number of times that users accessed external sites from any of the APEX applications, which can provide crucial data on how your APEX users interact with the world outside of your applications.

There is another very useful source of information about your APEX environment — the Application Express Views. A view is a collection of data that may span several tables, and the APEX Views are specifically used to give you easy access to pertinent information about your workspace, applications and components, regardless of where that information is stored within the Oracle database. There are more than 70 APEX views that come with the environment.

Try It Out   **APEX Application Views**

One of the many ways that APEX Views come in handy is to understand what database tables and columns are used in your workspace, application, page or region.

1. Click on the Utilities tab of the APEX development environment, and then on the APEX Views icon.

2. You are presented with a long list of views. You can either go to the second page of views or simply enter Db into the search box and click Go to access the APEX Application Page Db Items icon.

3. Click on the APEX Application Page Db Items icon to bring up the page shown in Figure 10-17.

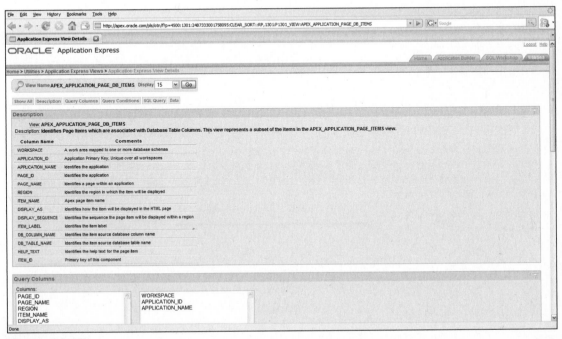

Figure 10-17

This page gives you some descriptive information in the top section, followed by list boxes you can use to select the columns from the view that you would like to see. The next section allows you to enter conditions for the query on the view, where you can limit the results to those for a smaller scope. The last two sections display the SQL query, which is actually used for the report and the data returned.

4. Add the DB_TABLE_NAME and DB_COLUMN_NAME columns to the right-hand list box, and click the Go button. Scroll down to the bottom of the page to see the results, as shown in Figure 10-18.

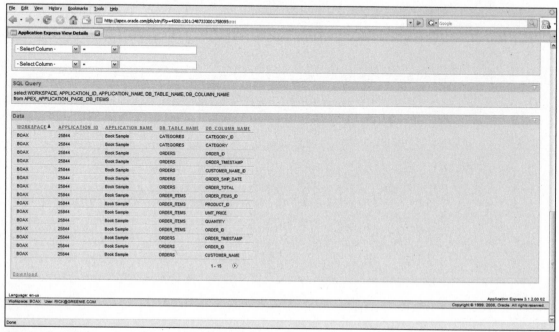

Figure 10-18

There, that's what you were looking for. You can click on the column headings to sort the data in the report by those column values.

The raw output of this report may not be exactly what you are looking for, but you can take the SQL query text listed in the page and use it in any standard Oracle tool, such as SQL Developer, which you will be learning about later in this book. You can modify the SQL any way that you like to shape the results to fit your exact needs.

Summary

Once your application is developed, you still have a number of tasks to perform. This chapter gave you an overview of some of those tasks, including:

❏ Understanding your deployment options

❏ Deploying an application

❏ Administrative roles in the APEX environment

❏ Administrative tools and utilities available

The next chapter will introduce you to the world of packaged applications, applications you can simply install and run in your APEX environment. As you might suspect, these applications will increase the value of your APEX world by delivering both functionality to your users and a source of examples for your future development efforts.

Packaged Applications

In the last chapter, you rounded out your understanding of the Oracle Application Express environment, learning how to administer the deployment of applications. This understanding may have started some thoughts in your head. Deployment of an application to another APEX environment seems pretty simple. Could you use your APEX instance to support multiple applications? Of course.

But the next question follows rapidly — are there existing applications that you could use to immediately install in your APEX instance? Once again, the answer is yes.

This chapter will focus on *packaged* applications, APEX applications that are available for you to use. The chapter will review the reasons as to why you would want to use packaged applications, provide a quick overview of some of the packaged applications currently available, and guide you through the capture and installation of a packaged application.

Packaged applications give you a way to increase the overall value of your APEX world, providing usable functionality for the cost of a free download.

The Benefits of Packaged Applications

Packaged applications deliver three main types of benefits:

- ❑ **Packaged applications deliver immediate value:** A packaged application includes everything you need to implement a particular strain of functionality. Whether that functionality is general, such as a Checkbox Manager, or specific, such as a bug-tracking system, you get it all when you load the application into your APEX instance. You and your users can immediately start to use this new functionality.

- ❑ **Packaged applications provide examples of APEX implementations:** Give a man a fish and he can feed himself for a day — teach a man to fish and he can feed himself for years. When you download and install a packaged application, you get access to all the objects and code used to implement the application. Grabbing packaged applications is a great way to learn how to implement functionality beyond the reach of this (or any) book. Since many of the packaged applications have been written by some of the top APEX practitioners in the world, you can use packaged apps to learn from the best.

❑ **Packaged applications provide a jumpstart for your own customized applications:** It is the way of the world that every particular organization is unique, with different needs and requirements. In fact, this fact of life creates work for all of us developers. The packaged application you acquire may provide most of the functionality your company demands, but certain aspects of the application need to be tweaked or enhanced. When you get a packaged application, the code and data structures are yours, so you can modify them in any way that you wish. This benefit of packaged applications is probably the most universal, so much so that you should make it a practice to consult the list of packaged applications before beginning any APEX project.

You can hopefully see how packaged applications can help to improve your APEX productivity. The next section describes where you can get APEX packaged applications and provides an overview of some of the currently available offerings.

Available Packaged Applications

You can go to a list of currently available packaged applications from your home for Oracle Application Express — `http://otn.oracle.com/apex`, the home page for APEX at the Oracle Technology Network, or from `http://apex.oracle.com`.

At the time of this writing, there are clusters of applications that deliver functionality grouped in the general areas of tracking and communications, as well as a number of applications that provide other types of functionality.

The tracking applications include:

❑ **Bug Tracker:** One of the most popular packaged applications. The Bug Tracker provides the ability to log and track bugs over their lifetimes, not that your applications would ever have any bugs. The application also includes a good range of reports to provide information on the status of bugs, as well as historical information on the performance of the bug fix team and its individual members, as shown in Figure 11-1.

❑ **Issue Tracker:** An application that allows users to define and track issues, as well as relate issues to specific projects. The Issue Tracker is the basis of an advanced APEX tutorial, which walks you through the creation of the application.

❑ **Customer Tracker:** A general contact manager style application, with companies, related contacts, and activities. You can also link contacts with companies, track customer-facing activities, and even add in links to relevant web pages for a customer. In Chapter 12, you will migrate a basic contact management system from Access — you might find it interesting to compare the results of that migration with this readily available packaged application.

❑ **Asset Manager:** An application that manages assets and provides an inventory history.

❑ **Task Manager:** An application where administrators define projects and users define tasks within those projects, assigned to either themselves or other users. Users can create a task from a list of standard tasks or create their own.

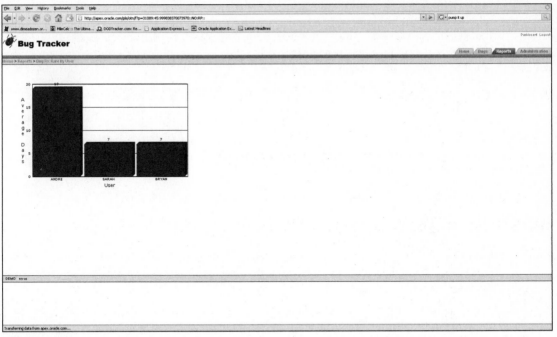

Figure 11-1

❑ **Software Projects:** A basic project tracker, oriented towards software projects. This application lets you manage software projects in terms of releases, tasks, and milestones within the projects. As with several other of these packaged apps, a version of this application is used inside Oracle — in this case by the Oracle Application Express development team.

❑ **Timesheets:** As its name implies, an application to track time across either a 5-day or 7-day week.

❑ **Artwork Catalog:** An application to manage image content, which includes the icons used in APEX itself.

❑ **Document Library:** An application that not only provides access to a set of shared documents but also allows users to add versions of a document, create tasks for themselves, and even create alerts for documents for proactive messages.

The applications which center on communications include:

❑ **Discussion Forum:** An application that implements a complete message board solution. The application includes a built-in email interface and text search features, based on the Oracle Text feature of the Oracle database.

❑ **Events:** An application which enables online registration for any number of events. Users can see and register for events, while administrators can specify emails to be sent to users who have registered.

❑ **Ask The Expert:** An application based on the site Ask Tom, where people can ask questions of well-known Oracle expert Tom Kite (http://ask.tom.com). The application uses the power of interMedia, an extension of the Oracle database that provides text search capabilities. In addition, the expert who is the target of this application can adjust parameters of the application, such as limiting how users communicate.

❑ **Aria Employee Directory Lookup:** An application used internally within Oracle that provides contact information for all global employees. The employees can modify information presented about themselves, as well as add an image for their profile, and includes Web 2.0 features, including the use of AJAX to implement partial page refreshes.

❑ **Subject Matter Experts:** Another application used by Oracle Corporation itself, this time to deliver a list of Oracle subject matter experts to the user community at large.

There are also a number of other miscellaneous applications, which include:

❑ **Checklist Manager:** One of the most popular utility applications offered. The Checklist Manager lets you create a checklist with any number of task columns. You can easily include indicators to show partial completion of tasks. Later in this chapter, you will install and use this application to see the type of functionality that a general-purpose application like this can provide for users.

❑ **Knowledge Testing:** An application which allows you to create tests on various topics. The application provides a user interface to these tests, which includes time tracking and history of results.

❑ **Loan Calculator:** A standard loan calculation application, complete with charts and reports to display loan schedules, as well as do "what if" analysis based on the payment amount for a loan. A good example of implementing a browser-based application with some significant calculation behind it.

❑ **Online Store:** An application that implements an online shopping cart. The application includes automatic registration for customers making their first purchase.

❑ **Sales Forecasting:** A basic forecasting system, which also includes the ability to define your own progression of steps to closing an opportunity, along with the corresponding probably of the sale for each step. The application also includes a set of reports to analyze the progress of opportunities.

All of these applications provide functionality you can put to immediate use, as well as provide examples of complete applications, including task lists on pages and attractive layouts, topics beyond the scope of this book.

Installing a Packaged Application

While scanning through the list of packaged applications described previously, your appetite to use one or more of these applications may have been whetted. You may be anxious to start using some of this free functionality. Wait no longer — in this section, you will download and install the Checklist Manager application and put it into immediate use.

1. Go to the packaged application section listed on the `http://apex.oracle.com` page.

2. Click on the Download link for the Checklist Manager, since you probably have a series of discrete tasks to perform, and this application can help you understand your workload and track your progress.

3. Save the ZIP file on your local hard drive, and then unzip the file into its own directory.

4. As you should with any installation, read the `checklist_readme` text file. This file contains instructions for loading the Checklist Manager application.

This application installs like any other Oracle Application Express application. You already performed this action in the previous chapter, when you deployed your application to another APEX environment. This time, you don't have to worry about building the package — the authors of this application already did this for you. You can simply perform the fairly simply load, as described in the text file.

1. Go to the home page of your APEX environment.

2. As you did in the last chapter, go to the home page of the APEX Application Builder and click Import.

3. In the next page, use the Browse button to navigate to the SQL file you unzipped from your downloaded Checklist Manager file and click Next. It may take a minute or two for APEX to import the script.

4. Once the script import is complete, you can click Next in the following page to install the application.

   The previous chapter details the import process, complete with screen shots of the relevant pages.

5. On the following page, select a schema to parse the new application, and leave the rest of the selections as defaults.

6. Click Install to begin the installation process.

7. Once the application is installed, you will be prompted as to whether you want to install the supporting objects for the application. Since this is the first time you will be installing this application, you should click Next on this page and then Install on the following page.

This final step will not take long at all. Once you have completed the installation of the supporting objects, you are given the standard option to run or edit your application.

8. Click on Run Application to bring up the page shown in Figure 11-2.

Figure 11-2

The page shown above has the advantage of looking like an APEX application, which means that your users will already know, for the most part, how to use the application.

1. Click on the Application Go Live checklist to bring up the page shown in Figure 11-3.

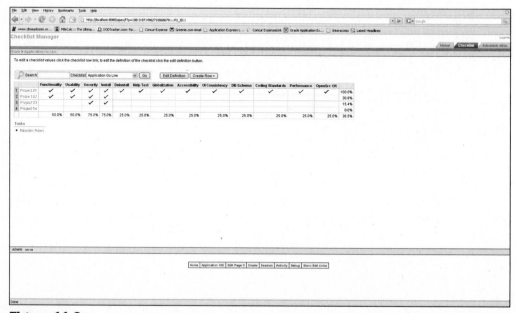

Figure 11-3

2. Once again, the checklist shown uses common APEX features. A user can simply click on the project name to go to the Edit page for the checklist, which is shown in Figure 11-4. Notice that the page has a collapsible section at the bottom that can display the definitions of the columns, providing online help for the user.

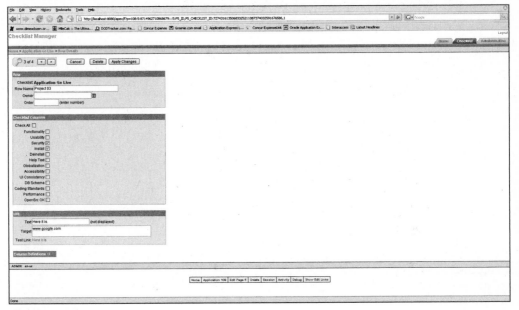

Figure 11-4

3. You can also see that the checklist page gives a user the ability to edit the definitions for the checklist. You could explore that option now, but you will see similar options when you create your own checklist, the next action in this section.

4. Return to the main page of the Checklist Manager by clicking on the Home tab.

5. Click Create Checklist, which will bring up the page shown in Figure 11-5, in its complete form.

6. You can create a rather simple checklist that you can use to track your progress as you read this book.

   Wish you had this when you started reading, right? Well, at least now you can use it for the next computer tutorial you read.

7. Give the checklist a name of Book progress and an appropriate description. Select Icons as the completion type.

8. Add Checklist columns of Read chapter, Do exercises, Play with application, and Clean up. Add a text column of Chapter Topic.

9. Click Create Checklist to put your definition into action. When you arrive back at the home page for the application, double-click on your new checklist to bring up your empty checklist. Click Create Row to add a row to the checklist for Chapter 2, as shown in Figure 11-6.

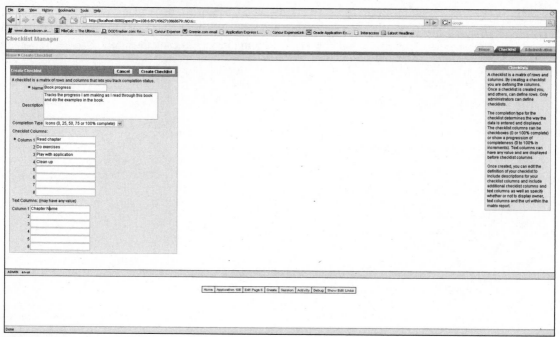

Figure 11-5

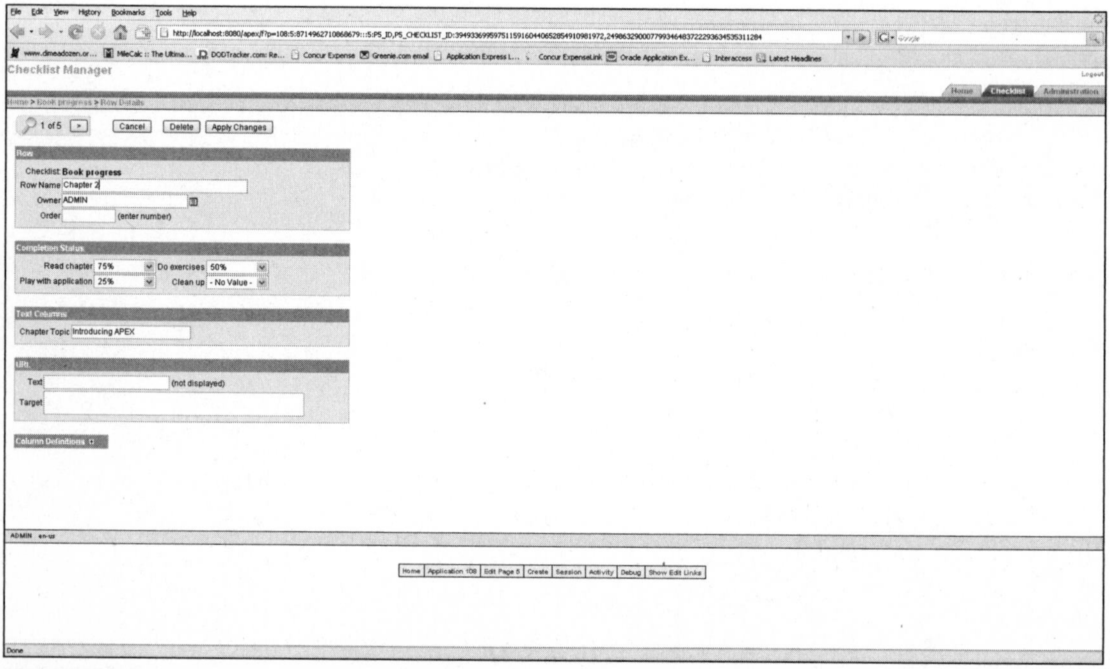

Figure 11-6

10. As you would have hoped, this page lets you name the row, in this case Chapter 2 and give a completion status for each column you defined. The choice of Icons in your checklist definition allows a user to define percentage values for their completion, which will display graphically, as you will see in a minute.

11. To see the graphics at work, select different percentages for each column and click Create to return to the main page for this checklist.

Figure 11-7 shows the checklist with a few more rows added. You can see that there are automatic totals for progress for each task and chapter. You can also see that a user could choose to reorder the rows to suit their needs. In this particular case, there was no need to give the rows an order indicator, since the natural sorting of values would place them in the correct order. However, a user could specifically order the rows with the Reorder Rows task at the bottom of the page.

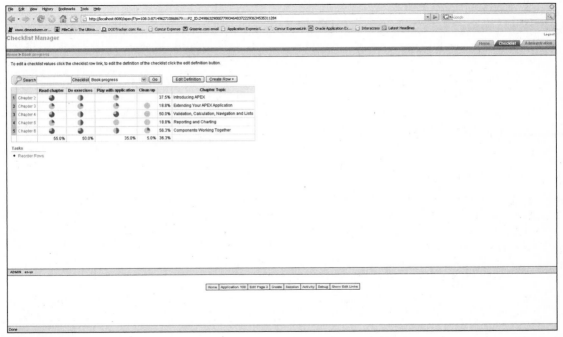

Figure 11-7

This Checklist Manager also provides administrative capabilities in the appropriately named tab. You can define administrators for the application, which will limit access to this tab to those users specifically defined — if you do not define any administrators, the Checklist Manager assumes that all users have administrative privileges. You can also export an individual checklist, to share with other APEX installations, or delete either of the two sample checklists included with the application.

Of course, you can also modify any packaged application you download from the site. The web site for this book has an example of modifying the Checklist Manager application at: www.wrox.com.

Using Sample Code

You have just seen how easy it is to import a packaged application and begin using its capabilities immediately. Once you download a packaged application, the application is entirely yours. You can limit or expand its functionality as you see fit.

You can use the code samples available on the page in the same way. The only real difference is that these samples are not complete in and of themselves. You can take the smaller chunks of functionality offered by these samples and integrate them into your applications, or simply grab the samples to get an insight into using a particular technique.

The code samples offered include:

❑ **Matrix Order Demo:** Which demonstrates how to implement a wizard-type interface to the order entry process.

❑ **Shuttle Demo:** Which demonstrates how to use two multiselect list boxes together, including user interface objects to move selections from one list box to the other. This sample code also allows you to specify that items are copied, rather than moved, and to turn sorting on and off.

❑ **Sticky Hide and Show:** You have already seen that one of the APEX themes includes hide and show regions, which users can expand and contract as they wish. This sample code makes it possible to save the state of a hide and show region, so the region will be in the same state as when the user last used the page. The code sample implements this capability using AJAX and APEX Collections.

❑ **Master-Detail PDF Report:** Includes a sample module for publishing a PDF which displays master-detail data.

❑ **Web Services Integration:** Contains code samples for integrating standard Web Services with your APEX application, including Amazon Store, Google Maps, and PayPal Payments Pro.

Summary

This chapter has given you a path to improved productivity — through simply downloading and using packaged applications and sample code.

You learned that both of these areas offer several benefits.

❑ You can add functionality with a simple import.

❑ You can learn tips and techniques on using APEX to address your issues through the examples in the applications and code.

❑ You can get a head start on your own development work with packaged applications and the modules in the code samples.

Through the standard device of exporting and importing applications and modules, you can quickly add plenty of power to your own APEX environment, which, in turn, makes the environment more valuable. You may reach the point where you want to start bringing some of your older, creaky applications into the APEX fold — a migration that is the subject of the closing chapter of this book.

Migration

You've come a long way in the course of this book. A handful of chapters ago, you were first introduced to Oracle Application Express. Now you have created a full-featured application, learned how to deploy that application and manage the APEX environment, and seen some of the packaged applications you can use for immediate results with APEX.

At this point, you may be looking at APEX as the destination for your new application development work, but this decision also has a hidden component — what are you going to do about your existing applications on other platforms, such as Access?

This chapter will discuss the migration task ahead of you, including the advantages of migrating your Access applications, as well as giving you the opportunity to explore the process you will use for a migration.

Why Migrate?

It's always good (although not required) to understand why you would want to do something before you leap into the task itself.

There are three broad areas where APEX has advantages over Access: administrator productivity, developer productivity, and the inherent strength of the Oracle stack versus Access.

Administrator Productivity

The first main area of APEX advantages is improved administrator productivity. As a developer, you may not necessarily give a lot of thought to the time and resources required to handle the administrative tasks necessary to support your applications and, more importantly, the data they use.

But you should remember that the source of value in information systems is, well, the information they store and present. This information stems from the underlying data and is shaped by the applications and reports you create. Lose your data, and you also lose all its stored value.

Administrators safeguard this value with maintenance and protection. Your data and applications must be regularly backed up, and those backups must be occasionally tested to insure that the backup routines are working properly. The larger the amount of data, the more value it represents, the more protection it needs, and the longer those tasks take. If you could combine the data from multiple applications into a single Oracle database, the backup procedures for all that data could be handled in a single job, and Oracle backup routines are optimized for large amounts of data. These two advantages mean that your administrators will have fewer tasks to perform, with those tasks completing faster.

If an Access application produces some real value, that value may result in the application becoming popular and being required to handle more and more data. At some point (a not too distant point), this very success will run right into the overall limitations for data storage in Access. This scenario could result in multiple instances of Access, with the related administrative task to somehow combine data across those instances.

Your data and applications have to have proper security controls, and these security settings must be implemented and maintained for all users. If users are working with several different Access databases, the security procedures will have to be repeated for all of these databases. And Access databases are stored as simple files, making them easy to copy by malicious individuals.

This usage of multiple Access applications, typical in many organizations, leads to one of the most problematic aspects of administering an Access application. One of the virtues of Access is that there is an easy ramp to using the product for applications and data storage. But this virtue can turn into a curse, as Access applications proliferate throughout an organization. Each application needs its own care, so the administrative burden rapidly multiplies. Given the reality that new instances of Access are often installed without the knowledge of the administrators, the administrators themselves may not even be aware of basic information such as the owner, file location, and the like, which will often leave the given Access application completely vulnerable.

Access applications often start out as small applications to meet some business requirement that the corporate IT applications were not addressing. This often involves copying sensitive data around the organization. This presents two profound issues. First, when sensitive information is moved around the organization without any proper controls, it is exceedingly difficult to identify the single source of truth. Second, these small applications often grow in importance to the point where they become mission critical, and the cost to the organization of losing data, or having it compromised, rises accordingly.

With APEX, you can have hundreds of schemas in a single Oracle database, and dramatically cut the number of administrative tasks required to support the environment, while still increasing its security, scalability, and reliability. In addition to this practical reduction in administrative overhead, this approach addresses the reality of dealing with multiple departments within large corporate IT environments. Corporate IT may have been reluctant to take on the burden of supporting such a large number of Access applications. However, corporate IT is often already performing maintenance and administration on their enterprise Oracle databases. Adding another Oracle instance into their overall procedures is typically not a big issue, but shifting the load will not only free up time of developers and local administrators but also improve the regularity with which necessary operations are performed.

Developer Productivity

Oracle Application Express, as you have seen in this book, offers a highly productive environment for creating applications. Access also offers some good tools, which you may be familiar with.

Oracle Application Express, however, like all Oracle products, was designed for all development organizations, from large to small. Even though APEX gives you the sort of personal development power you would expect, the APEX development environment is capable of supporting larger efforts.

You have already seen how you can share components across applications in a workspace, as well as the ability to export components and applications across workspaces. APEX reports include the ability to track changes made to your applications over time, by application, component and developer, which is vitally important when you are creating applications that will grow and evolve over their useful life.

Finally, Oracle Application Express applications can be exported as simple script files, files, which can be used with almost any version control system to manage and compare different versions of an application. These tools are designed to increase the efficiency and reliability of an ongoing development effort, which is exactly the sort of process that your most valuable applications will be continually undergoing.

APEX combines the best of both development worlds: personal productivity and enterprise strength features to allow larger development efforts to proceed efficiently.

Advantages of Oracle Stack

Probably the most compelling advantage of Oracle Application Express versus Access is the enterprise power of the Oracle stack.

Scalability and Performance

Although Oracle APEX is a powerful development and deployment tool, the tool is built using standard Oracle technologies, such as PL/SQL. Because of this basic fact, APEX is extremely robust and proven in enterprise scenarios.

Microsoft Access, unfortunately, comes with some inherent limitations in terms of scalability. Access includes significant limitations in terms of database size (2 GBs) and number of users (255). The Oracle database can support thousands of users and many terabytes (1,024 GBs) of data, with hundreds of customers using these high-demand production environments.

But even this comparison doesn't completely illustrate the vast differences in scalability and performance that come from the internal implementations of Access and Oracle APEX. You may have noticed that Access has trouble supporting a lot of users who are trying to update the database at the same time. Early versions of Access only supported page-level locking, where a page of data, typically containing multiple rows, was locked during write operations to protect data integrity. This broad locking introduced a great deal of contention, meaning that users inserting or updating data would have to wait until other users were finished with their write operations.

With version 4.0 of the Jet engine, the database engine underlying Access, Microsoft introduced record locking, which lessens the performance impact of contention while increasing overall resource usage, leading to reduced performance, albeit for a different reason.

The source of these locking issues is easy to understand, since Access is primarily designed to be a desktop tool for individual users. The Oracle stack, on the other hand, was designed from the beginning to support very large user communities. The Oracle database has included the most advanced locking implementation for more than 20 years. Oracle's locking strategy is implemented on individual rows. However, there is no increase in resource usage, since a feature known as Multi-Version Read Consistency (MVRC) allows Oracle to ensure data integrity without placing a lot of locks on the database.

MVRC is one of the great strengths of the Oracle database, but it is totally transparent to users and developers. You don't have to do anything to reap the performance benefits of MVRC; it just works, providing much greater performance and scalability.

Finally, the Oracle stack can not only scale up but also down. The Oracle database comes with a variety of licenses, ranging from the free developer version available for downloading from `http://otn.oracle.com` to the largest database implementations in the world. The Oracle stack can happily exist in the same limited environments as Microsoft Access, while still offering much more room for growth.

Advanced Features

The Oracle technology stack also boasts an incredibly wide range of advanced features to allow you to grow your systems and multiply the business value they produce.

There are far too many features to discuss individually, but a few areas stand out. The Oracle database gives you access to a host of features designed to support advanced analytics and data warehousing. These features include:

❑ Built-in analytic functions, which can produce sophisticated calculations with SQL syntax.

❑ Materialized views, which deliver precalculated summaries to dramatically speed up SQL statements that include aggregate values, without any change in the SQL.

❑ Additional index types, such as bitmapped indexes, which provide high performance in data warehouse environments.

❑ Tools to make building a data warehouse easy, like the Warehouse Builder, included with every edition of the Oracle database.

Oracle databases also include the ability to handle many different types of multimedia storage. You already got a taste of this capability when you used graphics in your APEX application, but Oracle can go far beyond this simple use to support large and complex files and provide the functionality needed to manipulate them.

Finally, the Oracle database can include a capability called Real Application Clusters, near and dear to this author's heart, since he helped to market this feature when it was first introduced. Real Application Clusters, commonly referred to as RAC, deliver the twin benefits of transparent scalability and high availability with the same solution. You can simply add more low-end servers into a RAC cluster to increase the overall scalability of your Oracle database, while increasing the availability at the same time.

Although not all of these features are available with all versions of the Oracle database, you can rest assured that you can grow into these areas as the demands of your users increase — something completely unavailable to users of desktop databases such as Access.

Open Platform

Last, but certainly not least, is the ability of the Oracle stack to run on virtually any platform. Access is, of course, limited to use on Microsoft platforms. In the past, this limitation did not seem like much of a problem, since Microsoft operating systems were virtually ubiquitous on the client side.

Today's world of IT infrastructure has evolved. Linux has become an inexpensive option for enterprise-strength server operating systems, on-demand computing is eliminating the requirement for a Windows-based client operating system, and even the Mac is making a bit of a comeback. With Access, Microsoft technology is a prerequisite, which may lock you out of these other conditions.

The Oracle database runs on all popular server operating systems, and APEX applications are both developed and run from a browser, making the entire stack completely open and transportable. With the Oracle stack, your choice of operating environments, on both the server and the client, is completely open, a sharp contrast with Microsoft Access.

Single Environment

All of the reasons mentioned above are valid starting points for considering application migration, but the most important one has not yet been stated. Supporting one environment for custom application development is a more efficient approach than supporting two environments.

If you see the advantages of using Oracle Application Express for your new application development, you will probably want to consider a plan for transitioning from your current environment to APEX. Some of that plan will involve creating new applications to replace older ones. However, a fair amount of work has gone into some of your existing applications, so you could reduce the overall cost and effort and make the transition smoother by migrating applications from your current environment to APEX. The process of migration is the subject of the next section.

Migrating Your Applications

With that brief overview of the reasons behind migration, it's time to jump into the migration process itself.

This chapter will focus on migration of Microsoft Access databases and applications, for three reasons. First, Access is one of the most popular database application development tools in the world, and yet it still has some limitations in terms of scalability and robustness that might prompt users to look for alternatives. The second reason is that Access combines both a database and an application development and deployment environment, much like the combination of Oracle APEX and the Oracle database. The third reason is that Oracle has provided a pretty rich set of tools specifically aimed at migrating Access applications to the APEX stack.

However, the steps and tools used for this migration could also be employed for moving data structures and data from other databases. Your methods might differ from other databases, such as targeting moving the data structures and data and developing applications quickly from scratch with APEX, rather than migrating applications themselves.

The remainder of this chapter will focus on presenting a high-level overview of the process of migrating a typical Microsoft Access application. You can get more details on migration from Access in general in an excellent paper on migration on the Apex web site, as well as the chapter on migration in the *Oracle Application Express Application Migration Guide*, available on the Apex site.

Migration Stages

Migrating an Access application to the Oracle Application Express environment consists of three basic stages:

❑   You have to get the data structures and data from your Access database into your Oracle database.

❑   You have to move your Access application components to your Oracle Application Express environment.

❑   You can then customize and supplement your application components.

Oracle has tools to help you through each of these three stages. SQL Developer, which you have heard about earlier in this book, can help you to migrate your data from an Access database, as well as many other types of relational databases.

With Oracle Application Express, you create migration projects. The Migration Wizard will convert those Access components to the corresponding APEX components, as well as flagging those Access components that cannot be automatically converted.

The entire process is highly automated, making your migration experience straightforward and simple. Between SQL Developer and APEX, the majority of your Access data and objects are automatically replicated into a scalable, robust APEX application.

You should always keep in mind, however, that any migration will, at best, bring over your existing application and data structures. You may decide that a migration is an ideal time for a rethinking and redesign of your application. For instance, you might want to redesign your data structures for more efficient and flexible data access, and then simply create an APEX application on top of your enhanced structure.

Your Migration Tasks

The previous section described the stages in a migration effort. For the remainder of this chapter, you will migrate an actual Access application to an APEX environment.

Your effort will involve seven steps:

1.   Export Access metadata.

2.   Migrate the Access database to Oracle Database. You will use SQL Developer to create the database structures in your target Oracle database.

3.   Create an Oracle Application Express workspace.

4.   Create a migration project.

5.   Review your recovered objects.

6.   Generate the Oracle Application Express application.

7.   Customize your Oracle Application Express application.

As noted previously, you will have to create a new workspace for your migration. The exercises in this chapter assume that you will be migrating the Access application to an APEX environment running on a local instance of Oracle, rather than the hosted version you used in earlier chapters.

Prerequisites

SQL Developer has been mentioned several times in this book, and you will use this tool to help to migrate your Access data and application components.

This chapter will assume that you have SQL Developer, version 1.5 or later, installed in your environment. You can get SQL Developer from the Oracle Migration Technology Center on the Oracle Technology Network (OTN), located at www.oracle.com/technology/tech/migration/index.html at the time of this writing.

The first time you run SQL Developer after installation, you may be prompted for the appropriate Java runtime before SQL Developer starts up. You should select the runtime that came with the SQL Developer install.

When you initially bring up SQL Developer, you will be presented with a page like Figure 12-1.

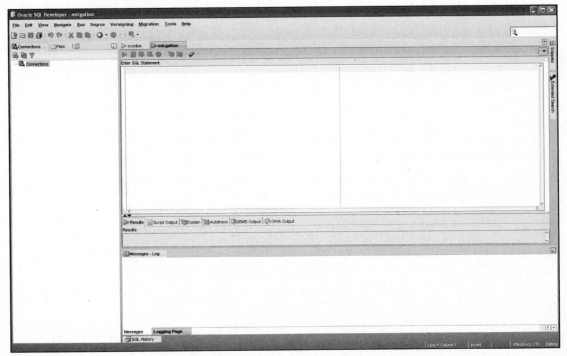

Figure 12-1

1. Once you start SQL Developer, create a connection to the target Oracle database by right-clicking on the Connections entry in the left hand navigator panel and select New Connection. The connection definition panel is shown, in its completed state, in Figure 12-2. Use the SYS user

connecting as SYSDBA, as shown in the figure. Click Connect to use this connection for the database, which will also save the connection.

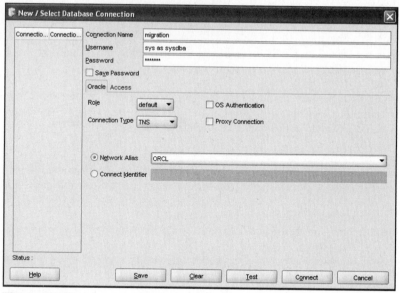

Figure 12-2

You can expand the connection shown in the left-hand panel to see the listing of all the available schemas and entities.

2. You will need a user who will be used to perform the migration. Right-click on the Other Users choice, and select Create User to create a user named MIGRATION.

3. Once the user is created, right-click on the user, and select the Edit menu to give the user the proper privileges. Click on the Roles tab, and grant the user the RESOURCE role. Click on the System Privileges tab, and grant the user CREATE SESSION, CREATE VIEW and CREATE USER privileges. Click Apply.

4. Create a connection for the MIGRATION user, save it, and connect to the database with this user.

5. For now, you will have to create a migration repository. Click on Migration in the main toolbar, and then Repository Management and New Repository. Select the current connection as the destination of the repository, and click Create.

6. Once the repository has been created, you will see two new panes in the left-hand panel, Captured Models and Converted Models, as shown in Figure 12-3.

You have properly prepared your Oracle database to handle the conversion of the Access application. You only have to perform these startup tasks once, since your migration repository can hold many different migration models.

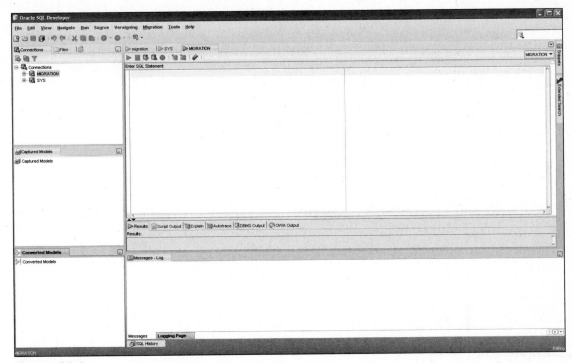

Figure 12-3

Export Access Metadata

The first task of your migration effort is to export metadata from your Access application. This metadata describes the data structures and application components that make up the Access application.

You accomplish this export process with the Microsoft Access Exporter, an Access application supplied by Oracle. The easiest way to get this tool is through the Migration menu in SQL Developer, but you can also get the program from a task listed in the migration process in Oracle Application Express, which you will be using shortly.

This output from the export process creates two files — an XML file that includes the metadata describing the Access database objects, and an SQL file that contains the metadata for the application components. For the purposes of this example, the Access metadata has already been exported, and the two files are available at the web site for this book, which is under www.wrox.com.

Migrate the Access Metadata and Data

With the XML and SQL files that were the product of the Microsoft Access Exporter, you are now ready to start the process of replicating your Access application in Oracle APEX.

1. Return to SQL Developer and connect with the connection you previously created.

2. Click on Capture Microsoft Access Exported XML. In the dialog box that appears, use the Browse button to locate the XML file that contains the metadata for the data objects from the Access database. For this sample migration, the file is named `contact.xml`.

3. Click OK, which will begin the import process.

As the import progresses, the Messages Log in the lower panel will be filled with messages indicating the progress of the import. The import process will proceed quickly, with a list of object types appearing in the message table as the process proceeds.

Once the process is complete, SQL Developer will put an entry into the Captured Models pane of the left-hand panel, as shown in Figure 12-4.

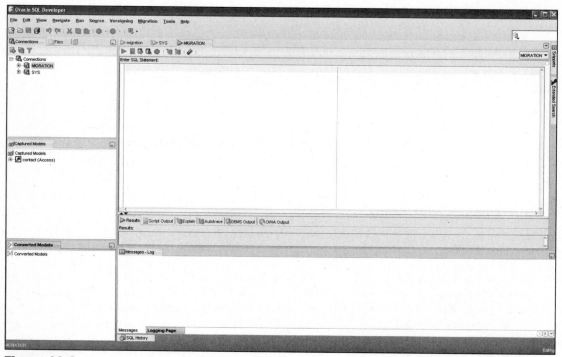

Figure 12-4

The previous step collected the metadata about the Access data structures and created a captured model. Your next step is to convert that model into a set of Oracle structures.

4. Right-click on the captured model and select Convert to Oracle Model. You will get a dialog box with a set of basic conversion rules. You could edit the existing mapping rules or add your own, but for this first migration exercise, you can simply use the defaults. Click Apply to begin the conversion process.

5. When the conversion process completes, click Close in the dialog box.

You can see that there is now a converted model shown in the lowest pane in the right-hand panel. You could expand the model to show the objects contained within the model, such as the tables, shown in Figure 12-5.

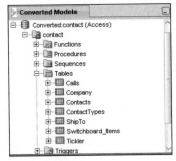

Figure 12-5

Your next step is to generate SQL scripts to create these objects in their own schema.

6. Right-click on the converted model contact, and select Generate. This choice will generate an SQL script, which will appear in the main window of SQL Developer, as shown in Figure 12-6.

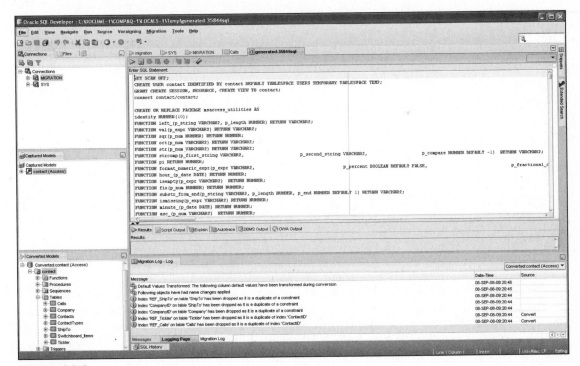

Figure 12-6

The script that was generated contains the Data Definition Language (DDL) to recreate the Access data structures in your Oracle database. As you can see at the top of the script, the tables and associated object will be created in a schema for the user CONTACT, with a password of CONTACT.

Of course, you could edit the generated script, to either change the destination for the Access data structures or any other aspect of the object generation. For the purposes of this chapter, you can leave the script as it is.

1. At the top of the script window, you can see a set of eight icons, with some greyed out. Click on the second icon, a green arrow over a page icon, to run the script.

2. You will be prompted for a connection to use to run the script. Select the connection you create for the SYS as SYSDBA user, since that user has the privileges required to run the DDL script.

3. Click OK after selecting the user, and then enter the password for the user.

The script should run successfully — you will be able to tell the script has completed when the time required for the script appears at the end of the line of icons, as shown in Figure 12-7.

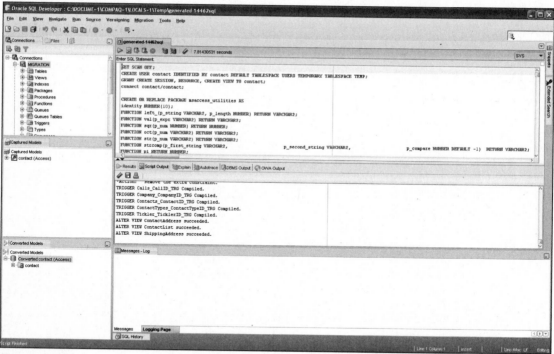

Figure 12-7

This figure also shows the Script Output pane below the DDL script window. In Figure 12-6, you could only see the tabs for this pane. The pane has been enlarged to display the feedback returned from your Oracle database as a result of the script.

1. You have now created the CONTACT user, with a password of CONTACT, and the Access database tables and related objects within the schema for that user. You can see this result by going to the navigation panel, clicking on Other Users for connection SYS, and then expanding the CONTACT user and the Tables underneath that user, as shown in Figure 12-8.

You may have to refresh the Other Users under the SYS connection.

Figure 12-8

You last task in this step of the migration process is to load the data that was exported from the Access tables into their new home in your Oracle database.

You will use SQL Developer again for this task, first creating a connection to the Access database for the application you are migrating.

2. In SQL Developer, right-click on the Connections heading in the left-hand navigation panel to define a new connection. Click on the tab in the center of the dialog box to change the connection type from Oracle to Access and define a connection to the Access database, as shown in Figure 12-9.

3. Connect to the contact.mdb database, which is available at www.wrox.com. Click Save to save the connection and Cancel to leave the connection definition dialog.

4. Go to the Migration choice on the SQL Developer menu, and select the Migrate Data choice. You will get a dialog box where you must select the Source Connection, the Access database connection you just defined, the Target Connection, which should be the SYS connection, and the Converted Model, which will be the Converted contact (Access) model. Click OK to migrate the data.

5. When this task has completed, click Close in the dialog box and click on any of the tables for the CONTACT user. Click on the Data tab in the main panel to show you that your data has migrated successfully, as shown in Figure 12-10.

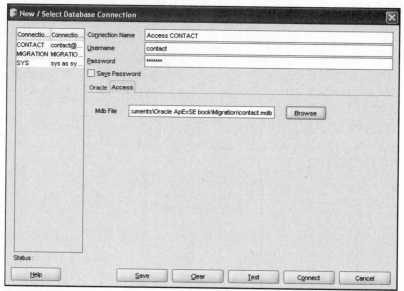

Figure 12-9

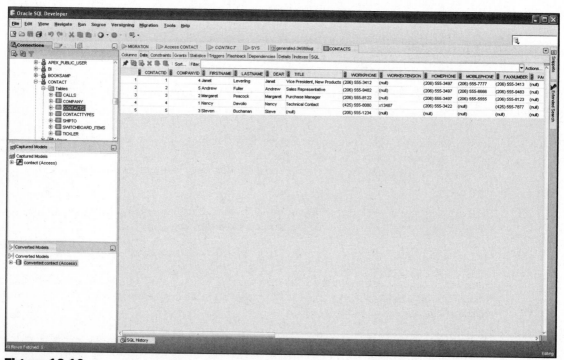

Figure 12-10

You have now migrated the data structures and the data from the Access database to your Oracle database. Now back to APEX to migrate the application.

Create an Oracle Application Express Workspace

You will be using Oracle Application Express to complete the remainder of the Access migration. The next step in the migration process is to create a workspace to hold the new application.

1. Go to the APEX Administration interface for your Oracle installation. You can reach this application through the URL of `http://instance:port/apex/apex_admin`, as described in Chapter 10.

2. Log in as a user with administrative privileges for the APEX instance.

3. Use the cascading menus from the Manage Workspaces icon to create a new workspace.

4. Give the new workspace a name, such as `ContactAccess`, and a relevant description. Click Next.

5. Select Yes at the Re-use an existing schema? prompt, and then select the `CONTACT` schema you just created with the Access data structures and data. Click Next.

6. Give the `ADMIN` user for this new workspace a password, a first and last name, and an email address, and click Next.

7. On the final page, click Create to create the new workspace, and then Done.

With this bit of housekeeping complete, you can move on to the real task of migration.

Create a Migration Project

Oracle APEX comes with a Migration Assistant to help you move the forms and reports of your Access application. This migration process will convert the majority of your Access objects into corresponding components in APEX.

1. Go to your APEX environment and log in to the workspace you just created, as the administrative user.

2. On the left-hand side of the main page of the environment, click on Application Migrations in the Migrations section of the tasks.

3. The main page for migrations will not show any migration projects, since none have been created. Click Create Project to bring up the page shown in Figure 12-11.

4. Give your migration project a name, and choose Access as the Type. The Description of the project is optional, but you should enter some appropriate text.

5. Use the Browse button to select the .SQL file you downloaded from the web site for this book, or any .SQL file created by the Exporter Tool.

Notice that you can download the Exporter Tool with the task listed on this page.

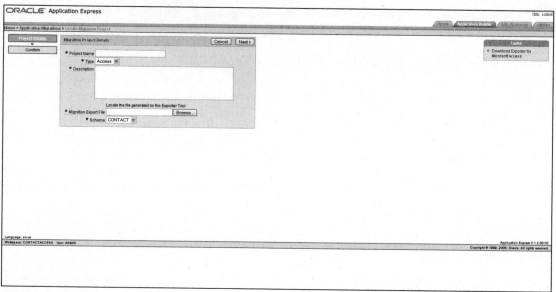

Figure 12-11

6. Click Next to bring up the confirmation page and then Finish to perform the actual migration.

The migration process may take a few minutes, depending on the complexity of the application you are trying to migrate and the speed of your environment. When the migration completes, APEX will display a page similar to Figure 12-12.

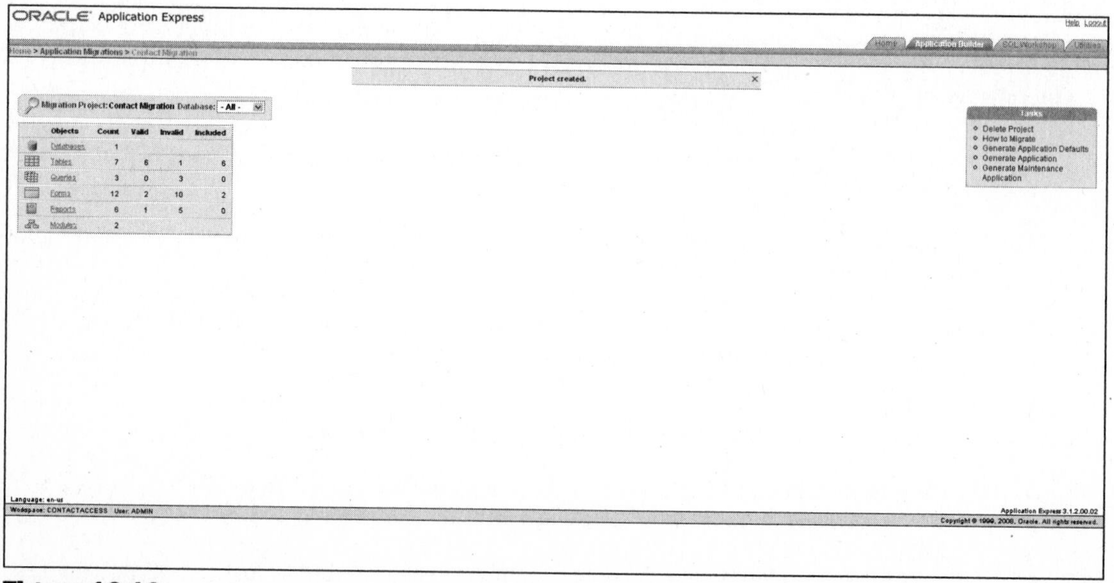

Figure 12-12

Review and Correct Your Recovered Objects

The results shown in Figure 12-12 contain quite a bit of information. You can see that the applications definitions loaded properly, but also note that not all of the Tables, Queries, Forms, and Reports were created as valid APEX objects.

You should revel in the good news — many of the objects did convert successfully — and then start to explore the issues with some of the invalid objects. As you will see, many of the problems are quite minor and easily fixed.

1. Click on the `Tables` link in the Migration Project summary. On the resulting page, shown in Figure 12-13, you can see that the `Tickler` table did not convert successfully. You can also quickly identify the reason for the problem — the table has no primary key, which is not only a best practice, but a requirement for tables used for APEX applications.

2. Click on the link for the `TICKLER` table. The next page gives you a summary of the table information and includes a link in the Tasks box on the right-hand side labeled Create Primary Key. Click on this link.

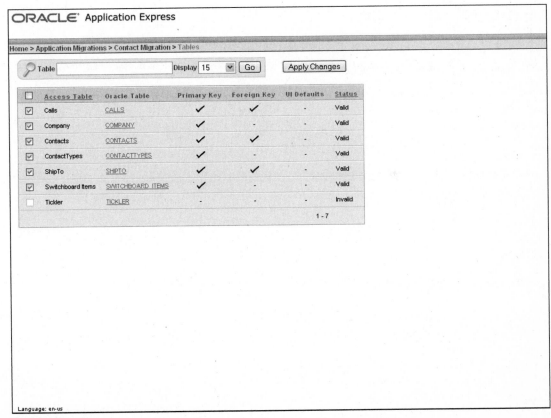

Figure 12-13

3. On the next page, select the TICKLERID column as the primary key and click Next. Click Finish to complete the creation of the key.

4. Once the key has been created, click on the breadcrumb for the migration project. You can see in the new summary that all seven tables are now valid. However, only six are included.

5. Click on the Tables link in the summary. Select the check box in front of the TICKLER table and then click Apply Changes to add the newly valid table to your migration project.

Your next step is to take a look at the invalid Queries for the project.

1. Click on the Queries link to bring up a list of the Access queries in the migration project. Click on the CONTACTADDRESS query to bring up the page shown in Figure 12-14.

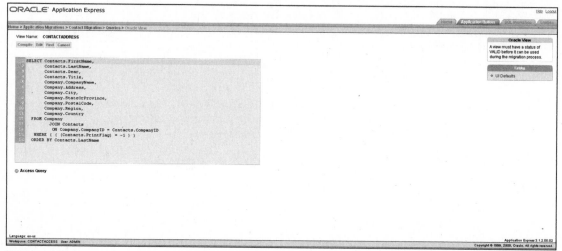

Figure 12-14

2. Click on the Compile button at the top of the page. Lo and behold, the query compiles successfully.

3. Click on the Queries breadcrumb to return to the summary page for the queries in the migration. You can see that the ContactAddress Access query is now valid.

4. Perform the same steps for the other two queries — they will compile as valid also. On your last trip to the Queries summary page, select the check box for all three queries, and click Apply Changes.

Now, that was easy. Time to move on to the forms, which will present a bit more of a challenge.

1. Click on the Forms link in the migration summary page to bring up the page shown in Figure 12-15.

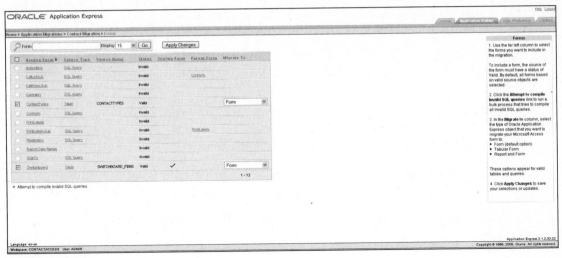

Figure 12-15

You can see quite a few forms, based on a number of different sources.

2. Click on the SQL Query link for CallListSub. On the next page, click Validate for the same pleasant surprise you have already experienced — the query is valid.

3. Click on the migration breadcrumb to go to the summary table, which now lists three forms as valid.

4. Follow the same process with CallNotesSub, Contacts, and ShipTo queries.

So far, so good — half the forms have been easily converted. You can get a couple more forms into shape with a simple change in their SQL.

5. Click on the SQL Query link for the Company form. For this query, the SQL syntax is:

```
SELECT Company.* FROM Company WHERE (((Company.CompanyID)=[forms]![Contacts]!
[cboCompany]));
```

You can probably spot the problem immediately — that function's WHERE clause. The WHERE clause you see is how Access does some of its joins, and it is easy to fix.

6. Click on Edit to modify the SQL Query, and edit the query to read:

```
SELECT Company.* FROM Company, Contacts WHERE Company.CompanyID = Contacts.CompanyID;
```

You simply added the Contacts table as one of the target tables and rewrote the WHERE clause to properly describe the join condition.

7. Click Validate for the new query, and another issue bites the dust.

8. Perform the same type of transformation on the SQL query for `ActionItems` to produce the following SQL:

```
SELECT Tickler.TicklerID, Tickler.ContactID, Tickler.TicklerDate,
Tickler.TicklerText FROM Tickler, Contacts WHERE Tickler.ContactID =
Contacts.ContactID;
```

9. Click Validate for this query, and then return to the listing of the Forms.

The last repair job for forms will address the issue in the `Reminders` SQL query.

10. Click on the SQL query for the Reminders form. Click Validate to see that the statement is not valid.

The interface to the query here is a bit concise, so you might have a bit of trouble seeing what the real problem is.

11. Copy the SQL statement, and click on the SQL Workshop tab. Click on the SQL Commands icon, and paste the statement into the command window.

Ah, there's the problem. Looks like Access uses a nonstandard implementation of the `Length` function.

12. Edit the query to read as follows:

```
SELECT Tickler.TicklerDate, Tickler.TicklerText, Contacts.LastName, Contacts
.FirstName, Company.CompanyName FROM (Company RIGHT JOIN Contacts ON Company
.CompanyID = Contacts.CompanyID) INNER JOIN Tickler ON Contacts.ContactID =
Tickler.ContactID WHERE (Length(ticklertext)>0) ORDER BY Tickler.TicklerDate,
Contacts.LastName, Contacts.FirstName;
```

The change you made was fairly simple — you only changed the specification for what was the `Len` function to the proper implementation of the `Length` function.

13. Copy the SQL and use the `Back` button in your browser to return to the page for the `Reminders SQL Query`, which is now blank. Click the Edit button and paste in your SQL code, and then click Validate.

14. With this correction, you have fixed enough of the forms for the purpose of this migration. Return to the Forms summary page, select all valid forms for inclusion, and then click Apply Changes.

Your last task is to take care of the Reports. As shown initially in Figure 12-12, most of the reports were not valid, but when you click on the link from the migration summary page, you can see that three of the reports are now valid, but not included. The newly valid reports became valid when you fixed the problems with the SQL Queries upon which the reports were based.

You can fix one more query problem with a little syntax problem.

1. Return to the migration summary and click on the `Reports` link.

2. Click on the SQL Query link for ActionItems.

3. In the SQL for the query, you can see the keyword DISTINCTROW, which is not a part of Oracle syntax. Click Edit, and change that word to DISTINCT.

4. Click Validate to confirm that you fixed the problem, and then return to the Reports summary page.

5. Return to the Queries page for a final time, select the four valid Reports, and click Apply Changes.

For now, you can simply leave the other reports as invalid.

Before you take the final step of creating an application, you should take a look at one more outcome of the migration process.

6. On the migration summary page, click on Modules. The page that appears lists all the Visual Basic code that was a part of the Access application.

7. Click on basContactHelpFunction to bring up the page shown in Figure 12-16.

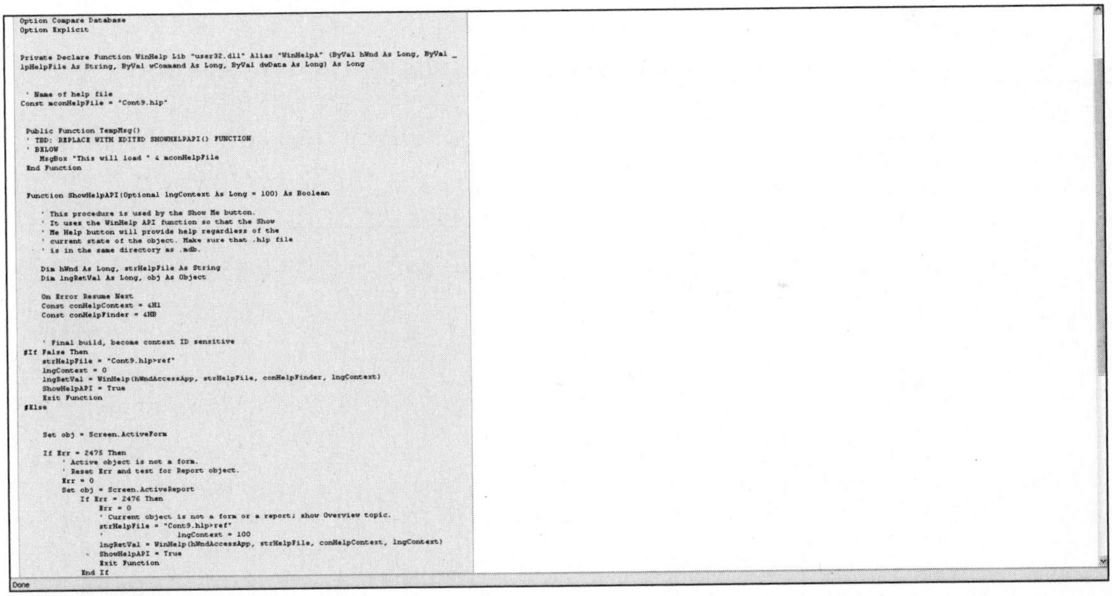

Figure 12-16

The listing is for a function that was created with Visual Basic to allow the Access application to use the Windows Help subsystem. You will not need this function in your application. The Access Migration Workshop does not convert any Visual Basic code, but the Modules section of the migration summary does point you towards functionality you may have to implement in another way in your APEX application. It's also handy to have this code within your new APEX environment, so you do not have to go back to the original Access application to see it.

You have completed your examination and the repair work on the converted Access code. The next step is to generate an APEX application based on these Access components.

Generate the Oracle Application Express Application

You have made most of the Access components valid, so you can move to the final step of your migration, generating the APEX application.

If you look at the Tasks list on the right-hand side of the migration summary page, you can see a task to generate the application, along with two other generation options. You can also generate application defaults or generate a maintenance application.

The option to generate application defaults allows you to select the default choice for the number of tab levels, the authentication scheme, the theme, and the globalization option for your generated applications. These options will act as the defaults for all migration projects, so if you were going to be converting many Access applications, you could use this choice to reduce the selections for each migration, as well as increase the standardization across all the new APEX applications.

The second choice creates maintenance forms and reports to interact with every valid and included table in the migration project. This type of application is certainly something that would come in handy in your production environment, and the process of generation only takes a minute or so. You could execute this task if you wished on your own.

For now, though, you can simply generate the APEX application you have just prepared.

1. Click Generate Application from the Tasks list, which will bring up the page shown in Figure 12-17.

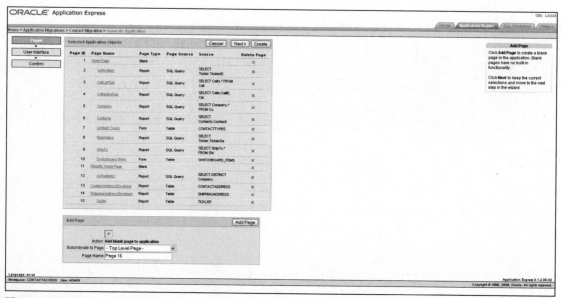

Figure 12-17

You can see the pages that will be generated laid out in a hierarchy, similarly to the way pages were assigned to the application you first created way back in Chapter 2. At the bottom of the page, you can choose to add a blank page to the application and make it subordinate to any existing page. For now, you do not need to do this.

2.   Click to choose a theme for the application. You could have immediately clicked Create, which would have used the application defaults.

3.   Select a theme for the application. In the screen shots for the rest of this chapter, Theme 16 has been selected.

4.   Click Next to confirm your choices, and then Create to create the application.

5.   Once the application is generated, click on the Run Application icon to bring up a login page. Log in with the username and password of the administrator for the workspace, which will reveal your new application, as shown in Figure 12-18.

Figure 12-18

The application looks quite a bit different from the original Access application, but a lot of the functionality is there. You can explore the functionality to see that the default application presents pages to interact with most of the tables in the application on the Home Page tab, and the valid reports on their own tab. The theme of the application provides breadcrumbs for navigation and collapsible display areas. But you might want to improve the overall application with some standard APEX features.

Customize Your Oracle Application Express Application

One of the most apparent issues with this migrated application is that the organization of the pages is very flat. You know that each company has contacts, but there are separate pages for the tables for each of these logical entities. It would be much better to link them together in a master-detail relationship.

In addition, if you look at the columns for the CONTACTS table, you are probably a bit overwhelmed. There is a lot of information, all of it useful sometimes, but much of it extraneous to most common tasks. The usability of the application would improve if each individual user could select the columns that they wanted to see, while still having access to all of the information if necessary.

Sounds like a job for a master-detail set of pages, with an interactive report. If you have been proceeding through this book from start to finish, creating these new pages will be a snap, so the following instructions will be presented at a rapid pace.

1. Go to the Application Builder development environment for the migrated application. On the home page for the application, Click Create Page, and then click on the Form icon to start the creation process.

2. On the next page, click on the Master Detail Form icon, which will take you to the next page in the Creation Wizard.

3. Select the COMPANY table and move all the columns to the Displayed Columns list box. Move the COMPANYID column back to the Available Columns list box, and click Next.

4. Select the CONTACTS table, move all the columns to the Displayed Columns list box, and then move the COMPANYID and CONTACTID columns back to the Available Columns list box. Click Next.

    Why all the columns? Because you will make the subsequent report into an APEX interactive report, which will allow users to limit the columns they see in their version of the report.

5. Choose the existing sequence of COMPANY_COMPANYID_SEQ for the COMPANY table and click Next; choose the existing sequence of CONTACTS_CONTACTID_SEQ for the CONTACTS table and click Next again.

6. Click Next on the next page to include the ability to navigate from the detail report to the complete record in your page. Click Next.

7. Select the choice to force editing of a detail on a separate page, and click Next again.

8. On the next page, change the Page Title for the Detail Page to Company Detail. Keep the breadcrumb active for this page, but change the Entry Name for the breadcrumb for the master-detail page to Company & Contacts. Click on the Home Page in the list at the bottom of the Create Breadcrumb Entry area to make that page the parent page in the breadcrumb trail. Click Next.

9. Choose to use an existing tab on the next page, and then click Next to accept the default tab set.

10. On the next page, select the Home Page tab and click Next.

11. Click Create to create your set of pages for companies and their contacts.

12. Click on the Edit Page icon to go to the attribute page for the company page. Note the number of the page.

13. Move to the next page, which is the master-detail page for a company and its contacts. Click on the `Report` region, and then the Region Definition tab.

14. Select the task to migrate the report to an Interactive Report, and then click Migrate.

You have one small task left — to tie your new pages to the list on the Home Page.

15. Go to edit `Page 1` in the application, and click on the `List` region.

16. Click on the `Company` entry in the list and change the Target for the link to the main page for the company that you just created.

17. Click Apply Changes, and then run the application.

18. Click on the `Company` link to see the master page you just created.

19. Click on the edit link for one of the companies to bring up the master-detail page, which will look like Figure 12-19.

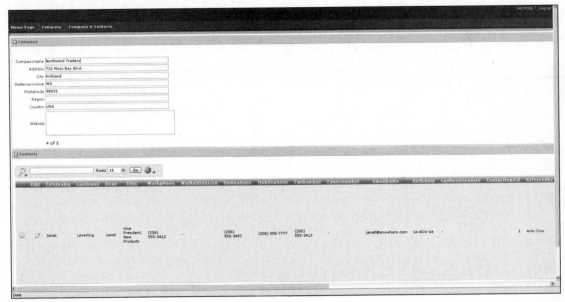

Figure 12-19

Whoa, that doesn't look too good. The reason is that the CONTACTS table has all of those fields. In reality, your users would probably come in to this page and immediately get rid of the columns that they did not want to see, making the page look much more like Figure 12-20.

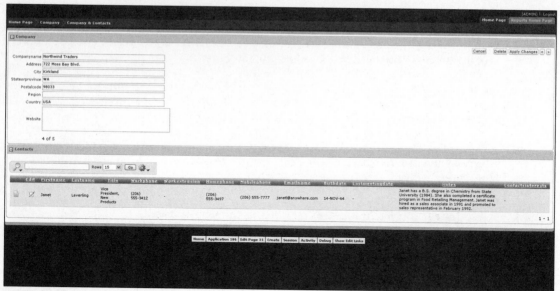

Figure 12-20

That's more like it. Notice the icon to the far left of the contact line. If users click on this icon, they will see all the fields for the record, as well as a button that will allow them to go back to this report view.

Of course, this new page includes an interactive report, which, as you saw in Chapter 5, provides an enormous amount of flexibility for your users.

The small modification you made is just one of many that you could quickly perform to give your users a better application than the Access environment they left. There is a lot more you could do with this application — in fact, a more fully modified version of the application is available for downloading from the web site for this book at www.wrox.com. Feel free to grab this enhanced example and load it up to see more modifications and a (hopefully) richer and easier to use application.

What Hath APEX Wrought?

You have walked through your first simple Access-to-APEX migration. The migration process exposes some good news — you can convert a great number of your Access components automatically, as well as migrating the data structures and data over to your new Oracle database.

But the news is not all good. There were some components that did not migrate easily. The underlying database design for the Access application was really not very good — the CONTACTS table, in particular, could have benefited from some reduction in the number of columns by splitting up the information into multiple tables. The extra Visual Basic code did not translate to the APEX environment. And, to be honest, the look and feel of the new application was not that close to the original Access application's look and feel — although you could have made the application look more like its Access ancestor with a bit more work.

All of these considerations raise a basic question — was it worth it to migrate your applications from Access in the first place? In the end, that is a question that only you can decide, based on your environment, the number of target Access applications, the resources available to create new applications, and how the entire process of change is seen within your organization.

Certainly, there are Access applications that are well designed, in terms of both data structures and application components. Just as certainly, there are Access applications that were not created with much consideration of design.

You can frequently complete a task with a higher level of quality the second time you attempt it. In a similar way, you can often take the basic functionality of an Access application, combine it with the knowledge gained from user feedback on the experience of using that application, and end up with a result that is more satisfactory to both sides when you recreate, rather than migrate, an Access application.

As you have already seen, with APEX, you can create robust applications very quickly. You may very well decide to migrate data structures and their associated data, redesign the data structures if required, and then create an APEX application to interact with the data.

Summary

This final chapter covered the last step in your embracing of Oracle Application Express — moving existing applications to your APEX environment.

When you move your Access applications to APEX, you get plenty of benefits:

- ❏ A highly scalable platform to grow your data and application functionality
- ❏ A way to integrate many different Access applications into a single environment
- ❏ A rapid development tool to supplement and augment existing Access functionality

APEX, along with SQL Developer, provides tools to simplify and automate the process of migrating databases and applications. This chapter led you through a sample Access migration, including moving data structures and data, converting Access modules, and supplementing the migrated application with APEX functionality.

This book has attempted to give you a firm grounding in using Oracle Application Express to address the information requirements of your organization. I hope that you will take this foundation and build fantastic application systems, making you a hero within your organization.

Index